Malinowski, Rivers, Benedict and Others

HISTORY OF ANTHROPOLOGY

Malinowski, Rivers, Benedict and Others

ESSAYS ON CULTURE AND PERSONALITY

Edited by

George W. Stocking, Jr.

HISTORY OF ANTHROPOLOGY
Volume 4

THE UNIVERSITY OF WISCONSIN PRESS

The University of Wisconsin Press
114 North Murray Street
Madison, Wisconsin 53715

The University of Wisconsin Press, Ltd.
1 Gower Street
London WC1E 6HA, England

5 4 3 2

Printed in the United States of America

Library of Congress Cataloging in Publication Data
Main entry under title:
Malinowski, Rivers, Benedict, and others.
(History of anthropology; v. 4)
Includes bibliographies and index.
1. Personality and culture. 2. Ethnopsychology—
History. I. Stocking, George W., 1928–
GN504.M35 1986   306   86-40061
ISBN 0-299-10730-2
ISBN 0-299-10734-5 (paper)

HISTORY OF ANTHROPOLOGY

EDITOR
George W. Stocking, Jr.
Department of Anthropology, University of Chicago

EDITORIAL BOARD
Talal Asad
Department of Sociology and Social Anthropology, University of Hull
James Boon
Department of Anthropology, Cornell University
James Clifford
Board of Studies in the History of Consciousness,
University of California, Santa Cruz
Donna Haraway
Board of Studies in the History of Consciousness,
University of California, Santa Cruz
Curtis Hinsley
Department of History, Colgate University
Dell Hymes
Graduate School of Education, University of Pennsylvania
Henrika Kuklick
Department of History and Sociology of Science,
University of Pennsylvania
Bruce Trigger
Department of Anthropology, McGill University

INFORMATION FOR CONTRIBUTORS

Normally, every volume of *History of Anthropology* will be organized around a particular theme of historical and contemporary anthropological significance, although each volume may also contain one or more "miscellaneous studies," and there may be occasional volumes devoted entirely to such studies. Since volume themes will be chosen and developed in the light of information available to the Editorial Board regarding research in progress, potential contributors from all areas in the history of anthropology are encouraged to communicate with the editor concerning their ongoing work.

Manuscripts submitted for consideration to HOA should be typed twenty-six lines to a page with 1¼-inch margins, with *all* material double-spaced, and documentation in the anthropological style. For exemplification of stylistic details, consult the published volumes; for guidance on any problematic issues, write to the editor. Unsolicited manuscripts will not be returned unless accompanied by adequate postage. All communications on editorial matters should be sent to the editor:

> *George W. Stocking, Jr. (HOA)*
> *Department of Anthropology*
> *University of Chicago*
> *1126 E. 59th St.*
> *Chicago, Illinois 60637 U.S.A.*

All communications relating to standing orders, orders for specific volumes, missing volumes, changes of address, or any other business matters should be addressed to:

> *Marketing Department*
> *The University of Wisconsin Press*
> *114 North Murray Street*
> *Madison, Wisconsin 53715*

Contents

CONTENTS

Malinowski, Rivers, Benedict and Others

Malinowski, Rivers,
Benedict and others
Show how common culture
   Shapes the separate lives:
Matrilineal races
Kill their mothers' brothers
In their dreams and turn their
   Sisters into wives.

Who when looking over
Faces in the subway
Each with its uniqueness,
   Would not, did he dare,
Ask what forms exactly
Suited to their weakness
Love and desperation
   Take to govern there.

Would not like to know what
Influence occupation
Has on human vision
   Of the human fate:
Do all clerks for instance
Pigeon-hole creation,
Brokers see the Ding-an-
   -sich as Real Estate?

When a politician
Dreams about his sweetheart,
Does he multiply her
   Face into a crowd,
Are her fond responses
All-or-none reactions,
Does he try to buy her,
   Is the kissing loud?

Strange are love's mutations:
Thus, the early poem
Of the flesh sub rosa
   Has been known to grow
Now and then into the
Amor intellectu-
-alis of Spinoza;
   How we do not know.

Slowly we are learning,
We at least know this much,
That we have to unlearn
   Much that we were taught,
And are growing chary
Of emphatic dogmas:
Love like Matter is much
   Odder than we thought.

—W. H. Auden

(Copyright 1945 by W. H. Auden. Excerpted from "Heavy Date," in *W. H. Auden: Collected Poems*, edited by Edward Mendelson, by permission of Random House, Inc., and Faber and Faber Ltd.)

ESSAYS ON CULTURE AND PERSONALITY

If the history of anthropology were to be made into a television miniseries, one of its "great moments" would surely be set on the Sepik River early in 1933. Reo Fortune and his wife, Margaret Mead, "starved for theoretical relevance" after two long bouts of fieldwork among the Arapesh and the Mundugumor, were just beginning their work among the Tchambuli; Gregory Bateson, Mead's husband-to-be, was "floundering methodologically" after months among the Iatmul (Mead 1972:209). "Cooped up together in the tiny eight-foot-by-eight-foot mosquito room, we moved back and forth between analyzing ourselves and each other, as individuals, and the cultures that we knew as anthropologists"—seeking a "new formulation of the relationship between sex and temperament" (216). During long hours of intense conversation—in which Bateson and Mead began the dialogue of their "amor intellectualis"—they worked out several typologies of temperament: one, in which Nijinsky and Diaghilev were opposed as east and west, and Fortune stood at the north pole (caring possessive) opposite to Mead and Bateson (careful responsive) at the south; another, in which the male and female temperaments of six different native groups were ranged around eight points of the compass (218; cf. Bateson 1984:161). Mead later recalled that their speculations were provoked in part by the draft of Ruth Benedict's *Patterns of Culture* (1934) they had just received, and that her own thinking drew on C. G. Jung's *Psychological Types*—which, one may note, seems also a likely stimulus for Benedict's use of Nietzsche's Apollonian/Dionysian opposition (Jung 1921:170–83; see also Modell 1983:192). But as Jung's account in fact suggested, theories of temperamental typologies were deeply rooted in both the psychological and the anthropological traditions of the West.

Thus when Linnaeus brought mankind within the *System of Nature* in the mid-eighteenth century (Bendyshe 1865), he distributed his four major races around an implicit geographical wheel of color, temperament, and body type, starting in the west and ending in the south: *Americanus—rufus, cholericus, rectus; Europaeus—albus, sanguineus, torosus; Asiaticus—luridus, melancholicus, rigidus; Afer—niger, phlegmaticus, laxus* (see Fogelson 1985). Linnaeus, of course, was drawing on a system of "humoral" thought that can be traced back through

3

Galen to the Hippocratic fragments on "Airs, Waters, and Places"—which, in the version of William of Conches, saw the choleric, melancholic, and phlegmatic types developing by degeneration from the original sanguine, as the result of "privations imposed . . . by life outside paradise" after the Fall (Klibansky et al. 1964:103; see also Temkin 1973). Although ethnological and psychological categories were rarely so neatly linked as in Linnaeus, for two thousand years thinking about human differences had been heavily influenced by the tradition of environmental humoralism: living for long periods in different geographical environments, different groups were assumed to have developed characteristic inborn temperaments (Greenwood 1984:25–43; Glacken 1967).

Although temperamental (and other psychological) typologies survived into the twentieth century—as Mead's debt to Jung testifies (see Allport 1937:55–97)—the tendency of anthropology after Linnaeus was to break down any such simple fourfold characterization. But far from reflecting a decline of interest in the mental differences among humankind, this represented rather an explosive proliferation of speculation (phrenological, ethnological, craniological) on the distinguishing mental characteristics of the various groups which in the nineteenth century were called "races"—and which even for "lumpers" were as likely to be reducible to three or five in number as to the Galenic/Linnaean four (see Odom 1967). And in the later nineteenth century, thinking about racial temperament tended to be reduced to a simple Spencerian polarity, in which the immediate, impulsive, and concrete responses of dark-skinned "savages" were posed against the mediated, considered, and abstract thinking of white-skinned "civilized" Europeans (see Stocking 1968:110–32; 1986).

It was to combat Spencerian evolutionary racialism that Mead's mentor, Franz Boas, offered his own interpretation of "the mind of primitive man" (1911). Drawing on his extended and intensive fieldwork among Northwest Coast Indians, he limned the possibilities of an alternative determinism of human mental differences: instead of reflecting differences in inborn temperament or intelligence between "races" at different points on an evolutionary scale, they were the product of a "common culture" that shaped "the separate lives" of the individuals in any human group (Stocking 1968). As British anthropology, too, turned more and more to the direct observational study of such groups, a similar argument for "cultural determinism" was advanced by Bronislaw Malinowski: if "matrilineal races" had different dreams of familial homicide and incest, it was because the Oedipus complex was not universal, but varied with the structure of the family (see Stocking, in this volume).

Thus by the 1930s, scholars in both streams of the double cultural tradition to which Auden spoke were well advanced in the process of "unlearning" much that nineteenth-century anthropology had taught on the matter of human psychic differences. But if resurgent Nazi racialism was to make them even more "chary of emphatic dogmas," anthropologists did not lose their fascination with the "mutations" and the oddities of human behavior, or their belief that these were deeply rooted, if not in the phylogeny, then in the ontogeny of human development—or even, in the case of Mead, the suspicion that some of them might have a foundation in "inborn differences between human beings" (Mead 1972:220). One might argue, even, that "culture and personality" became in a sense the functional anthropological equivalent of "race," explaining the same sorts of (presumed) psychological uniformities in very different terms, as "culture" took over the sphere of determinism that had been governed by "race." But the political implications were very different: on the one hand, the oddities of those whom Malinowski still called "savages" came to be treated more tolerantly as patterned selections from the arc of human behavior—or even as possible alternatives to the selections made by "civilized" Euro-Americans; on the other, those denied full participation in modern society on the grounds of "race" were argued to be equipotentially full participants, if only the barriers of prejudice and discrimination could be removed. "Culture and personality" was not without its own stereotyping potential, and its political implications in fact varied depending on the relative weight given to the particularistic/pluralistic and universalistic/assimilationist potential of cultural determinism in different ideological contexts. But by the end of the interwar period, the patterned products of this new determinism and the processes that patterned them had become a preoccupation of a number of members of the rising generation of academically trained anthropologists, especially in the Boasian tradition (see Stocking 1976; Jackson, in this volume).

If we focus primarily on the American scene, where the study of culture and personality became a major force in anthropology, it is evident that the movement may be interpreted in part as a development of the internal discourse of the discipline—as an approach to the problem of the integration of cultural elements once the study of their historical diffusion seemed no longer fruitful (see Stocking 1976; Manson, in this volume). But it is also clear that more was involved: the anthropological concepts at issue (or their equivalents in popular intellectual parlance) were matters of more widespread concern, and the anthropologists who discussed them spoke upon occasion to wider than professional audiences.

Although Auden did not settle in New York until 1939, his subway faces were in fact stock characters in the "spurious culture" that troubled Sapir and many other American intellectuals of the 1920s: the clerk, mindlessly reproducing the categories of rationalized bureaucracy; the broker, rendering ultimate reality in terms of real estate; the politician, reducing the fundamental human social connection to an illicit economic transaction. "Culture," of course, was only then beginning to carry the relativistic weighting of the modern anthropological concept; what was initially at issue was rather the nature of "civilization." Long synonymous with human evolutionary progress (as it had been with "culture"), "civilization" was now, in the aftermath of the Great War, intensely problematic: millions of young men, in the words of Ezra Pound, had been slaughtered "for an old bitch gone in the teeth, for a botched civilization." To a generation (or a generation and a half, since disillusion had in fact begun before the war) for whom Victorian values were no longer taken for granted as eternal or evolutionary verities, it seemed that "pretense [was] the key to modern civilization": "Men pretend to believe in God and sacrifice their lives to Mammon; they love liberty and persecute the champions of freedom [; they] bow down to virtue as holy, and stain the earth with prostitution and syphilis" (Calverton & Schmalhausen 1929:9)

The values of religion, work, and sexuality (which, not entirely by transatlantic coincidence, were the substantive foci of Malinowski's anthropology) no longer provided the integrating framework of a coherent vision of individual "character." Indeed, the "culture of character" itself was giving way to the "culture of personality." Individuality, which had been achieved through "self-control," "self-mastery," "self-sacrifice," and measured by a common standard of tradition-laden nominatives ("duty," "work," "honor," "morality"), was now to be realized through "self-fulfillment," "self-expression," "self-gratification," and captured by a changing array of adjectives ("fascinating," "attractive," "forceful," "creative") which could provide a measure of personal uniqueness in the mass society evoked by the New York City subway (see Susman 1984: 271–85).

Near the center of the "revolt against civilization" was the "sexual revolution," which, in the minds of many contemporary observers, was undermining an already weakened Victorian morality in the familial hearthland in which character (if not personality) was formed. In 1929, Havelock Ellis and the more than thirty contributors to a symposium on *Sex in Civilization* (Calverton & Schmalhausen 1929) ran through the litany of changes: the breakdown of the authority of the traditional family, the increase in adolescent sexual experimentation, the display of the body, the rise of the "New Woman," the birth-control movement, the increase in divorce and extramarital sex, the battle against prudery, secrecy, and censorship—all of this enhanced by and enhancing the growth of scientific knowledge in the sexual realm (as in all matters psychological and social). The Freudian revolution—following the Copernican and the Darwinian—had dealt the third great blow to the "peace of mind" of modern man (10), dethroning "the moralistic illusion which held sway for many centuries" (146).

If "new norms [had] not yet been created out of the luminous chaos that

[was] our contemporary morality," this did not mean that the "revolt against a decaying culture" (Calverton & Schmalhausen 1929:12) was simply the expression of disillusion and despair. As the indefinite articles here and in Pound's couplet suggest, the "revolt against civilization" implied the possibility of cultural alternatives: if Europe, which had stood alone at the pinnacle of evolutionary development, was "*a* botched civilization," then perhaps other civilizations (or, in a terminology that began to be more widely used in the social sciences, cultures) might offer new exemplars. And so they did: as Ellis noted, the Trobriand Islanders' "art of love [was], in the best sense, more 'civilized' than ours"; similarly, Samoa enabled us "to realize how rapidly a new sexual order, if on a reasonably natural foundation, may grow and become fairly stable" (Calverton & Schmalhausen 1929:20, 25). "Love's mutations" might be strange, but not so strange that Euro-Americans could not learn from them.

It was not the first time that South Sea islands had offered lessons in love, or alternative cultural styles, or different realizations of the human self, to discontented denizens of Western "civilization." When the "noble savage" Omai was brought back from Tahiti in 1774, poets made him the voice of a similar cultural criticism:

> Can *Europe* boast, with all her pilfer'd wealth,
> A larger store of happiness or health?
> What then avail her thousand arts to gain
> The store of every land and every main:
> Whilst we, whom love's more grateful joys enthrall,
> Profess one art—to live without them all.
>
> (quoted in Smith 1960:60)

Nor was it the first time that anthropologists had drawn lessons from the "primitive" or "savage" tribes they studied. But through most of the nineteenth century and especially in its evolutionary phase, the dominant ideological impulse of the anthropological tradition had been "progressivist" rather than "primitivist" (see Stocking 1986).

In contrast, the 1920s saw a resurgence of the motif of romantic cultural exoticism in the work of younger anthropologists, and their thinking about problems of culture and personality was motivated at least in part by their participation in the more general "revolt against civilization" (see Handler, in this volume; Stocking 1983). Although they were by no means all cultural radicals, they tended to be set apart by ethnic background, or gender consciousness, or political conviction from the culture of *Middletown* (Lynd & Lynd 1929). Not yet able (or in some cases, willing) to take for granted that their habitat (when they were not in Zuni or Samoa) was the university department, they retained an orientation toward the milieux of the literary intellectual—Greenwich Village, and the "little magazines" (to which a number of them contributed essays and poems). And like other intellectuals involved in "the revolt against civilization," some of them sought to influence more popular audiences—reaching out beyond Auden and those subway faces even to the Rotary Clubs of "Middletown." By exploring the different ways that separate lives had been shaped by common culture, they hoped to suggest, if not the possibility that lives might be shaped differently, then at least the need to be more "chary of emphatic dogmas" in evaluating different "visions of the human fate."

A half century further on, Auden's grouping of Malinowski, Rivers, and Benedict seems perhaps biographically idiosyncratic, if not metrically determined—especially in the case of Rivers, who was a particularly significant other for Auden's friend John Layard (see MacClancy, in this volume), but is scarcely thought of today as a contributor to the "culture and personality" movement. This reflects not only Rivers' death before the movement had begun, but also the fate of culture and personality, or more generally, of psychological anthropology, in the British tradition. With the exception of Layard (whose career mirrors the larger situation) and Bateson (who, like Auden, emigrated), the "others" in this volume are all Americans. Even Malinowski (an immigrant to Britain who died in America) illustrates the point: his argument about the modification of the Oedipus complex in the matrilineal Trobriands was less an interpretation of Trobriand culture and personality than a reinterpretation of Freudian theory. Far from initiating a movement, his approach was rejected by the relatively small community of British psychoanalysts and largely neglected by the community of social anthropologists, who turned instead to the social-structural analysis of Radcliffe-Brown (see HOA 2). From then on, "culture and personality" remained an alien territory for British anthropologists, and the same might on the whole be said of each of the two concepts taken separately.

It is tempting to suggest that this resistance is very deeply rooted: for the British, who stood so long at civilization's pinnacle, "culture" never completely lost its hierarchical and absolutist resonance; so also, "character," which had won them their place, was always to be preferred to "personality." Henry Buckle once remarked that savages *had* no "national character"—"all of them being equally vain, crafty, cruel, superstitious, and improvident" (quoted in Stocking 1986). After Buckle, evolutionism was to provide a unifying framework in which this undifferentiated base could be related to a singular peak, and while early-twentieth-century British anthropologists showed some interest in a variegated study of human culture, in the long run social structure was to provide an approach to human differentiation that was culturally and characterologically more congenial (see HOA 2).

Be that as it may, American anthropology has from the earliest times been oriented toward a psychological view of human differentiation (see Fogelson 1985). Paradoxically, this may reflect the fact that Euro-Americans, advancing across the continent, dispossessed a single grouping of humankind, instead of facing, at the bounds of overseas empire, all the "savages" of the world. The latter situation encouraged the development of a generalized "savage" Other; the former, a preoccupation with a particular type of "savage" character—which in the anthropological ideology of American expansion was seen as tragically flawed, and therefore justifiably expropriated (see School-craft 1857). Despite its institutionalized dominance in later-nineteenth-century American anthropology, evolutionism may be viewed as a temporary overlay on an earlier characterologically motivated study of the American Indian. In this context, Franz Boas' infusion of the Germanic interest in the "genius of peoples" simply reinforced and generalized an orientation that was already deeply rooted in American anthropology (see Stocking 1968)—and was no doubt further stimulated by the freshly problematic character of the multi-ethnic makeup of modern American society in the early twentieth century.

It is therefore quite appropriate that psychological anthropology should be perhaps the most "historied" of the subfields of American anthropology—albeit heretofore mostly in the mode of internal disciplinary history (see, among others, Aberle 1960; Bock 1980; Hallowell 1954; Kluckhohn 1944; Singer 1960; Spindler 1978). The more recent treatments, however, suggest that "culture and personality," as such, was an historically delimited phenomenon. Born in the aftermath of one world war, it was rushed still adolescent into national service in the second, remaining, figuratively, in uniform during the early years of the Cold War (and still largely premised on the assumption of cultural uniformity). Methodological elaboration rapidly overtook conceptual criticism: only months after Edward Sapir's worries over the "distributive locus of culture" were silenced by his death (see Darnell, in this volume), Mead, Bateson, and Benedict were already beginning to elaborate methods for the "study of culture at a distance" (see Yans-McLaughlin, in this volume)—methods which worked reasonably well in Benedict's study of Japanese national character (1946), but which began to be questioned in the aftermath of Gorer's interpretation of Russian national character in terms of the "swaddling hypothesis" (Gorer & Rickman 1949; Mead 1954; cf. Boon, in this volume). Coming "under severe fire by the 1950s," culture-and-personality was "declared dead during the 1960s"; since then a "whole generation of young anthropologists" has come of age with "a pervasive prejudice" against it, and "various misconceptions of its aims and methods" (Spindler 1978:3).

An approach so deeply rooted in the American anthropological tradition—and more generally, in the European construction of "otherness"—is not likely, however, to disappear entirely from the anthropological repertoire. The early 1960s witnessed efforts to distinguish the "old culture and personality theory" from the "new culture and personality theory" (Wallace 1961; 1962). Since then there have been a number of attempts to "rethink culture and personality theory" (Shweder 1979) and to establish on firmer foundations a broadened inquiry rechristened "psychological anthropology" (Hsu 1961; 1972). Whether that rethinking, broadening, and rechristening foreshadows the emergence of a major anthropological subdiscipline (equivalent to cultural, social, biological, or linguistic anthropology) from the current welter of adjectival anthropologies remains of course to be seen. The *longue durée* of American anthropology suggests that perhaps it will; in the meantime, the present essays may encourage a rethinking of its historical roots.[1]

Acknowledgments

Aside from the editor, the editorial board, the contributors, and Betty Steinberg and others on the staff of the University of Wisconsin Press, several other individuals and organizations facilitated the preparation of this volume. The Editor's efforts were sustained in part by a fellowship from the John Simon Guggenheim Memorial Foundation. The staffs of the Department of Anthropology (especially Kathryn Barnes), the Morris Fishbein Center for the History of Science and Medicine (Elizabeth Bitoy), and the Social Science Division Duplicating Service of the University of Chicago provided necessary assistance. Deborah Durham served as editorial assistant. Melissa Banta, May Ebihara, Margaret Gardiner, Daniel Gerould, Wendy Leeds-Hurwitz, Kevin Leonard, James Reed, Philip Sapir and Mary Wolfskill assisted in the pursuit of photographic and other materials. Raymond Fogelson provided bibliographic advice, conceptual orientation, and critical comments on the introduction. And with special gratitude now that its purpose seems to have been accomplished, we would like to thank Lita Osmundsen and the Wenner-Gren Foundation for the grant that helped to get *HOA* established.

1. In the light of the last sentence, which implies a greater degree of systematic purpose than has in fact been the case, it may be appropriate to make more explicit the way in which volumes of *HOA* are constructed. As a general rule, we have not commissioned articles, but have tried to discover what is "out there" within an initial rather broad thematic rubric. As manuscripts are offered (or located), and then evaluated and reworked, a more precisely defined theme gradually emerges, often crystallizing only in the later stages of the editing process. *HOA* 4 was originally announced as "Anthropology Between Two World Wars: 1914–1945"; its present more narrow theme was definitely fixed only several months before going to press; its title was chosen when most of the manuscripts were being copyedited (and one had, belatedly, been discovered "out there"). In this context, the thematic unity proclaimed by each title in the series is to a large extent a posteriori. Inevitably, important topics will not have been treated, and some less important ones given prominence—and deserving papers not included because they did not "work" so well in establishing a volume theme. But we mean the "essays" of our subtitles to be taken seriously: each volume is intended to open up, rather than to exhaust, a loosely defined historical area. So far, this approach has worked well enough to encourage us to continue; should it become too difficult to create this sort of problematic thematic unity, we reserve the right to try a different tack.

References Cited

Aberle, D. 1960. The influence of linguistics on early culture and personality theory. In *Essays in the science of culture in honor of Leslie A. White*, ed. G. E. Dole & R. L. Carneiro, 1–29. New York.

Allport, G. 1937. *Personality: A psychological interpretation.* New York.

Bateson, M. C. 1984. *With a daughter's eye: A memoir of Margaret Mead and Gregory Bateson.* New York.

Bendyshe, T. 1865. On the anthropology of Linnaeus, 1735–1776. *Mems. Anth. Soc. London* 1:421–58.

Benedict, R. 1934. *Patterns of culture.* Boston.

———. 1946. *The chrysanthemum and the sword: Patterns of Japanese culture.* Boston.

Boas, F. 1911. *The mind of primitive man.* New York.

Bock, P. K. 1980. *Continuities in psychological anthropology: A historical introduction.* San Francisco.

Calverton, V. F., & S. D. Schmalhausen, eds. 1929. *Sex in civilization.* Garden City, N.Y.

Fogelson, R. 1977. Notes on the history, status, and prospects of psychological anthropology. Paper for symposium on "Psychological Anthropology: A Perennial Frontier?" Am. Anth. Assn., Houston.

———. 1985. Interpretations of the American Indian psyche: Some historical notes. In *Social contexts of American ethnology, 1840–1984*, ed. J. Helm, 4–27. Washington, D.C.

Glacken, C. J. 1967. *Traces on the Rhodian shore: Nature and culture in Western thought from ancient times to the end of the eighteenth century.* Berkeley.

Gorer, G., & J. Rickman. 1949. *The people of great Russia.* New York.

Greenwood, D. J. 1984. *The taming of evolution: The persistence of nonevolutionary views in the study of humans.* Ithaca, N.Y.

Hallowell, A. I. 1954. Psychology and anthropology. In *Contributions to anthropology: Selected papers of A. Irving Hallowell*, ed. R. Fogelson, 163–229. Chicago (1976).

Hsu, F. L. K., ed. 1961. *Psychological anthropology: Approaches to culture and personality.* Homewood, Ill.

———, ed. 1972. *Psychological anthropology.* Cambridge, Mass. [new edition of Hsu 1961].

Jung, C. G. 1921. *Psychological types, or the psychology of individuation.* Trans. H. G. Baynes. London (1926).

Klibansky, R., et al. 1964. *Saturn and melancholy: Studies in the history of natural philosophy, religion, and art.* London.

Kluckhohn, C. 1944. The influence of psychiatry on anthropology in America during the past one hundred years. In *One hundred years of American psychiatry*, ed. J. K. Hall, G. Zilboorg, & H. A. Bunker, 289–318. New York.

Lynd, R. S., & H. M. Lynd. 1929. *Middletown: A study in American culture.* New York.

Mead, M. 1954. The swaddling hypothesis: Its reception. *Am. Anth.* 56:395–409.

———. 1972. *Blackberry winter: My earlier years.* New York.

Modell, J. 1983. *Ruth Benedict: Patterns of a life.* Philadelphia.

Odom, H. 1967. Generalizations on race in nineteenth-century physical anthropology. *Isis* 58:4–18.

Schoolcraft, H. R. 1857. *History of the Indian tribes of the United States: Their present condition and prospects, and a sketch of their ancient status*. Philadelphia.

Shweder, R. A. 1979. Rethinking culture and personality. *Ethos* 7:255–78, 279–311.

Singer, M. 1960. A survey of culture and personality theory. In *Studying personality cross-culturally*, ed. B. Kaplan, 9–90. New York.

Smith, B. 1960. *European vision and the South Pacific, 1768–1850: A study in the history of art and ideas*. London.

Spindler, G. D., ed. 1978. *The making of psychological anthropology*. Berkeley.

Stocking, G. W., Jr. 1968. *Race, culture and evolution: Essays in the history of anthropology*. New York.

————. 1976. Ideas and institutions in American anthropology: Thoughts toward a history of the interwar years. In *Selected papers from the* American Anthropologist: *1921–1945*, ed. Stocking, 1–44. Washington, D.C.

————. 1983. The ethnographic sensibility of the 1920s and the dualism of the modern anthropological tradition. Paper for symposium on "Margaret Mead and Samoa," Am. Anth. Assn., Chicago.

————. 1986. *Victorian anthropology*. New York.

Susman, W. I. 1984. *Culture as history: The transformation of American society in the twentieth century*. New York.

Temkin, O. 1973. *Galenism: The rise and decline of a medical philosophy*. Ithaca, N.Y.

Wallace, A. F. C. 1961. *Culture and personality*. New York.

————. 1962. The new culture-and-personality. In *Anthropology and human behavior*, ed. T. Gladwin & W. Sturtevant, 1–12. Washington, D.C.

ANTHROPOLOGY AND THE SCIENCE OF THE IRRATIONAL

*Malinowski's Encounter
with Freudian Psychoanalysis*

GEORGE W. STOCKING, JR.

When Sigmund Freud arrived in London in 1938 after Marie Bonaparte's ransom enabled him to escape from Nazi-occupied Vienna (Bertin 1982:200), one of the first English intellectuals to communicate with him was Bronislaw Malinowski. Describing himself as a "devoted admirer of your Father and his Work," Malinowski sent a short welcoming note to Anna Freud on June 18, recalling their "many common friends" in Vienna, offering any help he could give as a nearby London neighbor, and hoping that he could call and pay his respects (MY: I-3/207). Writing back four days later, Freud said that he was "pleasantly surprised" that Malinowski was "an adherer of Psychoanalysis," since he had previously been more aware of his "opposition and contradictions to our views" (ML: 6/22/38; see also Jones 1957:III, 234). The present essay attempts to recreate the history of Malinowski's ambivalent relationship to Freudian psychoanalytic theory, and in the process to illuminate the sometimes fruitful and often contentious relationship of two twentieth-century discourses that seek, in somewhat different ways, rational explanations of the apparently irrational.

The Progress of Reason and the Economy of Thought

We begin where Freud and Malinowski began: with nineteenth-century British evolutionism, which provided Freud with almost all of his anthropologi-

---

George W. Stocking, Jr., is Professor of Anthropology and Director of the Morris Fishbein Center for the History of Science and Medicine at the University of Chicago. His book on British social evolutionism, *Victorian Anthropology*, is in process of publication by The Free Press.

cal assumptions, and which—somewhat less obviously—provided also the starting point from which Malinowski developed his functionalist anthropology
(see Stocking 1986). Although some would have it that British evolutionism
in its more manifestly biological aspects was an ideological transformation
of the lived experience of early Victorian economic life, the case can also be
made that in its cultural form—that which Marett and Evans-Pritchard later
called the "English Intellectualist Tradition" (Evans-Pritchard 1933; Marett
1908b)—evolutionary anthropology was a kind of antiscience to English political economy. Whereas the latter was quintessentially the science of the rational utilitarian behavior of civilized men, evolutionism in its Tylorian-
Frazerian form was the science of the apparently irrational behavior of "savages"
—which was seen as a kind of "lost rationality," the surviving irrational resi-
due of behavior that had once been soundly reasoned, albeit (like that of
Locke's madmen), from false principles. The process was archetypified to the
point of parody in Frazer's "first theory of totemism": if one accepted the
primitive belief in an external soul, then it was rational to deposit it for safe-
keeping in a particular plant or animal; but since the animals or plants of
a single species are difficult to distinguish, the savage "does not know which
the dear one is," and is "obliged to spare them all from fear of injuring the
one"—thus creating the totemistic relationship (Frazer 1900:I, 351, 417). By
similar lines of reasoning from the principle of psychic unity, the mental world
of savages could be linked to that of children and neurotics—an equation which
was in fact the starting point of Freud's anthropology (see Wallace 1983).

The savage as failed philosopher-cum-madman, however, was not the only
view of primitive reason possible within a Tylorian evolutionary framework.
Another approach—more consonant with the view of evolutionism as economic ideology—may be found in the work of another fin-de-siècle Viennese
intellectual: the physicist, psychologist, and philosopher of science Ernst Mach.
Although he drew heavily from Tylor's work, Mach was much more consis-
:ently Darwinian in outlook, and he was not "ashamed" to base his epistemology on the "miserly mercantile principle" of the "economy of thought"
(Mach 1895:15–16): "When the human mind, with its limited powers, attempts
to mirror in itself the rich life of the world . . . it has every reason for proceeding economically" (186). For Mach, the history of human mentality was
characterized less by "lost rationality" than by "lost instinct": the instinctive
organically adaptive behavior of savages was the ultimate basis of science, which
was simply "the formulation, in clear, abstract, and communicable terms, of
what was instinctively known long before" (191). In his epistemological mag-
num opus, *Knowledge and Error*, Mach elaborated this viewpoint at greater
length, arguing that all the processes of the living individual were reactions
in the interests of self-preservation (1905:80). Knowledge and error proceeded
from the same source—observation, sometimes adequate, sometimes inade-

quate. But in general, "ideas gradually adapt to facts by picturing them with sufficient accuracy to meet biological needs" (120); and the formation of scientific hypotheses was merely a "further degree of development of instinctive and primitive thought" (180), once the simple biological goals had been met. Mankind's first rough attempts at finding his way about nature—demonic, poetic, and mythological thought—were progressively refined, and an "increasing restriction of expectations" accompanied the ever more precise adaptation of thought to the natural world (354).

Although it would of course be a considerable oversimplification, one could do worse than to characterize Malinowski's thought as the outcome of a confrontation between Mach and Freud—between the instinctive rationality of self-preservation, and the rationalized instinctuality of reproduction.

Neopositivism and Neoromanticism in the Formation of Malinowski's Thought

Growing up in that third of partitioned Poland that formed the Austrian province of Galicia, Malinowski would naturally have been oriented toward the metropolis of the Hapsburg Empire and—more important, perhaps, for young Polish intellectuals in the first decade of the century—the birthplace of cultural modernism (Janik & Toulmin 1973; Schorske 1980). In Malinowski's case, the major influence was that of Mach, who from 1895 on was Professor of Philosophy at the University of Vienna, and who—for those questioning all metaphysical assumption in the name of positive science—was surely the most important Middle European philosopher of the day (Janik & Toulmin 1973:133).

Malinowski's early studies after entering the Jagiellonian University in his native Cracow in 1902 were in physics and mathematics, but by the end of his undergraduate years he had moved toward the philosophy of science, which he continued to pursue for his doctoral training (Śrdniawa 1981). His three major professors have been described as "adherents to the 'second positivism' of Ernst Mach and Richard Avenarius" (Paluch 1981:278). One of them, Maurycy Straszewski, was the author of the only Polish-language work treating the principle of the economy of thought, which in turn became the topic of Malinowski's doctoral dissertation—a rather brief historical-critical essay that reveals him in the process of coming to terms with "two of the most eminent representatives of the anti-metaphysical movement" (1908:2–3).

Malinowski's main concern was whether the principle of economy of thought (or, in Avenarius' terms, "least exertion") contained within itself metaphysical assumptions, or whether it could be interpreted in a way consonant with "one of the most general scientific principles": "the law of unequivocal determina-

tion" (1908:1, 8–9). Avenarius clearly failed the test, and in the end, Malinowski concluded that "we do not yet have a general empirical foundation for
a philosophical view of the world" (48). But despite his discomfort with Mach's
tendency to make "direct inference from the field of biology to psychology"
(36), Malinowski was much more positive about Mach, whose work was not
open to the objection of falling "into conflict with the law of unequivocal
determination" (38). Mach's notion of adaptation left open the issue of whether
the validity of scientific laws was to be determined psychologically or objec-
tively. Rejecting the former approach, Malinowski chose instead a practical
criterion: even if only one normal man remained in the world, he would not
have to "despair of the values, both material and scientific, of the achievements of mankind," since their "enormous practical importance" would "allow
him to destroy his adversaries outright." In one of only two passages referring
directly to the traditional subject matter of anthropology, Malinowski noted
that this situation was "sadly and emphatically" illustrated by "the relation
of the white man to his less civilized colored brethren" (40–43).[1]

Despite Malinowski's somewhat critical posture in the dissertation itself,
it is impossible to examine Mach's major epistemological works without remarking resonances of Malinowski's later anthropological outlook. Like Malinowski, Mach was *au fond* a methodological individualist—he began his *Analysis of Sensations* with the famous drawing of the world as "presented to my
left eye" (Mach 1906:18). From such a starting point, Mach developed his view
of science: "From sensations and their conjunctions arise concepts, whose
aim is to lead us by the shortest and easiest way to sensible ideas that agree
best with sensations" (1905:105). Science was a description of the natural
world in biologically adaptive terms, with theory (not sharply separable from
observation) a matter simply of the mutual adaptation of thoughts previously adapted to the facts of nature (120). Beginning in the practical and instinctual world of direct biological adaptation, science became gradually lib-
erated for the pursuit of intermediate (i.e., secondary) goals (96). Central to
the scientific endeavor was the concept of "function"—which for Mach had
made "superfluous" the "ordinary concepts of cause and effect" (206, 210).
True, Malinowski's use of "function" was to be much broader than Mach's,
which was essentially that of mathematical covariation (see Stocking 1984b).
But this seems not inconsistent with the sort of diffuse intellectual influence
that is being asserted here. By temperament, Malinowski was inclined to want

---

1. My references to Malinowski's doctoral thesis were made possible by a former student,
Edward Martinek, who after research in Malinowski manuscripts in Cracow in 1975 prepared
a translation. My interpretation of the thesis differs somewhat from that of Andrzej Paluch (1981),
who suggests a Machian origin for the idea of culture as an instrumental whole, who tries to
dissociate Malinowski from Mach's radical empiricism, and who postulates a neo-Kantian influence on Malinowski.

more from philosophy in the way of Reality, Law, and Truth than Mach was willing to give. An intellectual opportunist, frankly willing "to accept all the risks which eclecticism carries" (MY: II-27/266), he remained open to a variety of influences, not in their full complexity, but as they offered straight-forward standpoints from which to approach the large philosophical and anthropological questions that preoccupied him. But it seems likely that behind all of these influences lay Mach, as a source less of specific concepts than of general assumptions to which Malinowski often later returned, albeit in a detextualized and recontextualized fashion.

Thus, it is to Mach that one must look for the philosophical source not only of Malinowski's methodological individualism, but also of his mooted "obsessional empiricism" (Leach 1957:121; see also, Symmons-Symonolewicz 1959). Its relationship to the empiricism of William James is a matter less of direct influence than of elective affinity—James and Mach having found themselves kindred philosophic spirits as early as 1882 (Hiebert 1976:xiii, xxvi). When Malinowski attempted systematically to work through his "Systema Philosophiae" in Melbourne in 1919, after returning from his second round of fieldwork in the Trobriands, he did read James. But while he found him intellectually congenial, he was critical of the "instrumental view of truth," and at one point equated "pragmatism" with the view that "our physical universe is constructed only for the sake of commodity." On the other hand, a Machian groundwork was still very much in evidence, although somewhat transmogrified by Malinowski's passion for Reality and Truth (MY: II-27/239).

Although critically important, the influence of Machian positivism was not the only major influence on Malinowski in his intellectually formative years. Malinowski was a person of strongly dualistic temperament, pulled between intellect and passion, science and art; and it has been convincingly suggested that he was a product as much of the "second romanticism" as of the "second positivism" (Strenski 1982; see also Firth 1981).[2] A recent Polish commentary suggests that Malinowski's "creative personality was shaped, both in its better and its worse manifestations," by his being "brought up in the very specific and unique atmosphere of Polish modernism"—a remark elaborated, unfortunately, only with the veiled suggestion that the "style" of his published diary is more understandable when "compared with some mannerisms" of "the Zakopane panopticon," as manifest in some "very controversial" individuals with whom Malinowski used to spend his summer vacations at the Tatras

---

2. Although doubtless correct on the general point, Strenski goes beyond documentary evidence in arguing the specific influence of Wilhelm Dilthey as the basis for Malinowski's concern in *Argonauts* with "spirit" and *Weltanschauung*; furthermore, the mid-1920s "shift" in "methodological ground" Strenski postulates (1982:769) seems to me better seen as a return to an underlying neopositivist scientism after a brief period in which Malinowski's romantic literary muse held sway.

Oil painting by Stanisław Witkiewicz, 1910: "Bronisław Malinowski appears as Xerxes Yakshma in [Tadeusz] Micinski's [novel] *Nietota.*" (From the collection of Eva Franczak and Stefan Okołowicz. Courtesy Daniel Gerould.)

Mountains resort (Paluch 1981:281, 284). Most prominent among these was Stanisław Ignacy Witkiewicz, who as "Staś" figures in the early pages of Malinowski's published diaries (1967), and who as "Witkacy" was to become one of the major figures in twentieth-century Polish painting, literature, and theater before his suicide in the face of invading Russian troops in 1939 (Gerould 1981).

Deliberately reared by his father, a leading Polish painter, as a Nietzschean genius who would confound the aesthetic establishment, "Staś" was Malinowski's closest friend in the years before World War I. As adolescents "they read plays and poetry, wrote mock scientific treatises, and invented bizarre names for one another" (Gerould 1981:6). Despite Staś's father's fear that formal artistic training (and Malinowski's personal influence) might distort his son's development, in 1905 Staś joined Malinowski in Cracow, where he spent a year at the Academy of Fine Arts. When Malinowski moved to London in 1910, Staś stayed with him for some time; in 1914, in the aftermath of his fiancée's tragic suicide, Staś accompanied Malinowski to the southwestern

Pacific, in a Gauguinesque search for primitive regenerative experience. There the friendship ended, for reasons the diary does not clearly reveal—"Nietzsche breaking with Wagner" (Malinowski 1967:33–34)—and their lives went in opposite directions. The two differed considerably in metaphysical temperament, especially in regard to the religious impulse in man; and it would surely be inappropriate to attribute to Malinowski the full range of experiences Witkiewicz recounted in *The 622 Downfalls of Bungo*—a sexually explicit fictionalized autobiography written in 1910 but withheld from publication until 1972. But it is fair to assume that the man who figures in it as Edgar, "The Duke of Nevermore" (and who was a subject for Staś's expressionist portraits), would have felt himself in the very forefront of the Polish cultural avant-garde, and that he would have been generally aware of the Freudian viewpoint—the more so since Staś underwent psychoanalysis with "the first Polish Freudian psychiatrist" in 1913 (Gerould 1981:11). Just as Mach's often-remarked intellectual anglophilia may have helped to preadapt Malinowski to the intellectual concerns of the British empirical and evolutionary traditions, so also is there evidence to suggest Malinowski's biographical and cultural experience may have preadapted him to the influence of Freud, even before he began to read seriously in the literature of psychoanalysis.

A Machian Between Westermarck and Durkheim

After completing his doctoral studies, Malinowski spent some time in Leipzig at the university where his father, late Professor of Slavic Philology at Cracow, had gone a half century before. There he studied with Wilhelm Wundt, the founder of experimental psychology, whose interests in both individual and collective mental phenomena (*Völkerpsychologie*) seem each to be reflected in Malinowski's early work (see Strenski 1982), and with the economic historian Karl Bücher, whose *Arbeit und Rythmus* helped shape Malinowski's lifelong interest in primitive economics (see Firth 1957b:210). The surviving reading notes from this period (largely in Polish), indicate that in addition to Wundt's linguistic writings and *Gefühlstheorie*, Malinowski read Simmel on the current state of German sociological thought (MY: II-27/260, 261, 268). Already by this time, however, Malinowski's fabled encounter with *The Golden Bough* (Frazer 1900) had "bound" him "to the service of Frazerian anthropology" (1926a:94; see also MY: II-27/244); and in 1910, he departed for England, where a strong tradition of empirical ethnographic investigation had been established by the members of the "Cambridge School" (see Langham 1981; Stocking 1983).

Given his prior sociological interest, and the greater cosmopolitanism of the London School of Economics—and the fact that Frazer did no teaching—it is not surprising that Malinowski became a student of Charles Seligman and Edward Westermarck, rather than of Alfred Haddon and William Rivers. Seligman seems primarily to have encouraged an impulse to ethnographic particularism; but Malinowski found in Westermarck's neo-Darwinian evolutionary sociology (Stroup 1984) an important theoretical resource, as he attempted, in the two major monographs of his armchair apprenticeship, to come to terms with the most important sociological influence on twentieth-century British anthropology: Emile Durkheim (see Stocking 1984a; 1984b).

By 1910, when Frazer's *Totemism and Exogamy* incorporated all three of his successive theories of totemism into four volumes of secondhand ethnographic data, it seemed clear to many that the categories and methods of classical British sociocultural evolutionism required some reconsideration (see Stocking 1983:91; 1984b). Malinowski entered the discussion in 1912 with a piece of Frazerian revisionism he contributed to Westermarck's festschrift. Taking off from Frazer's suggestion in *Totemism and Exogamy* that the division of labor embodied in the Australian *intichiuma* ceremonies was a good principle misapplied, which under totemism led to no positive results, Malinowski argued that the ceremonies were in fact a "collective and regular system of labor" involving a higher and more "economic" type of work than "savages" were normally capable of. Applying Bücher's distinction between "primitive" and "civilized" labor, Malinowski argued that the labor of the *intichiuma* ceremonies had all the characteristics of the latter: it was organized, collective, continuous, regular, periodical, and involved systematic planning and definite goals. In a manner resonant of the abortive protofunctionalism of Frazer's *Psyche's Task* (1909), Malinowski suggested that it required strong stimuli to force savage man into a work style repugnant to him, and that magic and religion had supplied the necessary "coercive forces." He rejected, however, "any universal scheme of evolution . . . among all the races of mankind" (1912:99): the aim of science was a "correct and exact description of facts," and the role of theory was simply to provide more precise concepts for the analysis of observed connections between facts, and for the formulation of new ones (103).

Recast in the methodological idiom of contemporary historiography and in the theoretical idiom of Durkheimian sociology, Malinowski's empiricism was rather differently manifest in his first book-length monograph. Although there were still numerous residues of evolutionary assumption, the strategy of *The Family Among the Australian Aborigines* was to evaluate certain widely held evolutionary notions (such as primitive promiscuity) by a consideration of all the available data for the most methodologically crucial (i.e., most "primitive") case, in order to confirm his mentor Westermarck's view of the universality of the individual human family (1913a:34–35; cf. Westermarck 1891). Malinowski prefaced his argument by suggesting that it would show the importance of theory as well as facts in sociological inquiry: thus, even if problems of origin and development were put aside and inquiry limited to the "actual working of aboriginal kinship organisation," there would still be plenty of subjects worthy of theoretical consideration (1913a:v). The Durkheimian chord was struck in the beginning, when Malinowski declared that "each social institution must be studied in all its complex social functions as well as in its reflexion in the collective psychology" (vi). And although Malinowski made a point of criticizing Durkheim's "exclusive stress on the legal aspect of kinship" (204), his main constructive argument clearly derived from his reading of the Durkheimian literature. Social (as distinguished from physiological) consanguinity was defined relativistically as "the set of relations involved by the collective ideas under which the facts of procreation are viewed in a given society" (182), and a key footnote made clear that the idiom of "social facts," "social morphology," and "collective ideas" derived from "the French school of Prof. Durkheim and his associates" (192; see also 300–302)— to which Malinowski, like some Anglo-American writers of this period, seems to have assimilated Lévy-Bruhl's ideas about the "prelogical mentality" of savages (214).

Even in this, his most Durkheimian work, Malinowski's use of the term "social function" was by no means consistently Durkheimian, and his future disagreements were foreshadowed in a footnote insisting that "collective mind" did not "postulate the existence of any metaphysical entity" (1913a:308–9). His subsequent response to Durkheim's *Elementary Forms* (1912) pursued further the fundamental issue of methodological individualism. Quoting liberally to establish his grammatical-cum-philosophical point, he argued that society was "the *logical subject*" of many of Durkheim's arguments, rather than merely "the atmosphere in which *individuals* create religious ideas"—although he insisted that in practice Durkheim frequently resorted to "individual psychological explanations" (1913b:285, 287–88).

Malinowski formulated his own approach to "the genesis of religion" in the other major monograph of his armchair period: a yet-untranslated Polish publication entitled "Primitive Beliefs and Forms of Social Organisation" (1915), a work which has been characterized as "the real *fons et origo* of [his] later theories of magic and religion" (Symmons-Symonolewicz 1960:4). Despite his refusal to "find the origins of religion in crowd phenomena" (1913b:286), Malinowski still drew heavily on Durkheim in his discussion of "the sociological side of religion" (1915:229). But although he clearly reflected the recent reaction against the intellectualism of Tylor and Frazer, he still insisted that religion, like all other cultural phenomena, must ultimately derive from individual psychic processes. Posing the issue in terms of "the crystallization of ideas from emotional states"—fear, love, anxiety, hope, expectation—"which compel us to grasp strongly a certain idea and desperately to cling to it," he suggested that "ideas born in this way radically differ from ideas born by simple contemplation, observation and other everyday experiences." The seminar notes in which these passages occur make it clear that though he was influenced by Ernest Crawley and Robert Marett (and perhaps thus indirectly by William James), his viewpoint was quite explicitly an extension of Westermarck's neo-Darwinian interpretation of the evolution of moral ideas into the "magico-religious" realm (MY: II-27/245; cf. Westermarck 1906–8).

Malinowski had already lost his early Roman Catholicism, and like Mach sought to purge himself of all metaphysical residues; but his anthropological readings (enlivened, perhaps, by all those conversations with Staś about matters of ultimate belief) had led him toward a view of human religiosity that rooted it firmly in the primitive nature of man. Although his last prefieldwork publication (1914) was in fact to call into question, on empirical ethnographic grounds, Durkheim's distinction between the sacred and the profane, the general import of his armchair speculation was to mark off, still in evolutionary terms, a realm in which instinctual irrational emotional impulses held sway—albeit subsequently rationalized and socialized in the form of religion: "Man, especially primitive man who lives in a constant struggle for survival, . . . is mainly emotional and active, . . . and it is easy to show that these very elements lead him to the performance of such acts and activities which constitute a germ of religion" (1915, as translated by Symmons-Symonolewicz 1960:5).

Malinowski never abandoned a Machian view of primitive human nature as pragmatically adaptive and instinctually rational; buttressed by his fieldwork experience, it was to characterize much of his later anthropological work. But already before he went into the field, he had marked off a human motivational domain governed—albeit still in adaptive terms—by an instinct much more passionately conceived. His experience in the field was also to confirm this view of man's primitive nature, not only in the religious but also in the sexual realm.

The Freudianism of Fieldwork Experience

Although one can indeed find in Malinowski's immediate prefield writings premonitory manifestations of his future theoretical development, we must still take very seriously the role of his fieldwork experience in defining his mature theoretical point of view. Malinowski himself at several points suggested something of its impact in further attenuating the influence he had imbibed of French writers. It was "experience in the field" that had persuaded him of the "complete futility" of Lévy-Bruhl's hypothesis that the mental processes of "savages" were "prelogical"; it was fieldwork experience also that had carried him "entirely out of touch with Professor Durkheim's philosophical basis of sociology": because "in the field . . . one has to do with the whole aggregate of individual souls, and the methods and theoretical conceptions have to be framed exclusively with this multiplex material in view," he had concluded that the "postulate of a collective consciousness" was "barren and absolutely useless for an ethnographical observer" (1916:273–74). The most illuminating such acknowledgment, however, is perhaps the suggestion that "nothing surprised me so much in the course of my sociological researches as the gradual perception of an undercurrent of desire and inclination running counter to the trend of convention, law and morals" (1925b:205)—for the revelation of a similar "undercurrent of desire" in Malinowski himself is one of the most striking aspects of his Trobriand diary.

The extent to which Malinowski's fieldwork experience represented a departure from the immediately prior experiences of a dozen other post–Torres Straits ethnographers has been dealt with elsewhere (Stocking 1983). Suffice it to say here that although he began in October 1914 following in Seligman's tracks with the Rivers edition of *Notes and Queries* in hand, by the time he left Mailu in February 1915 he clearly had glimpsed the possibility of a much more actively participatory ethnographic style; and that although there are discrepancies between his subsequent practice and its prescriptive mythologization, he seems to a remarkable degree to have implemented such a style during his two expeditions to the Trobriands. However, because the first left no diary record, we must rely on his account of the second Trobriand expedition for some insight into the inner personal meaning of an ethnographic mode Malinowski himself characterized as Conradian.

It is this diary, properly, that is the "Diary in the Strict Sense of the Term" —not simply a narrative of events, but "a moral evaluation, [a] location of the mainsprings of my life" (1967:104). Perhaps because reaction to the diary has not got much beyond the disillusioning shock of its references to Trobriand "niggers" (Stocking 1983:71, 102; see also 1968), there has been no serious attempt yet to extract a "plot" from its unindexed Joycean (or Witkacian) stream of consciousness—despite the clues provided by its abrupt closing, months before Malinowski left the field. Only indirectly "about" his fieldwork, it is best viewed as an account of the central psychological drama of his life— an extended crisis of identity in which certain Freudian undertones were obvious to Malinowski himself.

Save Malinowski, the major characters are all female. Back in Poland, threatened by the flow of battle on the eastern front, was his mother, widowed since Malinowski was fourteen. An only son, Malinowski seems to have had a rather strong oedipal attachment, as indeed his own later variant of Freudian theory might suggest. His Viennese friend Paul Khuner (to whom he dedicated *Sex and Repression*) suggested that the reason he had difficulty in making emotional attachments with women was that all his emotions were centered on his mother (MY: PK/BM 8/17/18; see also Wayne 1985); and his relations with women clearly evinced a characteristic oedipal tension between the spiritual and the erotic—evident in the Mailu diary in the contrast between Zenia and Toska, the "incomparable mistress" (1967:133) with whom he had broken at the time of his mother's last prewar visit to London (68).

In Australia, Malinowski had become successively involved with two other young women, both of them daughters of leading figures in the country's rather small scientific community: N. S. (Nina Stirling), whom he had met after his return from Mailu and was "thinking seriously of marrying" (1967:99); and E. R. M. (Elsie Rosalin Masson), whom he met in 1917 and did eventually marry. Although he had stopped seeing Nina in 1916 at her parents' insistence, her serious illness constrained him from breaking off their continuing correspondence, or telling her about the relationship he subsequently began with Elsie (MY: BM/Seligman 6/21/18; see also Wayne 1985). When he left for the Trobriands in the fall of 1917, Malinowski regarded Elsie as his fiancée, but in January, while watching a dying native woman hemorrhage, he was struck with remorse about his "betrayal" of Nina, and momentarily decided that he wanted to be with her "at any cost, to allay her sufferings" (1967:192). The psychological complexities of the situation are suggested by the fact that although Elsie was later explicitly equated emotionally to his mother—with a parenthetic reference to "Freud's theory" (245)—Malinowski also dreamed that his mother reproached him for not marrying Nina (202).

Closely bound up with this unresolved emotional involvement was the problem of national identity. There was more than a bit of ambivalence in Malinowski's wartime sympathies, and at times he was moved by a "strong hatred for England and the English" (1967:218). He feared that if he married Elsie, he "would be estranged from Polishness" (174); and as late as mid-April he proclaimed: "I shall go back to Poland and my children will be Poles" (253).

The last half of the diary recounts the resolution of this extended crisis. After three months of vacillation, Malinowski finally decided he must write "an absolutely irrevocable letter" to Nina (1967:265)—although in fact it was Nina herself who broke things off in the summer of 1918 (Wayne 1985:534). By May 13, Malinowski had brought himself "round to the knowledge" that "physical contact, frenzied self-surrender is valuable only against [the] background of true spiritual communion"—and that Elsie was "the only woman for whom I have this feeling" (274). Although she was not "the fulfillment of all the potentialities of woman" (279), she was "the ideal wife" for him (283); on June 4 he decided that "de facto" they were married (288). A week later, he received news of his mother's death (291), and after two weeks in which he could bring himself to write nothing, the diary rushed to a conclusion.

The "shadow of death," which in January had threatened to separate him from Elsie (1967:192), now drew them closer together. Life had been "pierced

Bronislaw Malinowski with Trobriand women, 1917. (Courtesy the London School of Economics and Helena Wayne Malinowska.)

with the arrow of grief, guilt feelings, irretrievable things" (295), and Poland now stood on the other side of a "black abyss, a void," in his soul (293). Even in his grief, "external ambitions ke[pt] crawling" over him "like lice," and these were now clearly linked with England: F.R.S., C.S.I., even *Sir* Bronislaw Malinowski (291). Although thoughts about Elsie were painful, she was now the anchor of his future and the redeemer of his past. In the diary's last paragraph, Malinowski recalled how his last evening with his mother in London had been "spoiled by that whore [Toska]," and suggested that "if I had been married to E. R. M., I would have behaved very differently" (297).

Although necessarily schematicized, this biographical detail is by no means a detour from the intellectual-historical point, which has to do with the way in which a particular experiential situation helped shape Malinowski's theoretical orientation. Indeed, to make the point we must for a moment venture even further into the realm of his emotional life. Malinowski was clearly a highly erotic individual, who at times suffered from "the metaphysical regret" of "you'll never fuck them all" (1967:113–14). His ethnographic style placed him in very close daily proximity to grass-skirted native women, whose bodies excited him, and whose relatively uninhibited sex lives were in fact a primary subject of his study. However, he had deliberately chosen to restrain his erotic

energy throughout the period of his fieldwork, having resolved to remain
faithful to Elsie in both deed and thought. He seems to have managed the
former, but his impulses were quite another matter; the attempt to cope with
them is in fact a primary psychological theme of the diary.

At a certain level, these erotic impulses separated him from the Trobrianders, provoking at one point his "regret that this incompatibility can exist:
physical attraction and personal aversion. Personal attraction without strong
physical magnetism" (1967:273). And in general, we may offer the aside that
many of the references to "niggers" occur in close relation to thoughts about
Elsie and his own problematic and momentarily frustrated love life (see Stocking
1968). But his realization, in the context of his "sensual arousal" by native
women at a spring, "of the gulf between me and the human beings around
me" (273) was not the ultimate meaning he drew from his field experience.
Quite the contrary, it was rather an appreciation of the basis of their shared
humanity.

When Malinowski formulated "the deepest essence" of his ethnographic
work in November 1917, he echoed the goal he had set for his own diary:
"to discover what are [the native's] main passions, . . . his essential deepest
way of thinking."[3] In doing so, "we are confronted with our own problems:

---

3. The elision in the quoted passage is not one of the many in the published diary—which
one suspects may have to do with autoerotic sex—but was introduced by me. Included in the
elided portion was a parenthesis worthy of comment: "(Why does a *boy* 'sign *on*'? Is every *boy*,
after some time, ready to 'sign *off*'?)." The reference, one assumes, is to "signing on" for a term
of plantation labor overseas. In the present context, this seems at first starkly disjunctive: why
should Malinowski, plumbing the depths of human nature, suddenly introduce what seems such
a blatant bit of colonial economic pragmatism? Since the argument of this essay did not seem
structured to facilitate explanation at this point in the text, I elided the parenthesis. But there
are other contexts (including perhaps a more elaborated rendering of the present argument) in
which the parenthesis seems very relevant.

The most obvious is that of Malinowski's active role a decade later in developing a "practical
anthropology" directed to problems of colonial administration and economic development (see
Stocking 1985; James 1973). When Malinowski testified in October 1916 before an Australian
parliamentary commission investigating the impact of the war on "British and Australian Trade
in the South Pacific," his expertise had to do specifically with the topic of the elided parenthesis:
why it was that "the native Papuan is not very keen on working for the white man." Malinowski's testimony can indeed be read as his contribution to the solution of a problem of practical
anthropology—and one that had a sexual as well as an economic aspect, insofar as it was related
to the issue of Melanesian depopulation, which was becoming a matter of widespread concern.
Speaking from "the natives' point of view"—his empathy heightened, perhaps, by his own experience—Malinowski suggested that it was "almost impossible to think that a young native would
spend three years of his life without having sexual intercourse without degenerating into sexual
abnormality." It is worth noting, however, that although he offered advice on how best to handle
the plantation labor problem, Malinowski's conclusion was "that it would be best to leave them
to their own conditions"—i.e., not to ask them to "sign on" (Malinowski 1918).

If we recall Malinowski's contribution to the Westermarck festschrift (1912)—and look forward what is essential in ourselves?" (1967:119). In seeking the mainsprings of his own life, Malinowski resolved to watch himself "right down to the deepest instincts" (181). Alone in the heart of darkness, he tried to penetrate the darkness of his own heart, and was confronted there by instinctual forces common to all men: "Now I often have the feeling of being 'at the bottom of consciousness'—the feeling of the physical foundation of mental life, the latter's dependence on the body, so that every thought that flows effortlessly in some psychic medium has been laboriously formed inside the organism" (294). There, at "the bottom of consciousness," behind what he later called "the ever-imperfect wall of culture" (1925a:81), all men were motivated by the same biologically based drives he felt so acutely in the course of his own psychological drama in the Trobriands.

It was in this context that Malinowski conceived the notion of a "New Humanism" centered on "living man, living language, and living full-blooded facts" (1967:255), for which he planned to organize a "kind of humanistic R[oyal] S[ociety]" when he got back to England (267). Although the "Society of Modern Humanism" did not materialize, the "New Humanism" was explicitly echoed in an article published after his return, in which he explained the currently debated "Depopulation of Melanesia" in psychobiological terms. Convention-bound "morality mongers" and parochial middle-class "petty inquisitors of primitive life," in their "fanatical zeal to prune and uproot," had choked off the natives' "joy of living" by suppressing the institutions that gave "zest and meaning to life"—the flute playing of the Dobu, the drums around Port Moresby, the dancing of the Trobrianders. Malinowski was particularly incensed by attempts to tamper with "the most powerful human instinct"—the sexual instinct—and with the system of regulations and liberties which "a natural biological and social development has built around it" in a particular

---

to the argument of *Sex and Repression* (1927)—it is also possible to reintegrate the elided passage more directly into the broader themes of Malinowski's anthropology, both intellectually and experientially. His first contribution to anthropological literature had to do with the transition from "savage" to "civilized" labor; so also, in a way, does the elided parenthesis. Yet the argument of *Sex and Repression* makes it clear that the passage from savagery to civilization was also a passage away from a relatively easy and harmonious genital sexuality. For mankind as a whole, the long-run evolutionary consequences of "signing on" might be interpreted as involving loss as well as gain—and the loss might be even more sharply felt by a European living on a tropical island, but denying himself the sensual pleasures that cultural exoticism usually associated with such primitive realms. Denied the compensating gains of civilization, why, indeed, would the native "boy"— or anyone else—"sign on"?

All of which suggests that two of the major domains of Malinowski's anthropology—the domains of sex and work (of Freud and Mach?)—may articulate in Malinowski's thought in a more systematic way than as the sequential ethnographic and theoretical foci of his work. They surely did in Victorian anthropological ideology—to which Malinowski was certainly reacting (see Stocking 1986).

culture. In this context, he offered one of his earliest published statements of the functional integration of culture, expressed in essentially psychobiological instrumental terms:

> every item of culture . . . represents a value, fulfils a social function, has a positive, biological significance. For tradition is a fabric in which all the strands are so closely woven that the destruction of one unmakes the whole. And tradition is, biologically speaking, a form of collective adaptation of a community to its surroundings. Destroy tradition, and you will deprive the collective organism of its protective shell, and give it over to the slow but inevitable process of dying out. (1922b:214)

Thus, we must understand Malinowski's gradual perception of an "undercurrent of desire" not simply in terms of the opposition of individual impulse to societal "convention, law, and morals," but also as a deepened appreciation of their grounding in the regulation of instinct by tradition. If Westermarck— and in a somewhat different fashion, Mach—had prepared him to see cultural life as founded in human instinct, it was his field experience of human sexuality (his own and that of the Trobrianders) that prepared him to see this relationship in a specifically Freudian context.

The Problem of Social Psychology

It was not until four years after he left the field that Malinowski began to read seriously in the literature of psychoanalysis. His first book-length approach to the ethnographic interpretation of his fieldwork experience has nothing in it of depth psychology and relatively little of Trobriand sexuality, beyond references to the "promiscuous free love" of native adolescents and the "ceremonial license" initiated by women during the gardening season (1922a: 53–54). Clearly a product of Malinowski's "neo-romantic" strain, its attempt to penetrate "the inner meaning and the psychological reality" of a particular native institution representing a "fundamental type of human activity" was cast in the Germanic mode of *Weltanschauung* and "spirit" (514, 517; see Strenski 1982; Thornton 1985). Despite Malinowski's preparatory avowal of "theoretical ambitions quite as far reaching" as Rivers' (MY: BM/C. Seligman 1/21/19), it is essentially pretheoretical, explicitly referring to the idea of functionalism only in its final call for "a new type of theory" (515). While its narrative structure and style play an important role in validating his general ethnographic method, the book is more a product of Malinowski's artistic than his scientific muse—as indeed his own retrospective view of it confirms (Stocking 1983; Malinowski 1937:xxii).

While Malinowski was off in Tenerife writing *Argonauts*, however, psychoanalysis was beginning to enjoy something of a fad in British intellectual life. Indeed, an editorial in *Psyche* spoke of it as "almost without parallel in the history of scientific progress" (1921 [2]:97; see also Jones 1959:230). A perusal of the contents of and the advertisements in *Psyche* suggests that it provided a forum in which the broad realm that had once been called the "spiritual" could now be explored from a variety of viewpoints by intellectuals for whom the Great War climaxed a long disillusioning of the foundation verities of the Victorian era. Along with such ventures as the *International Library of Psychology, Philosophy and Scientific Method*, it marked off a discursive space in which philosophers, psychologists, spiritualists, students of literature and language, and social scientists of various sorts could try to redefine the meaning of meaning in a number of areas—including that of human sexuality.

Among those who had by this time become interested in psychoanalysis were two of Malinowski's anthropological mentors: C. G. Seligman and W. H. R. Rivers. Rivers' career helps to place Malinowski's Freudianism in the context of the more general relationship of British anthropology and psychology (see Pear 1960). After coming to anthropology from medicine, psychiatry, and experimental psychology, Rivers continued to do some experimental neurophysiological research; but in his early anthropological work he seems to have adopted the evolutionary associationist assumptions characteristic of the "intellectualist" tradition. His turn from evolutionism to historical ethnology around 1910 involved a momentary retreat from psychological interpretation in anthropological inquiry. Rivers' brief withdrawal was a particular manifestation of a more general feeling among certain British anthropologists that the psychological assumptions of social evolutionism were inadequate to the interpretation of the growing body of more directly experienced ethnographic data. In Marett, and even more so in Radcliffe-Brown, this mood led toward Durkheimian sociology—which, because it interpreted human motivation in other than individualistic rationalistic terms, was initially seen as a form of social psychology. Somewhat problematically exemplified in the instinct theory of William McDougall (1908)—which in turn drew on the notion of "sentiment" developed by Alexander Shand (see Shand 1914) —social psychology was itself part of the reorientation in British psychological thought that led Radcliffe-Brown in 1914 to accuse Rivers of implicitly accepting psychological assumptions long since rejected by professional psychologists (Stocking 1984b; see also Langham 1981; Soffer 1978).

But if social psychology offered one alternative to the now questioned assumptions of the intellectualist tradition, another alternative was available in the new Freudian psychology of the unconscious. Within a year or so after Rivers and Brown had debated the relation of psychology and sociology, Rivers' encounter with Freud's writings in the course of treating shell-shocked soldiers at Maghull Hospital led to the reintroduction of explicit psychological

W. H. R. Rivers (seated) and his colleagues Dr. William Brown (left) and Grafton Elliott Smith (right) at the Maghull Military Hospital, 1915. (Courtesy Beth Dillingham.)

concerns into his anthropology (Rivers 1917a). Rivers would not follow Freud on the primacy of the sexual motive, and he had a much more optimistic view of the role of instinct in human evolution. But although he tended to interpret the dream work in rather immediate problem-solving terms, he was very much influenced by Freud's *Traumdeutung*, and by April 1918 had made his own attempt to show how such processes as condensation and displacement were at work in the myths and rituals of "savage peoples" (Rivers 1917b; see also 1920; 1923).

By that time, Seligman, who had joined Rivers in wartime psychiatric work, had sent Malinowski a "short account of dreams" (presumably Rivers' "Dreams and Primitive Culture") and a book on "insanity from the modern point of view" (unnamed), encouraging him to collect dreams from his Trobriand informants (MY: CGS/BM 12/2/18; see also B. Z. Seligman/BM 6/19/18). Malinowski responded that he had already a "fair idea" of Freud's theory—having read part of the *Traumdeutung*, and several ethnological articles in *Imago*—but he assured Seligman that he would indeed spend some time on dreams (MY: BM/CGS 4/29/18?). He later recalled that Seligman's letter had stimulated reflections on how the Oedipus complex might manifest itself in a matrilineal community (1927a:6), but the contemporary evidence suggests that it was some time before he turned seriously to reading the Freudian literature. Although by January 1919 he assured Seligman that he had finished reading Rivers' "Dreams and Primitive Culture," he added that he was not "very up yet" on the subject (MY: BM/CGS 1/21/19).[4]

Malinowski's circle of intellectual intimates in Australia were very much concerned with a range of issues not dissimilar to those that were to define the discourse of *Psyche*, including the interpretation of religion "in the Freudian manner" as the reflection of "imperfectly repressed infantile tendencies" (MY: E. Mayo/BM 5/10 & 11/23/18; see also Wayne 1985). But while psychological issues were at the center of Malinowski's immediate postfield readings, they seem to have been of a more general philosophical sort. He apparently attended a philosophical seminar early in 1919, in which he attempted to redefine the bases of his own scientific point of view. It was in this context that he read William James and reread Mach, and took as his own metaphysical starting point the "Absolute Value" of "naive realism" or "naive empiricism." Dividing experience into the "objective" and the "subjective," and ranging the sciences in a hierarchy (Physics, Biology, Evolution, Psychology, Sociology, Humanistic), he suggested that psychology—conceived

4. In 1927, Malinowski recalled that he had first heard of Freud at the age of eighteen, by which time he already knew that he had an "Oedipus complex"—having been very frequently distressed in adolescence by incest dreams and dreams of his father's death (MY: II-26/218, pp. 9, 10, & 28 of "Notes").

as an awareness or mastery "of our own body from within" by "the coordination of our brain & other nervous systems"—was "the basis of all other disciplines" of the subjective realm (MY: II-27/239).

Central among these was "social psychology," which was the focus of much
of his reading after he completed *Argonauts* in April 1921. Over the following
year Malinowski gave occasional lectures at the London School of Economics, where Seligman hoped to obtain for him a permanent appointment. To
reacculturate himself intellectually, Malinowski for a while immersed himself
in the current British social psychological literature, including works by Con-
way, Ginsberg, Hobhouse, McDougall, Trotter, and Wallas—as well as Bagehot
on "the cake of custom," and Gabriel Tarde, whom he described as the "starting point of the most important investigations in Social Psychology" (ML:
Box 7).

While sorting out the body of largely undated notes from the early 1920s
is a task that must await his biographer, one can get a sense of how Malinowski's viewpoint was shaped by this intellectual interaction. Although he was
considerably influenced by those currents of social psychological thought that
emphasized the biological and instinctual bases of human behavior, he was
critical of all notions that seemed to postulate the existence of supra-individual
entities like the "herd," the "crowd," or the "group mind" (see Malinowski 1921).
He insisted that the basis of all social organization was "a common stock of
ideas," which he spoke of in terms of the *Kultur* of each particular group.
Defining *Kultur* in functional terms as the "means of satisfying human needs
through general social cooperation," he argued that "the real problem of Social Psychology is for me [how] the Group through its social organisation
achieves unity of Action, which implies a definite coordination of ideas, as
well as of functions" (ML: Box 7; see also MY: II-26/221, 258). His goal—as
suggested in some undated early notes toward his never realized theoretical
book on kinship—was to solve "the fundamental Mystery of the Social": "When
we understand how this system [kinship] comes into being, how it imposes
the prototype values of future social morals: respect for authority, personal
loyalty, subordination of impulses to feelings—when we discover that, we have
really answered (in a concrete instance, but one which allows of a simple gen-
eralization by extension) the main question: how does society impress its norms
on the individual?" (ML: Box 28, "General Idea of Ksp Book").

It was in this context that he approached the writings of Sigmund Freud,
who by providing "the first concrete theory about the relation between instinctive life and social institution," offered an inspiration for the "exploration
of the difficult borderland between social tradition and social organisation"
(1923b:116)—which of course had been a central concern of Malinowski's since
his prewar encounter with the Durkheimians (see 1913a:210).

Malinowski's explorations in Freudian literature were not, however, simply a response to central issues of his theoretical concern; they had also a certain pragmatic aspect at this phase in his intellectual career, which coincided with a moment of indeterminacy in the development of British anthropology. Rivers, who for a decade had been its dominant figure, had just died in his prime, and the intellectual leadership of the discipline was there for the capturing— more easily, perhaps, by picking up one of the central strands of Rivers' own anthropological interests. The strongest immediate candidates were Elliot Smith (Rivers' literary executor) and William Perry, who from an institutional base at University College were carrying forth the banner of a diffusionism even more extreme than Rivers had adopted (see Langham 1981). Malinowski was one of several who—in different fashions—were to pursue the central Riversian problems of kinship and social organization. His initial approach, however, was to follow yet a third strand of Rivers' interests: the problem of "psycho-analysis and anthropology." As the early psychoanalytic fad among English intellectuals moved toward its crest in 1924, that issue seemed, momentarily, at the head of the intellectual agenda of British anthropology.

Malinowski as Freudian Revisionist

Appropriately, Malinowski's Freudian readings were undertaken back in Central Europe, where he spent much of the time even after he took up a regular appointment at the London School of Economics in the fall of 1924 (MY: BM/H. Carter, n.d., 1926; see also Wayne 1985:536). In July 1922, his publisher expressed satisfaction that he was going to turn to "Studies in Erotics and Psychoanalysis among Savages"—warning him not to expect much from Freud, who was "largely swayed by Ernest Jones"; early in 1923, he responded to Malinowski's inquiry regarding the firm's publications on psychoanalysis (MY: W. S. Stallybrass/BM 7/25/22, 1/9/23). At about the same time Malinowski was also getting bibliographic advice from Seligman (MY: CGS/BM 1/6/23). He seems also to have had conversations with at least one member of the Freudian inner circle in Vienna on one of the trips he took there from the modest Tyrolian villa he acquired in 1923 (ML: O. Rank/BM 2/5/34, referring to talks ten years before). He later acknowledged also a considerable debt to his wife, whom he described as "more enthusiastic of the virtues of P.A." than he had been, and to Paul Khuner, "whom I first convinced that P.A. is not all nonsense" (MY: II-26/218).

Insofar as one may judge from the surviving materials (two annotated books and several folders of manuscript notes), Malinowski approached Freud through three major works: *Three Contributions to the Theory of Sex, Introductory Lectures on Psychoanalysis* (both in the German editions of 1922), and *Totem and Taboo* (in the English translation of 1919). Despite Seligman's interest in dreams,

Bronislaw Malinowski and his wife Elsie Malinowska with their three daughters (left to right), Jozefa, Wanda, and Helena, near their villa in Oberbozen (Soprabolzano) in the Dolomite Alps. (Courtesy Helena Wayne Malinowska.)

it was primarily Freud's libido theory that engaged Malinowski's attention. From the beginning, he seems to have been critical on a number of issues. Although he later recalled that his favorable "bias" toward psychoanalysis was due to its "honest and direct manner" in regard to sexual matters (MY: II-26/218), he felt that Freud construed libido in too narrowly sexual terms: "his whole *problem-stellung* is futile." According to Malinowski, "a theory of sexuality must be based on [a] sound view of instinct"—which must include not only the sexual, but also other biologically based needs (notably the nutritional) (MSC: Freud 1922a, p. 346). On the other hand, if he wanted to "push back Freud's boundaries" to include a fuller range of instincts, Malinowski felt that Freud "still embraced an enormous field and his contribution [was] was most valuable" (MY: I-10/714). And his early reading of *Totem and Taboo* evinces surprisingly little of the criticism that he was later to develop. In commenting on Freud's assumption of a "mass psyche," he suggested merely that Freud's reasoning did not "entail this assumption"—explaining its adoption by the fact that Freud was "at sea regarding psychosociological method." Similarly, while accepting the resemblance of taboo to compulsion neurosis, Malinowski added: "I think he does not sufficiently lay stress on the dynamic value of social atmosphere in belief" (MY: II-26/217).

Late in 1923 Malinowski stepped forward as prospective Freudian revisionist, seeking simultaneously to apply psychoanalytic concepts to anthropology and to modify them in the light of ethnographic evidence. Although the preceding May he had submitted some of the opening chapters of his proposed book to his "Viennese friends," who felt they would "interest the public there," his early contributions in fact appeared in *Psyche*. The first was essentially a straightforward ethnographic account of beliefs about procreation and parenthood in the matrilineal Trobriands (later republished virtually without change as *The Father in Primitive Psychology* [1927b] and as chapter 7 of *The Sexual Life of Savages* [1929]—of which it was already projected as a part). The theoretical implications of its title—"The Psychology of Sex and the Foundations of Kinship in Primitive Societies"—were no more than hinted at in the opening and closing paragraphs, where Malinowski noted "the dependence of social organisation in a given society upon the ideas, beliefs and sentiments current there," and affirmed his conviction that the "ignorance of paternity" he had found among the Trobrianders was "an original feature of primitive psychology, and that in all speculations about the origins of Marriage and the Evolution of Sexual Customs, we must bear in mind this fundamental ignorance" (1923a:98, 128; see also 1916).

The significance of this data for Freudian theory was suggested, however, in a letter on "Psycho-Analysis and Anthropology" the following month in *Nature*: "when we come to examine in detail the original constitution of the human family—not in any hypothetical primeval form, but as we find it in actual observation among present day savages," we find not the "tyrannical and ferocious father" of *Totem and Taboo*, but a situation in which "the two elements decisive for psycho-analysis, the repressive authority and the severing taboo, are 'displaced,' distributed in a manner different from that in the patriarchal family." Assuming that "Freud's general theory [was] correct," Malinowski argued that "the repressed wish formation ought to [and did] receive a shape different from the Oedipus complex" (1923b:115–16).

That possibility was pursued more systematically in a second article in *Psyche* published in April 1924—at a point when the relations of "Psycho-Analysis and Anthropology" had already become matters for discussion before the Royal Anthropological Institute (Jones 1924a; Seligman 1924). The article was clearly written from an outsider's perspective, with Malinowski glossing the notion of "complex" in the idiom of Shandian "sentiment" (1924a:294, 327, 330). But it is also clearly intended as a contribution to psychoanalytic theory, which by emphasizing the "libidinous nature" of primitive man, had "given the right foundation to primitive psychology" (296). Distinguishing between the psychological, the biological, and the sociological aspect of Freudian thought, Malinowski largely accepted the first, was somewhat critical of the second, and saw the third as a field still untouched (save for some suggestive hints in J. C. Flugel's *Psycho-Analytic Study of the Family* [1921]). Although he presented his contribution as simply a sociological "Introduction" and "Epilogue" to the "psychological treatment of the nuclear complex," Malinowski's goal was quite ambitious: it was in fact no less than to confront "the main task of psycho-analytic theory," by showing how the formation of the "nuclear complex" would vary with the varying "constitution of the family" in different forms of society (294–95), as well as within the various social strata of our own society (300). Along the way, he hoped to offer a more precise scheme of ontogenetic stages—since although it had been one of the "chief merits" of psychoanalysis to show the "stratification of the human mind, and its rough correspondence to the stages in the child's development," not even Freud's *Three Contributions* had clearly defined those "successive stages" (300–301).

In the body of the article, Malinowski traced the formation of the nuclear complex in "the two most radically different types of family known to empirical observation"—the "matrilineal family" of the Trobriands and the "patriarchal Family of modern civilisation" (with occasional asides on the peasantry and working classes)—through the stages of infancy, babyhood, childhood, and adolescence (1924a:297, 301). Although his view of the development of the European Oedipus complex did "not differ to any extent" from that of psychoanalysis, the "interplay of biological impulse and social rule" was quite different in the Trobriands. Whereas "the institution of father-right crosses and represses a number of natural impulses and inclinations," the "social arrangements of Trobriand matriliny" were "in almost complete harmony with the biological course of development" (327–28). The Trobrianders, however, paid a cultural evolutionary price: whereas the latency period of the European upper classes represented "the triumph of other cultural and social interests over sexuality," the harmonious continuity of sexual development among "savages" was "destructive culturally," since genital sexuality, early and easily established "foremost among the child's interests, [was] never to be dislodged again" (329). While there was no friction between the father and the son, and "all the infantile craving of the child for its mother" gradually spent itself "in a natural spontaneous manner," the Trobriand child was nevertheless eventually "submitted to a system of repressions and taboos"—in the form of the matriarchal authority of his mother's brother and the strongly asserted prohibition of all contact with his sister, who became, respectively, the objects of a young man's homicidal and incestuous wishes (329–30). Having thus discovered for the first time a hitherto unsuspected alternative "type of nuclear complex," Malinowski described his contribution as "a notable confirmation of the main tenet of Freudian psychology." The major revision required was "to draw more systematically the correlation between biological and social influences; not to assume the universal existence of the Oedipus-complex, but, in studying every type of civilisation, to establish the special complex which pertains to it" (331).

Having offered an account of "the sociological nature of family influences," Malinowski turned to the "analysis of the consequences for society of the nuclear complex" (1924a:294) in an article on "Complex and Myth in Mother-Right" which appeared in *Psyche* the following January. He began with a few comments on the influence of childrearing on adult personality, contrasting the "hearty" Trobrianders with the "community of neurasthenics" he had found in the more sexually repressive Amphletts. He then discussed the expression of the matrilineal complex in "the social culture and organisation" of the Trobrianders, looking specifically at their dreams, their folklore, and their mythology. Eschewing "roundabout or symbolic interpretations"—which he granted might facilitate a more traditional Freudian gloss—he argued that all these cultural forms clearly reflected the matriarchal complex. But although he insisted that "the foundations of psycho-analytic explanations of myth we have in no way shaken," a final comment rejecting the interpretation of myth as "the secular dream of the race" seems to foreshadow the more pragmatic view of the relation of myth to social organization he was to elaborate in his Frazer lecture later that year (1925a:212, 216; see also 1925b).

It may be that in writing this Malinowski was already aware of the response his attempt to revise Freudian theory had elicited from the guardians of orthodoxy. If ever there was a propitious moment in the early history of psychoanalysis to call into question the Oedipus complex, 1924 was not that time. One of the major rifts in the movement was just beginning to be manifest: Otto Rank's *The Trauma of Birth* (1924)—which Malinowski had cited, and to which he may have been referred by Rank himself—had raised the possibility that "all mental conflicts concerned the relation of the child to its mother, and that what appeared to be conflicts with the father, including the Oedipus complex, were but a mask for the essential ones concerning birth" (Jones 1957:III, 58; see also Taft 1958). Rank had developed his argument in phylogenetic as well as ontogenetic terms, and would surely have regarded Malinowski's argument as ethnographic validation (Karpf 1953:88). As director of the Freudian publishing house in Vienna, Rank must have played a role in the reprinting of Malinowski's April article (along with Jones's February lecture) in *Imago*, and as a separate publication of the *Internationaler Psychoanalytischer Verlag*, under the somewhat more pointed title "The Matriarchical Family and the Oedipus Complex" (Malinowski 1924b). It was in this context that Freud's Lord Lieutenant in England took up the prob-

lem of "Mother-Right and the Sexual Ignorance of Savages" in November of
that year (Jones 1924b).

Although describing Malinowski as a fieldworker of "remarkable acumen"
whose observations inspired "great confidence" (1924b:153–54), Ernest Jones
wondered if savage ignorance of paternity was "after all so genuine and complete as it would appear" (157)—suggesting that the "tendentious denial of paternal procreation" served the "function of unloading affect in a relationship
where it might have unpleasant consequences and depositing it at a safer distance" (162–65). Malinowski's suggestion that the nuclear family complex might
vary with family structure, while ingenious and even plausible on the surface,
was—for those with a more "intimate knowledge of the unconscious"—in fact
the opposite of the truth. The matrilineal system with its avunculate complex arose "as a mode of defense against the primordial Oedipus tendencies"—
which were, for the psychoanalyst, not a "late product," but the *fons et origo*
(169–70). Far from forcing a revision in Freudian theory, Malinowski's apparent ethnographic exception merely proved the universal oedipal rule.

Instinct and Culture

"Psychoanalysis and Anthropology" was one of a number of contributions
Malinowski offered to theory in anthropology in the middle 1920s. With the
beginning of his regular teaching at L.S.E., he stepped forth as candidate for
the leadership of anthropology in a moment of "acute crisis." And he did so,
not as an advocate of the "new anthropology"—the diffusionism of Smith and
Perry—but as one whose "theoretical bias makes him remain faithful to the
old school" (1924c:299–300). Indeed, a year earlier he had written a highly
laudatory review of the new one-volume edition of Frazer's *Golden Bough*—
although rather from the viewpoint of its "empirical fecundity" than its specific
evolutionary argument (1923c). Granting that "the principle of evolution" might
require modification, Malinowski made a bow to the importance of taking
into consideration "historically established facts" (1924c)—but in the context
of having earlier insisted that "the obvious, common-sense and essentially scientific way of proceeding is to get firm hold of the fundamental aspects of
human nature" so that we could analyze "each fact as we meet it" (1922c:120).

The theme that draws together Malinowski's works of the middle 1920s,
however, is not simply the problem of human nature per se, but also that
of its modification by culture and its subjection to the forces of social cohe-
sion. It was to these large questions, very much in the evolutionary tradition,
that Malinowski applied the rich empirical data gathered by the ethnographic
method he had validated in *Argonauts*—the work that had thrust him to the
center of the anthropological stage. And it was in the course of their con-

sideration that he moved toward the definition of his "functional anthropology" (1926c).

At the very beginning of this burst of creativity, Malinowski had announced a small book "on certain questions of interest to Psycho-analysis" (1924a:293), and almost until he penned the preface of Sex and Repression in Savage Society in February 1927, he had in mind a more ambitious volume evaluating Freudian theory from an anthropological perspective—several of the sheaf of notes summarized by a ten-part outline for such a work are dated that January (MY: II-26/218). At the last minute, he settled for republication of the two earlier articles, followed by two new ones responding to Jones's critique—a four-part pattern that in fact duplicated that of Totem and Taboo, which was now the focus of his attention, and from a much more critical point of view.

The first new essay carried somewhat further a range of criticisms A. L. Kroeber (whom Malinowski had met while in the United States in 1926) had first raised in 1920 (Kroeber 1920). The central point was that Freud's argument was circular: that the origin of culture in the aftermath of the primal parricide in fact assumed the prior existence of culture, since the guilt feelings that led to the imposition of totemic sacrifice and sexual taboo must themselves have been "imposed upon man by culture" (1927a:165). "The actual transition from the state of nature into that of culture was not done by one leap" but was a "very laborious and very slow process achieved in a cumulative manner by infinitely many, infinitely small steps integrated over enormous stretches of time" (165–66).

Because all reasoning as to origins had to be based on processes observable in the present, Malinowski's own discussion of that transition was cast in somewhat discontinuous terms. In contrast to Freud, he found his beginning not in the deed, but the need: an adequate understanding of culture could be founded only on an adequate understanding of the role of instinct in man. From his first reading of Freud, Malinowski had regarded libido theory as a powerful instrument too narrowly conceived, and he had read widely on the problem of instinct (MY: II-26/218, 223). Much of his later argument had already been limned in 1924, in a review of Forel on the social world of ants and men, in which Malinowski had argued the "plasticity" of human instincts in the "secondary milieu" of culture (1924d). But his fully elaborated approach to the problem was cast within a developmental framework that was, broadly, Freudian; and if the primacy that Malinowski gave to the nuclear family as "the starting point of all human organization" (1927a:24) could be traced to Westermarck, it was his reading of Freud that had made critically problematic precisely what Westermarck took for granted: the repression of incestual impulses (cf. Malinowski 1922c; 1927a:244). If he now disagreed more sharply with Freud on the issue of infantile sexuality (1927a:36), the problem of incestuous sexuality was nonetheless central to the genesis of culture—in its socially constraining, as opposed to its individually creative, aspect. Drawing evidence from Havelock Ellis on sexual periodicity in animal and man (193, 196), Malinowski saw sexuality as "the original sin of man." Because it was the "most difficult to control" of all human instincts, its channeling was essential to "the establishment of the first foundations of culture." Without the incest taboo, "at maturity we would witness the breaking up of the family, hence complete social chaos and an impossibility of continuing cultural tradition" (251–52).

The repression of incestuous sexuality, however, was only one of two fundamental problems of cultural continuity; the other "main peril of humanity," the "revolt against authority," had also to be dealt with if the "new type of human bond" for which there was "no prototype in the animal kingdom" was to be maintained (1927a:223–24). Although Malinowski insisted on the instinctual basis of paternal love (just as he insisted on the cultural conditioning of maternal love), he saw its transformation into a "principle of force, of distance, of pursuit of ambition and of authority" as culturally essential (257). Furthermore, it is worth noting that despite his insistence that "male authority is not necessarily that of the father" (258), he in fact tended to see the supercession of male tenderness by male coercion in phylogenetic evolutionary as well as ontogenetic familial terms. Mother-right, in which the two principles were embodied in two different men, was a "more useful principle of social organization" at a "level of human organization where kinship plays a paramount sociological part"; but "as culture advances . . . the principle of father-right naturally becomes dominant" (271–72).

Rebuffed by the most loyal guardian of Freudian orthodoxy, Malinowski abandoned the revisionary hopes he seems at first to have entertained for psychoanalysis. The republished texts of his earlier essays contain several footnotes highlighting the shift (as well as reflecting his more intimate experience of English and American family life, which he now marked off as a distinct, and less patriarchal, variant of the general European model [1927a:239–46]). His unpublished notes contain a number of more explicit disavowals: he was not and never had been an adherent of psychoanalysis; he had neither been analyzed nor practiced analysis; he rejected 90 to 95 percent of its doctrine, much of which he professed not to understand; he wished that he had not used psychoanalytic terminology in the first place—and indeed, he expended considerable effort in *Sex and Repression* in a more systematic recasting of the ideas of complex and repression into the conceptual idiom of Shandian sentiment (MY: II-26/218; cf. 1927a:175–78, 240–42). But despite all of this distancing, and despite all of the modification of specific Freudian doctrine, he ended *Sex and Repression* by noting that throughout he had been dealing "with the central problems of psycho-analysis," and that his conclusions were "not entirely subversive of psycho-analytic doctrine"—especially if it were "taken as an inspiration and a working hypothesis and not as a system of dogmatic tenets" (277–79).

The Passing of the Psychoanalytic Moment in British Social Anthropology

There was another side of Malinowski's concern in this period with the dynamics of instinct and culture: a more individual actor-oriented view, in which the instinct served was that of self-preservation rather than reproduction, and the approach was often more at the level of conscious pragmatic purpose. Here the pre-Freudian (and indeed prewar) influences were more in evidence, although there was sometimes a strong Freudian element, when "the repressive forces of law and morality are broken by the repressed passions" (1925b:199–200)—as in the last half of *Crime and Custom* (1926b). In the longer run, this more Machian side of Malinowski came again to the forefront (see 1931). While the retrospective systematization of his viewpoint in *A Scientific Theory of Culture* was recognizably derivative from the last essay of *Sex and Repression*, "reproduction" was now only one of eight "basic needs," most of them clearly of a self-preservational character ("metabolism," "safety," "growth," etc.) (1944: 91). The psychological assumptions, too, had changed. Shand had disappeared entirely, and Freud was given rather brief acknowledgment—their place taken by the stimulus response psychology of the behaviorists at Yale, where Malinowski spent the last months of his life (22–23, 133).

This fading of Freud from the forefront of functionalist theory may be placed in several contexts. Already in 1927, Malinowski had felt that the fad of psychoanalysis was passing, and hoped that what was suggestive in it might somehow "merge" with mainstream social science (MY: II-26/218). But despite his rebuff by the guardians of Freudian orthodoxy, he made a second offer of interdisciplinary cooperation. Acknowledging the help anthropology had received from "the psychoanalytic school," he suggested in the last paragraph of *Sex and Repression* that "it would be a great pity" if psychoanalysts "refused to collaborate, to accept what is offered in good faith from a field where, after all, they cannot be at home" (1927a:238). As it happened, the most important early attempt at such domestication—Roheim's researches in Australia—was carried on in rather doctrinaire Freudian terms; the development of a more flexible collaborative approach was a slightly later contribution of neo-Freudians in the United States (Wallace 1983:159–61, 199; cf. Manson, in this volume). Although Malinowski briefly noted the possibility of future "fruitful collaboration" in *A Scientific Theory of Culture* (1944:22), by that time the moment of his own serious involvement with psychoanalysis had passed.[5]

5. Malinowski's work on Trobriand sexuality seems to have had some influence on Wilhelm

If Malinowski is more often remembered as the person who "disproved" (or failed to disprove) the universality of the Oedipus complex than as a contributor to "Neo-Freudian" psychoanalytic anthropology (Lasswell 1931; Fine 1979:189, 466; Wallace 1983:138–40; cf. Spiro 1982), it is also because he himself did not systematically pursue the issues he had raised in the 1920s. Although his writings on problems of sexuality, marriage, and kinship made him the outstanding spokesman for anthropology on major issues of contemporary popular intellectual concern (Lyons & Lyons n.d.), Malinowski did not produce a major theoretical statement on these topics to sustain his authoritative position on them within the discipline itself. No doubt this is to be explained in part by the pragmatic attitude to theory exemplified in his praise of Westermarck for refusing "to construct out of meagre and insufficient evidence a vast, hypothetical building, through the narrow windows of which we would have to gaze upon reality, and see only as much of it as they allow" (1922c:120). But there is also clearly a retreat even from more limited theoretical statements in this area.

Malinowski's first announcement of *The Sexual Life of Savages* suggested that it would include "a theoretical analysis of Primitive Erotics" (1923a:98); subsequent statements separated the ethnographic presentation from two theoretical contributions, one on psychoanalysis and one that was to have been entitled *The Psychology of Kinship* (1924a:293). The former appeared only in truncated form; the latter survives only as a series of outlines, notes, and chapter drafts in his manuscripts. While their detailed analysis must await a biographer, the earliest outline of "the theoretical part of [the] sex book as conceived in 1922–23 in Oberbosen" clearly reflects Malinowski's psychoanalytic preoccupation at that time; in the later outlines, he is preoccupied rather with "the puzzles of the classificatory system" (ML: Box 7). And whereas he had seen himself as contributing constructively to a psychoanalytically oriented theory of kinship, his attitude to the systematic study of kinship terminology in the tradition of Morgan/Rivers/Radcliffe-Brown was fundamentally unsympathetic. His notes are full of derogatory references to "kinship algebra," "the pseudomathematics of kinship," and the "classificatory obsession." For a time Malinowski saw himself in a united front with Radcliffe-Brown for functional anthropology, but he was fundamentally at odds with him on this issue. Both men had in the early 1920s used an "extensionist" vocabulary, but Malinowski, like Meyer Fortes after him, recognized a difference between his own extensionism and that of Radcliffe-Brown—who "pre-

Reich (Sharaf 1983:138, 197–98, 207). Mediated by Reich, it may also have had an influence on a more conventional neo-Freudian, Abram Kardiner (see Manson, in this volume). The possibility of a more general impact of his work on the emergence of neo-Freudianism remains obscured by the image—both contemporary and subsequent—of Malinowski as the putative disprover of the universality of the Oedipus complex.

sents us with the fait accompli, but not with the process of accomplishment" (ML: n.d.; see also 1930). Whether or not one accepts Fortes' view that Malinowski could not write his kinship book because "his theoretical premises ran counter to those on which any analytical study of . . . kinship must be based" (1957:162), it is clear that by the end of the 1920s Radcliffe-Brown had successfully claimed Rivers' place as the leading British student of such problems. By 1932, Malinowski had effectively withdrawn from the field of kinship study, turning his attention to the ethnography of Trobriand agriculture and issues of cultural change—problems much more in the tradition of Mach than of Freud (see Stocking 1984b).

Beyond the resistance of Freudians and the retreat of Malinowski from the field of kinship, the fading of Freud from functionalist anthropology must be seen against the more general background of the reception of psychoanalysis by British anthropologists. Despite the criticisms of Kroeber and others, psychoanalysis became an important undercurrent to mainstream anthropology in the United States, frequently breaking to the surface in writings on culture and personality (see Mark 1968). But in Britain, the response was much more contained. Other than Malinowski, the most important British figure to come under Freudian influence was Rivers. Perhaps because his somewhat delibidinized psychoanalytic ideas were never really integrated with his social organizational or historical concerns, Rivers left no coherent intellectual estate to British anthropology after his death in 1922. For a moment, it seemed as if the psychoanalytic portion might be picked up, especially given the interest of both the Seligmans. Early 1924 saw two addresses to the Royal Anthropological Institute on psychoanalytic topics: Seligman's presidential address "Anthropology and Psychology," and Jones's lecture on "Psycho-analysis and Anthropology." However, Seligman's psychoanalytic interest seems never to have gone beyond a rather superficial sort of dream interpretation, which at this point was cast in Jungian rather than Freudian terms. And aside from Malinowski, the main response to Jones seems to have been Hocart's impeccably scholarly, but fundamentally unsympathetic, questioning of specific detail from an historical viewpoint (1925). As for the man with whom the immediate future lay, Radcliffe-Brown (responding critically to the first half of *Sex and Repression*) insisted in 1927 that all that the Freudians had written on myth was "valueless." Although he later had contact with psychoanalysts in Chicago, the Freudian influences that have been traced in Radcliffe-Brownian social anthropology (in the area of avoidance customs, joking relations, and ceremonial role reversals) seem more obviously derivative from his underlying Durkheimian concerns (Barnes 1959; see also Stocking 1984a).

It is of course possible that closer biographical study will cast light on less obvious psychoanalytic influences. In the case of the archetypical Radcliffe-Brownian, Meyer Fortes, a subterranean Freudian current did in fact surface later in his career. Perhaps because he came to anthropology in the 1920s from psychology, where he had been close to J. C. Flugel, one of the leading British Freudians (Fortes 1978), Fortes had the keenest appreciation of the importance of Freud in the development of Malinowski's thought. In contrast to other writers, Fortes saw clearly that "psycho-analysis was the light by which he was able to make a new synthesis of his ideas and experiences" (1957:167–69).

Freud was not the only source for an "extensionist" approach to kinship that privileged the initial situation and ontogenetic development of individual actors in the derivation of kinship systems. But it was surely Malinowski's creative interaction with Freud, in the context of his fieldwork experience, that firmly fixed the "genetic conceptualization" as 'the first principle of [his] kinship theory" (ML: n.d.). And although "ambivalence" was in fact listed among the more dubious Freudian concepts in one of Malinowski's several summary evaluational notes, there is no doubt that the Oedipus complex, as formulated by Freud and as he had experienced it in his own life, was a powerful influence on the way Malinowski formulated his genetic conceptualization. More generally, the notion of "repression"—which Malinowski had early queried from the point of view of its social process—was central to his view of culture as both the shaper of human instinctual urges and as "a seething mixture of conflicting principles" (1926b:121) Although Malinowski's summary notes show him critical of each of the major components of Freudian theory—the libido, the unconscious, infantile sexuality, and ontogenetic development—in each case he also found something of value. And despite his rejection of specific concepts (the censor, the ego, etc.), other notes make clear that the "bad" in Freudian theory was for him more than balanced by the "good": psychoanalysis had provided a "concrete" and "dynamic" psychology which, by focusing on sexuality and emphasizing the importance of early experience in the evolution of the individual, made possible the linking of psychology with sociology and the science of culture (MY: II-26/218).

Despite his intellectual withdrawal from Freudian theory, Malinowski continued to maintain personal contact with figures in the world of psychoanalysis into the 1930s. Flugel remained one of his intimates; and during a stay with his family in the south of France in 1932, he established a close friendship with Princess Marie Bonaparte, with whom he corresponded over the next few years, often about matters relating to psychoanalysis and anthropology (Bertin 1932:186). Through Princess Marie, he became briefly involved in helping Geza Roheim settle in the United States, and later he made efforts on behalf of Wilhelm Reich in England. It was apparently as a result of conversations with Princess Marie after Freud's arrival in London that he became involved in an anti-climactic epilogue to his association with psychoanalysis: an attempt to win a Nobel prize for its founder. Because the prize in medicine was decided in Stockholm, where medical opinion was hostile, the goal was the Nobel Peace Prize, which was decided in Oslo, where Princess Marie had contact with the circle of the royal court (MY: BM/MB 9/6/38). Although Princess Marie thought that Freud might feel the Peace Prize inappropriate (MY: MB/BM 9/15/38), the chairman of the Peace Prize committee—a personal friend of Malinowski's—thought it "within the limits of possibility" (MY: BM/E. Jones 9/29/38). Previously, Freud had discouraged any such efforts on his behalf (Jones 1957:III, 233–34). Jones, however, felt that a case for the Peace Prize could be made on the grounds that there could be "no stable security until we have far more knowledge of the explosive psychological forces" Freud had been the first to investigate"—suggesting that "it would certainly brighten his last years, and also help him financially, if you were able to succeed in your laudable aim" (MY: Jones/BM 9/30/38). Four days later—after the outbreak of another war seemed to have been forestalled by the Munich Pact—Jones had second thoughts: "it looks to me . . . as though the next Peace Prize is heavily booked, namely for Chamberlain" (MY: EJ/BM 10/1/38). And there the matter ended—an appropriately ambiguous conclusion for an intellectual relationship that had always been ambivalent.

Acknowledgments

I am indebted to Edward Martinek for his translation of Malinowski's doctoral dissertation, and to Krzysztof Brozi and Andrzej Paluch for helping to place it in context. David Goodman wrote an interesting seminar paper on the "discursive space" of the psychoanalytic moment in England, and David Koester helped in various ways with research. I am especially grateful to Dr. George Moraitis, of the Chicago Psychoanalytic Institute, who joined me in rereading Malinowski's *Diary* and other documents as part of his own investigation of the nature of scholarly creativity, and to my colleague Raymond Fogelson, who co-taught a course on "Psychoanalysis and Anthropology." An earlier version of the section on "The Freudianism of Fieldwork Experience" was previously incorporated into an unpublished paper, "Sex and Aggression in Savage Society," first presented in 1972 at the University of Texas, and on several occasions since. In its present form, this paper was first presented at the Malinowski Centenary Conference ("Rationality and Rationales") of the Association of Social Anthropologists, held at the London School of Economics, April 9–13, 1984—where I found the comments of Ernest Gellner particularly helpful. I would also like to thank the librarians and archivists who have facilitated this project.

References Cited

Barnes, J. 1959. Anthropology after Freud. *Australasian J. Philos.* 13:14–27.
Bertin C. 1982. *Marie Bonaparte: A life.* New York.

Durkheim, E. 1912. *The elementary forms of the religious life.* Trans. J. Swain. New York (1965).

Evans-Pritchard, E. E. 1933. The intellectualist (English) interpretation of magic. *Bul. Fac. Arts, Cairo* 1:1–21.

Fine, R. 1979. *A history of psychoanalysis.* New York.

Firth, R. 1957a. Malinowski as scientist and man. In Firth 1957c:1–14.

———. 1957b. The place of Malinowski in the history of economic anthropology. In Firth 1957c:209–28.

———, ed. 1957c. *Man and culture: An evaluation of the work of Bronislaw Malinowski.* New York.

———. 1981. Bronislaw Malinowski. In *Totems and teachers: Perspectives on the history of anthropology,* ed. S. Silverman, 103–37. New York.

Flugel, J. C. 1921. *The psycho-analytic study of the family.* London (1939).

Fortes, M. 1957. Malinowski and the study of kinship. In Firth 1957c:157–88.

———. 1978. An anthropologist's apprenticeship. *Ann. Rev. Anth.* 7:1–30.

Frazer, J. G. 1900. *The golden bough: A study in magic and religion.* 2d ed. 3 vols. London.

———. 1909. *Psyche's task.* London.

———. 1910. *Totemism and exogamy.* 4 vols. London (1968).

Freud, S. 1919. *Totem and taboo.* Trans. A. A. Brill. London.

———. 1922a. *Drei Abhandlungen zur Sexualtheorie.* 5th ed. Leipzig.

———. 1922b. *Vorlesungen zur Einführung in die Psychoanalyse.* 4th ed. Leipzig.

Gerould, D. 1981. *Witkacy: Stanislaw Ignacy Witkiewicz as an imaginative writer.* Seattle.

Hiebert, E. 1976. Introduction. In Mach 1905 (1976):xi–xxx.

Hocart, A. M. 1925. Psycho-analysis and anthropology. *Man* 25:14–15, 183–84.

James, W. 1973. The anthropologist as reluctant imperialist. In *Anthropology and the colonial encounter,* ed. T. Asad, 41–70. London.

Janik, A., & S. Toulmin. 1973. *Wittgenstein's Vienna.* New York.

Jones, E. 1924a. Psycho-analysis and anthropology. In Jones 1974:II, 114–44.

———. 1924b. Mother-right and the sexual ignorance of savages. In Jones 1974:II, 145–73.

———. 1957. *The life and work of Sigmund Freud.* 3 vols. New York.

———. 1959. *Free associations: Memories of a psycho-analyst.* New York.

———. 1974. *Psycho-myth, psycho-history: Essays in applied psychoanalysis.* 2 vols. New York.

Karpf, F. B. 1953. *The psychology and psychotherapy of Otto Rank.* New York.

Kroeber, A. L. 1920. *Totem and taboo:* An ethnologic psychoanalysis. *Am. Anth.* 22: 48–55.

Langham, I. 1981. *The building of British social anthropology: W. H. R. Rivers and his Cambridge disciples in the development of kinship studies, 1898–1931.* Dordrecht.

Lasswell, H. 1931. A hypothesis rooted in the preconceptions of a single civilization tested by Bronislaw Malinowski. In *Methods in social science,* ed. S. Rice, 480–88. Chicago.

Leach, E. 1957. The epistemological background to Malinowski's empiricism. In Firth 1957c:119–38.

Lyons, A. P. & H. D. Lyons. n.d. Savage sexuality and secular morality: Malinowski, Ellis, Russell. Wilfred Laurier Univ. Res. Pap. Ser. No. 8351. Waterloo, Ont.

Mach, E. 1895. *Popular scientific lectures.* Trans. T. J. McCormack. Chicago.
———. 1905. *Knowledge and error: Sketches on the psychology of inquiry.* Trans. T. J. Mc-
Cormack & P. Foulkes. Dordrecht (1976).
———. 1906. *The analysis of sensations and the relation of the physical to the psychical.*
Intro. by T. Szasz. New York (1959).
Malinowski, B. 1908. O zasadzie ekonomii myślenia [On the principle of the economy
of thought]. Trans. E. Martinek. Diss. Ms. Jagiellonian Univ. Archives.
———. 1912. The economic aspect of the Intichiuma ceremonies. In *Festkrift tillegnad
Edvard Westermarck*, 81–108. Helsinki.
———. 1913a. *The family among the Australian aborigines.* New York (1963).
———. 1913b. Elementary forms of religious life. In Malinowski 1962:282–88.
———. 1914. A fundamental problem of religious sociology. In Malinowski 1962:266–
67.
———. 1915. *Wierzenia pierwotne i formy ustroju społecznego* [Primitive beliefs and forms
of social organization]. Polish Acad. Sci., Cracow.
———. 1916. Baloma: Spirits of the dead in the Trobriand Islands. In Malinowski
1948:149–274.
———. 1918. [Evidence by Malinowski, October 27, 1916]. In *British and Australian
trade in the South Pacific* (Rept. No. 66, F 13489, Parl. Commonwealth Aust.), 107–8.
———. 1921. Review of W. McDougall, *The group mind. Man* 21:106–9.
———. 1922a. *Argonauts of the western Pacific.* New York (1961).
———. 1922b. Ethnology and the study of society. *Economica* 2:208–19.
———. 1922c. Sexual life and marriage among primitive mankind. In Malinowski
1962:117–22.
———. 1923a. The psychology of sex and the foundations of kinship in primitive
societies. *Psyche* 4:98–128.
———. 1923b. Psycho-analysis and anthropology. In Malinowski 1962:114–16.
———. 1923c. Science and superstition of primitive mankind. In Malinowski 1962:
268–74.
———. 1924a. Psychoanalysis and anthropology. *Psyche* 4:293–332.
———. 1924b. Mütterrechtliche Familie und Oedipus-komplex: Eine psycho-analytische
Studie. *Imago* 10 (2/3).
———. 1924c. New and old anthropology. *Nature* 113:299–301.
———. 1924d. Instinct and culture in human and animal societies. *Nature* 114:79–82.
———. 1925a. Magic, science and religion. In Malinowski 1948:17–92.
———. 1925b. Complex and myth in mother-right. *Psyche* 5:194–216.
———. 1926a. Myth in primitive psychology. In Malinowski 1948:93–148.
———. 1926b. *Crime and custom in savage society.* Paterson, N.J. (1964).
———. 1926c. Anthropology. *Encyc. Brit.* 1:131–40.
———. 1927a. *Sex and repression in savage society.* Cleveland (1965).
———. 1927b. *The father in primitive psychology.* New York. (1966).
———. 1929. *The sexual life of savages in north-western Melanesia: An ethnographic account of courtship, marriage and family life among the natives of the Trobriand Islands,
British New Guinea.* New York (n.d.).
———. 1930. Kinship. *Man* 30:19–29.
———. 1931. Culture. *Encyc. Soc. Scis.* 4:621–45.

———. 1937. Foreword. In *Coming into being among the Australian Aborigines*, by M. F. Ashley-Montagu, xix–xxxv. London.

———. 1944. *A Scientific theory of culture and other essays*. New York (1960).

———. 1948. *Magic, science, and religion, and other essays*. Garden City, N.Y. (1954).

———. 1962. *Sex, culture and myth*. New York.

———. 1967. *A diary in the strict sense of the term*. Trans. N. Guterman. New York.

Marett, R. R. 1908a. *The threshold of religion*. London.

———. 1908b. A sociological view of comparative religion. *Soc. Rev.* 1:48–60.

McDougall, W. 1908. *An introduction to social psychology*. London.

Mark, J. 1968. The impact of Freud on American cultural anthropology, 1909–1945. Doct. diss., Harvard Univ.

ML. See under Manuscript Sources.

MSC. See under Manuscript Sources.

MY. See under Manuscript Sources.

Paluch, A. K. 1981. The Polish background of Malinowski's work. *Man* 16:276–85.

Pear, T. H. 1960. Some early relations between English ethnologists and psychologists. *J. Roy. Anth. Inst.* 90:227–37.

Rank, O. 1924. *The trauma of birth*. London (1929).

Rivers, W. H. R. 1917a. Freud's psychology of the unconscious. *Lancet* 95:912–14.

———. 1917b. Dreams and primitive culture. *Bul. John Rylands Library* 4.

———. 1920. *Instinct and the unconscious*. Cambridge.

———. 1923. *Conflict and dream*. London.

Schorske, C. E. 1980. *Fin-de-siècle Vienna: Politics and culture*. New York.

Seligman, C. G. 1924. Anthropology and psychology: A study of some points of contact. *J. Roy. Anth. Inst.* 54:13–46.

Shand, A. F. 1914. *The foundations of character: Being a study of the tendencies of the emotions and sentiments*. London.

Sharaf, M. 1983. *Fury on earth: A biography of Wilhelm Reich*. New York.

Soffer, R. N. 1978. *Ethics and society in England: The revolution in the social sciences, 1870–1914*. Berkeley.

Spiro, M. E. 1982. *Oedipus in the Trobriands*. Chicago.

Śrdniawa, B. 1981. The anthropologist as a young physicist: Bronislaw Malinowski's apprenticeship. *Isis* 72:613–19.

Stocking, G. W., Jr. 1968. Empathy and antipathy in the heart of darkness. *J. Hist. Behav. Scis.* 4:189–94.

———. 1983. The ethnographer's magic: Fieldwork in British anthropology from Tylor to Malinowski. *HOA* 1:70–120.

———, ed. 1984a. Dr. Durkheim and Mr. Brown: Comparative sociology at Cambridge, 1910. *HOA* 2:106–30.

———. 1984b. Radcliffe-Brown and British social anthropology. *HOA* 2:131–91.

———. 1985. Philanthropoids and vanishing cultures: Rockefeller funding and the end of the museum era in Anglo-American anthropology. *HOA* 3:112–46.

———. 1986. *Victorian anthropology*. New York.

Strenski, I. 1982. Malinowski: Second positivism, second romanticism. *Man* 17:266–71.

Stroup, T. 1984. Edward Westermarck: A reappraisal. *Man* 19:575–92.

Symmons-Symonolewicz, K. 1959. Bronislaw Malinowski: Formative influence and theoretical evolution. *Polish Rev.* 4(4):1–28.
———. 1960. The origin of Malinowski's theory of magic. *Polish Rev.* 5(4):1–9.
Taft, J. 1958. *Otto Rank: A biographical study.* New York.
Thornton, R. J. 1985. "Imagine yourself set down . . .": Mach, Frazer, Conrad, Malinowski and the role of imagination in ethnography. *Anth. Today* 1(5):7–14.
Wallace, E. R. IV. 1983. *Freud and anthropology: A history and reappraisal.* New York.
Wayne [Malinowska], H. 1985. Bronislaw Malinowski: The influence of various women on his life and works. *Am. Ethnol.* 12:529–40.
Westermarck, E. 1891. *The history of human marriage.* London.
———. 1906–8. *The origin and development of the moral ideas.* London.

Manuscript Sources

This paper is based on extensive research in the two major bodies of Malinowski manuscript materials, at the London School of Economics (cited ML) and at Yale University (cited MY, followed by series, box, and folder, e.g., II-28/208), as well as several items from Malinowski's library that are at the University of California, Santa Cruz (cited MSC). There are, however, limitations that should be specified. The body of potentially relevant materials is very large, dispersed through many folders on a variety of topics, and often very hard to read (although with some exceptions in the case of earlier materials, diaries, and field notes, the vast majority of the surviving materials are in English). My major research was done in 1969 and 1973, long before I had the present essay in mind—since which time, it should be noted, the London Malinowski papers have been reorganized. In writing this essay, I have been able to obtain additional microfilm copies and photocopies of relevant materials in the Yale papers, where most of the psychoanalytically oriented materials are preserved—a fact which may itself be significant, if one were inclined to argue that Malinowski would take with him to America materials that were especially important in the formation of his theoretical viewpoint. But while I believe that I have examined most of those manuscript materials directly relevant to psychoanalysis, I would not make the same claim in regard to more indirectly relevant materials. Although I do not feel that additional research in his social theoretical readings (or in his lecture or field notes) would modify the major outlines of the present account, there is a lot more work to be done. Until it is, the present essay must be regarded as tentative.

UNCONVENTIONAL CHARACTER AND DISCIPLINARY CONVENTION

John Layard, Jungian and Anthropologist

JEREMY MacCLANCY

To study unconventional characters is to throw into relief the conventions of their day; to define the nature of their eccentricity is to illuminate the central concerns of their more orthodox colleagues; to detail the reasons for their failure (if indeed they fail) is to make plain how others were held to have succeeded. If this be true of modern social life, it is no less so for the smaller social orders constituted by professional disciplines—and especially, perhaps, in the earlier periods when their intellectual conventions and institutional structures are being molded. For modern social anthropology in Britain, that process took place between the wars, when the fieldwork tradition we associate with Malinowski was informed by the social structural concerns of Radcliffe-Brown—culminating in the formation of the Association of Social Anthropologists at Oxford in 1946 (see *HOA* 1 & 2, passim).

Although John Layard was among the thirteen present at the founding meeting, he was already then marginal to social anthropology, despite the fact that he had finished a year's intensive fieldwork before Malinowski arrived in the Trobriands. As a student of Rivers and a colleague of Jung, Layard was both anthropologist and analytical psychologist. Like Rivers, he thought that anthropology could provide materials for the consideration of mental processes; unlike Rivers, he thought of these processes in terms of "archetypes,"

Jeremy MacClancy is an Economic and Social Research Council Postdoctoral Research Fellow in the Institute of Social Anthropology, Oxford University. His major previous publications include *To Kill a Bird with Two Stones: A Short History of Vanuatu*. He is currently at work on the confrontation between Basque nationalism and Navarran regionalism.

which "anthropologists, although surrounded by them in every aspect of their work, have so curiously ignored through concentration on external factors as opposed to internal ones which always go hand in hand . . ." (Layard 1956:353). Toward the end of his life, Layard attributed his difficulty in putting over his ideas to anthropologists to the fact that "they didn't know psychology" (n.d.a). But the state of affairs Layard lamented was the outcome of an historical process; and although that process proceeded largely independently of Layard, his life—which he called the "Study of a Failure"—may help to illuminate it.

The Scenes of a Life:
Cambridge, Malekula, Berlin, London, Oxford

The Layards, of Huguenot stock, were "gentlefolk" rather than "landed gentry"—"South Kensington," not "Mayfair people" (Layard n.d.a:96). John's greatuncle, Sir Austen Henry Layard, was the famous archeologist who discovered Nineveh in the 1840s; his father—with whom Layard seems to have had a difficult relationship—lived the life of a "literary gentleman" of private means. Born in 1891, John was educated at Bedales, a progressive boarding school, and after spending a year abroad learning French and German, went up to Cambridge in 1909. While at King's College, he read Modern Languages, and joined a "humanistic, anti-establishment" group called the Heretics Society, which met in the rooms of C. K. Ogden and discussed such issues as the psychological basis of linguistics. Through a friend in the Heretics, Layard became involved in, and later secretary of, the university's "Anthropological Club," at which W. H. R. Rivers was a frequent speaker (Langham 1981: 202–3). Rivers, trained in neurophysiology and psychology, had become involved in ethnology while on Haddon's expedition to Torres Straits, going on to achieve recognition as the premier fieldworker of his day; by 1912, his analysis of data collected in Melanesia had led him to abandon the still-prevailing evolutionary interpretations for a "diffusionary" view of the development of culture. Layard was "overwhelmed . . . by the aura of this marvellous man," who "could do anything"—and whom he soon "adored" and "worshipped" as a "kind of male mother" (n.d.a:16, 44, 100). Rivers persuaded Layard to stay in Cambridge for a fourth year to study anthropology. To Layard, this was one of the most pleasant times of his life; although he attended some of Haddon's lectures on race distribution, he later recalled avoiding anthropology for more hedonistic pursuits.

In 1914, Layard (like Malinowski, who was with Haddon on another boat) took advantage of the British Association meetings in Australia to go out for fieldwork. Although he traveled with Rivers, Layard recalled that his mentor spent all his time correcting proofs for *The History of Melanesian Society*, in which he interpreted the varieties of Melanesian social organization as the end product of a series of invasions by "relatively small bodies of immigrants" (Rivers 1914:II, 5), each with different social institutions and cultural practices—including sun worship and the building of large monuments of stone. Although Layard later recalled finding the proofs "quite incomprehensible" when he tried to read them (n.d.a:13), he was in fact to be much influenced by the book; and it is clear that he also got from Rivers some idea of what was involved in Rivers' "concrete method" for the study of culture through the collection of kinship data. While they were on board ship, war was declared in Europe, and Rivers decided to delay his return to Cambridge—which he expected would be disorganized by mobilization—in order to mount an expedition to the New Hebrides (Vanuatu), where a Swiss ethnologist had recently described a living megalithic culture (Spieser 1913). Rivers invited Layard to accompany him, and on Haddon's advice, Layard accepted.

After consulting with the British Resident Commissioner, they went to work in Atchin, one of the Small Islands, off the northeast coast of Malekula, where native culture was least corrupted by European influences—and from which an Irish trader had recently been forced to flee. The Atchinese concluded that Layard was the trader's brother, and kept well away from the two researchers. Rivers, unused to such sustained unfriendliness, decided to leave on a mission boat that happened to call ten days after their arrival. Although Layard "expected Rivers to come back" (n.d.a: 27), he never did—carrying on his fieldwork instead from the relative comfort of a mission station on another island.

Layard, deserted and isolated, gradually began to make friends among the Atchinese, especially the younger men, and to carry on fieldwork as best he could with the minimal training he had received from Haddon and Rivers— who had refused to discuss such matters while they voyaged together. He started to learn Atchinese by writing down the names for material items and transcribing myths from informants; he also surveyed the villages on the island, collecting genealogies as a basis for the study of their social organization. Reading his autobiography, it is patent that he delighted in the life that he led: transcribing their songs, participating in the male initiation ceremonies as an honorary novice, pleasuring in the complex rhythms beaten out by slit-drum orchestras, thrilled by their dancing—in which he once joined, painted black with charcoal and clad only in a penis wrapper. There is none of the ambivalence of Malinowski's diary, none of the aggression, none of the yearning for white womanhood. As Layard later remembered it, Atchin was "my paradise—the one place I'd been really, really happy . . . , living with these natives and enormously enjoying life with them" (n.d.a:331). Except for a month's holiday in Norfolk Island over Christmas, a sojourn in southwest

Malekula, and brief trips to Vao, the neighboring Small Island to the north, he lived on Atchin for a year, until October 1915.

Though Layard remembered Atchin as a tropical island paradise, he also found fieldwork very tiring. Exhausted, he returned to a civilization in violent upheaval and a nation engaged in a war from which he was excluded (the recruiting authorities in Sydney having turned him down for flat feet). It seems that he suffered severe cultural shock, which was aggravated by the mental breakdown and subsequent death of his father. Layard later concluded that his father's illness had somehow been transferred to him; be that as it may, he experienced a series of severe mental crises and long bouts of feebleness that left him physically unable to cope. The next several decades of his life may be regarded as a series of efforts to cope with his recurrent psychic difficulties, through which, working with a series of therapists, he achieved both an ambiguous personal adjustment and a hybrid intellectual style.

The first of these therapists was in fact Rivers, whose contribution to the British war effort took him back from ethnology toward psychology. In the course of treating shell-shocked soldiers, Rivers developed his own somewhat desexualized and pragmatically oriented version of psychoanalysis, which emphasized the problem-resolving function of dreams (Rivers 1923). Rivers' approach worked very well for the poet Siegfried Sassoon, whom the war had made pacifist, but whom Rivers "bucked up" to rejoin his regiment (Sassoon 1936:3–72). But it did not work so well for the culture-shocked young anthropologist, who later claimed that Rivers exacerbated his condition of nervous exhaustion by suggesting that he start to write up his field notes. Furthermore, Rivers would not "take the transference": he would not respond emotionally to Layard's statements. When Layard, during one of his crises, declared his love for his mentor, Rivers, "blanching" and "almost trembling," left the room, never to return. "Rivers had obviously not recognized the whole homosexual content of our relationship, probably on both sides" (n.d.a:116). Layard, practically bedridden, spent the next few years being looked after by friends in Hertfordshire.

In 1924, Layard began a period of consultation with the unorthodox American psychologist Homer Lane, at the suggestion of one of Lane's former patients. Lane, who had gone from railroading to grocery clerking to working with delinquent boys, had settled in England in 1912 to become superintendent of the Little Commonwealth, a self-governing reformatory school in Dorsetshire. Although his unorthodox methods worked very well for a time (and seem to have been an important influence on the progressive educationalist A. S. Neill), the school was forced to close in 1918 when two runaway girls charged Lane with assault. For the next few years, Lane supported himself as a therapist, melding the influences of Freud and Jung into his own American romantic celebration of the release of impulse and the fulfillment of the natural creativity of man (Bazeley 1928:7–24). Here was a very different pragmatism from Rivers': when Layard complained that he could not walk, Lane suggested that he should buy a car. And, within three months, Layard was leading an active life. He could "relate" to Lane, and was deeply influenced by his theories, which included the idea that all disease was psychosomatic in origin, and that every external event had an internal cause (Layard n.d.a:137–60). Layard edited a collection of Lane's "lectures on the self-determination of small people" for publication, although owing to disagreements with other Lane supporters, his contribution was not acknowledged in the published version (178; cf. Lane 1928).

Layard's treatment by Lane was abruptly terminated in 1925 when Lane, suspected of sleeping with female patients, was forced to leave England on an immigration-law technicality; he died soon after. Although Layard worked for a brief period in the Museum of Anthropology at Cambridge, arranging Malekulan materials, the aftermath of Lane's departure and death saw the return of his psychic and physical symptoms. Dissatisfied with analysts he was seeing in London, he left for Vienna, where he was treated by the heterodox Freudian Wilhelm Stekel, before moving on for three years in Berlin, where he tried unsuccessfully to write up some of his field notes.

While there, Layard seems to have become part of the late Weimar bohemian and homosexual scene immortalized by Christopher Isherwood—the "Cosy Corner" in which he and W. H. Auden found an uninhibited "amusement park for the flesh" (Mendelson 1981:55). Younger than Layard by almost twenty years, the two poets were for a time held spellbound by his "X-ray eyes, his mocking amusement, his stunning frankness, and his talk about Lane" (Isherwood 1977:6). But there was no relief for Layard's depression, and when the painful memory of an earlier unrequited love for a female patient of Lane's was compounded by the failure of a homosexual relationship, he put a pistol in his mouth and pulled the trigger. Coming to consciousness with a bullet lodged in his forehead, Layard staggered to Auden's flat and asked him to finish the job; Auden refused, and took him to a hospital, where the bullet was extracted. With his brain miraculously undamaged, and his immediate obsessions dispelled by the suicide attempt, Layard soon recovered and returned to Britain (Gardiner 1976).

Back in London, he began working on his Malekulan material—"pouring over my anthropological notes and writing them out on a typewriter, all day long, until I got absolutely exhausted and couldn't go on anymore" (n.d.a:212). In order to talk about his anthropology, he started visiting the University College seminar of Grafton Elliot Smith and William Perry, who in the brief anthropological interregnum after Rivers' death in 1922 had caused quite a stir with an extreme diffusionism that saw all human culture in terms of the migrations of seafaring Egyptian megalithic sun-worshippers (Langham 1981:

John Layard with his son Richard, ca. 1936. (Courtesy Margaret Gardiner and Richard Layard.)

160–99). Until the early 1930s, the University College seminar attracted as many students as Malinowski's competing antidiffusionist seminar at the L.S.E., which Layard also occasionally attended, although he was not "particularly interested."

Among the people he became friendly with at University College was Doris Dingwall, the Demonstrator in Human Anatomy, who was in fact "the moving spirit" in the actual organization of Smith's department and the organizer of its seminars (Layard n.d.a:213). Layard's return to academic anthropology was largely due to the attention that she paid to him; her encouragement helped him to give his first paper at the Royal Anthropological Institute (Layard 1930a). He found new strength from being with her (n.d.a:220), and within several years they were married.

After years of isolation, Layard was becoming a participant in the small band of academically oriented British anthropologists; in his own words: "I was waking up, I was beginning to come into the world" (n.d.a:218). With Dingwall's encouragement, he applied for and won a two-year fellowship from the Leverhulme Foundation to write up his field notes—overcoming his inter-

viewers' concern that he might have forgotten a lot in the intervening years
by reassuring them that the experience he had since had of life had enabled
him to understand ethnographic statements he had not understood at the
time he collected them (288).

That same experience had also made him "intensely interested" in the anthropological relevance of psychology. But he was not satisfied with "the conventional schools," and "certainly not [with] the Freudian sort" (n.d.a:218).
It was not until he suffered another breakdown in 1936 that he found a theory that satisfied his intellectual curiosity. This time he was treated by H. G.
Baynes, who had been a supporter of Lane, and who, "more than any other
individual, established the roots of [Jungian] analytical psychology in Britain" (Prince 1963:41). As before with Rivers, Layard could not "relate properly" to Baynes, who seemed simply an imitator of Jung; so he got Baynes
to introduce him to the master when Jung came to London to deliver a lecture on "The Concept of the Collective Unconscious" in October 1936 (Prince
1963:45; Layard n.d.a:300). This meeting was to be the first of many between
Jung and Layard over the years immediately before and just after World War
II, Layard often taking a house in Zurich so that he could be even closer
to the founder of analytical psychology. Although Jung agreed to accept Layard as a patient, he was interested more in learning about anthropology than
in the state of Layard's psyche. He would see Layard only during term, no
more than twice a week, and refused to discuss sexual matters. Like Rivers,
he refused to "take the transference" (Layard n.d.a:313); Layard reciprocated
by regarding Jung as "quite an unpleasant person" (n.d.b). After a series of
conversations in 1950, consisting mainly of a Jungian monologue about his
intellectual distinctions and his triumph over the myopia of Freudian psychotherapy, their relationship was finally ruptured by Jung's refusal to see or to
speak to Layard. Although Layard later claimed that the only thing he got
from Jung was the idea of archetypes, which he then applied both to himself
and to his ethnography (Layard n.d.b), it is clear that Jung's ideas were a tremendous intellectual stimulus.

Indeed, Layard, when he was not in Zurich, practiced privately as an analytical psychologist in London or in Oxford, where he held weekly meetings
of an "Analytical Psychology Club." Although he also played an active part
in the Oxford University Anthropological Club (of which he was president
and his wife secretary in 1941), the bulk of the publications of his later years—
including the ethnography of Vao discussed below—were oriented toward
Jungian psychology. In addition to the mythological study he published in
1944 (*The Lady and the Hare*), a number of his postwar articles, based on papers
he gave at the (Jungian) Eranos Institute in Zurich, were Jungian analyses
of Malekulan rituals. Although he also found time to write a lengthy introduction to Homer Lane's psychology, exhaustive case histories of two of his

patients, an introduction to "primitive kinship" for psychotherapists, and a Jungian analysis of Welsh mythology, only the last was published (Layard 1975), and that after his death.

The Diffusion of Archetypes Among
The Stone Men of Malekula

The ethnography of Vao, where he had in fact worked only a few weeks, was to have been the first of a four-volume series on the people of the Small Islands. Although Layard did write up much of his field notes (including an 800-page manuscript on kinship of Atchin, where he had spent the bulk of his time), the other three projected volumes did not appear. Even so, *The Stone Men of Malekula* is a very impressive book—not least for its size (despite wartime restrictions, its 800 pages managed to achieve the volume and the density of a brick). Writing in a leisurely discursive style, Layard detailed the full range of Vao cultural fashions, including social organization, kinship, and ritual life —all the while arguing his diffusionist and Jungian points. The volume closes with three chapters of comparative survey which have the world as their limit.

The core of the book is an account of initiation rites and of the *maki*, the Vao version of the graded society then common to most of the north and central islands of Vanuatu, which had become the main interest of Layard's fieldwork. He characterized the *maki* as "a propitiatory rite in which, through the sacrifice of tusked boars," the sacrificer took in the *ta-mat* (soul, spirit, ghost) of the boar, so ensuring against annihilation by the Guardian Ghost after death. "In so doing he at the same time honours the ancestral ghosts, and gains for himself a place by their side in the hereafter by gradually rising in rank through each successive sacrifice." Each sacrifice represented a rebirth signified by the assumption of a new name and title, and was followed by a period of seclusion (Layard 1942:270). The rite itself took from fifteen to twenty years to perform and was "divided into two main parts, each part culminating with the same set of ceremonies, at the end of which all the sacrificers" took new names and began a period of seclusion (271). The two parts were called *ramben* and *maki ru*: in the former the only stone monument erected was a single large dolmen; in the latter the main stone monument was a stone platform. Both dolmen and platform were used in the respective parts of the *maki* as "sacrificial altars" (272). In Vao, the *maki* was performed by each village, where each "line" (as Layard called the unnamed groups consisting of alternating generations in the male line of descent) performed the rite in alternating succession. The "*maki*-men" were the candidates and their "fathers and sons" were the introducers who organized the *maki* for their fathers and sons (294).

Life on Vao, or elsewhere in north and central Vanuatu, however, was not suspended in some mythical ethnographic present, but was in constant flux, its rate accelerated by the indigenous institution of cultural "copyright." Every rite, subrite, dance routine, song, and many other cultural aspects, was owned. Since prestige, when performing ritual, came from staging some innovation, people preparing to undertake a ceremony had to buy the copyright to perform some cultural novelty, or invent one themselves. So the content of rituals changed rapidly and, for Malekulans, "hardly a single element of megalithic culture is indigenous" (15).

Though Layard wrote his ethnography more than two decades after his fieldwork, time enough for his approach to have been affected by many influences, that of Rivers was still clear, especially in Layard's diffusionist passages. Layard thought that since there was a "close similarity" between Vao stone monuments and their associated ideas and similar combinations in Indonesia and Nagaland, Assam, and since many of the "most important" words used in the *maki* had Indonesian roots, there could "be no doubt whatever of the immediate origin of the megalithic culture of Malekula and the surrounding islands from the Malay archipelago and the neighbouring mainland of South-Eastern Asia" (20). Even in his seventies, Layard remained convinced that the elements of civilization were taken round the world by a maritime megalithic culture originating "somewhere" in the Near East (Layard n.d.a:19). To him, parallels between biblical mythology and Malekulan statements about the journey their dead had to make "point so clearly to a generic connexion with Near Eastern practice and belief that I have no hesitation, where any given element in this layer of Malekulan culture receives no local explanation, to seek one in those areas in which the culture-complex to which it belongs appears to have originated" (1936:127).

Layard argued, following Rivers' *History of Melanesian Society* (1914), that "a megalithic stream" of "dual nature" had come to the New Hebrides, "representing in all probability two separate migrations, having their origins in the ancient centres of civilization"—the first, predominantly matrilineal, the second, predominantly patrilineal (1942:340). Thus he argued that the present twelve-section system of matrilineal and patrilineal moieties plus patrilineal trisections derived from a hypothetical, earlier twelve-section system which had matrilineal trisections: matrilineal descent "is less obvious on the surface but nevertheless forms the foundation of the whole social system" (104).[1] Since Vao Islanders "affirm that at one time the dolmen was the only stone monument erected [in *maki*] and that in those days the rite was similar

1. Layard admitted that he was unable to explain how this transformation occurred (1942: 153). I do not, unfortunately, have space here to examine Layard's treatment of Vao kinship. However, for a critical discussion of his use of "moieties," see Dumont 1966 and Blackwood 1981.

to that practised at the present time in the matrilineal island of Malo immediately to the north," Layard argued that the dolmen was the chief sacrificial monument for the matrilineal culture, and hence the stone platform was the main monument for the patrilineal culture (274, 340). Similarly, because on Atchin it was said that the dead live in the volcano on Ambrym, an island nearby, whereas on Vao the dead were said to live both in a cave on the east Malekulan coast and in the Ambrym volcano, Layard argued that "when the matrilineal element predominates the Home of the Dead is conceived of as being in a cave; while in those areas where patrilineal influence was on the increase, the cave came to be looked on as a first stage in a longer journey to the volcano" (1937b). So also the circumcision and the organized homosexuality found in northwest Malekula were "an expression of the triumph of patrilineal descent over the former matrilineal system" (1942:489).

But other anthropologists had been diffusionist. What marks Layard out as distinctive is his marriage of analytical psychology and anthropology, his interpretation of social function in Jungian terms, his "structural Jungianism," as it were. To Jung, the psyche is a dynamic self-regulatory system, one in constant movement. The creative energy of the mind—the libido—travels between pairs of opposing poles, complementary opposites, which have a regulatory function. Unconsciously produced symbols attract libidinal excess and so possess overtones: their full significance cannot be understood in purely intellectual terms. Exactly what Jung meant by "archetype," however, is difficult to convey adequately. Storr, comparing it to a flexible mold, says it "does not correspond to the actual manifestation as produced by any particular culture; yet it underlies all manifestations produced by all cultures" (Storr 1973:40). Both myth and religion, fundamental expressions of human nature, are direct manifestations of the collective unconscious, which is the home of the archetypes. The central figures in all religions and myths are archetypal in character, though the archetypal material has been consciously modified to some extent. In "primitive cultures" there is less of this modification, making the archetypal character of their myth and religion that much clearer. For an individual, the point of all this activity, his (or her) supreme value, is the achievement of "wholeness"—a satisfactory conclusion to one's development (to Jung, "the process of individuation"), a sort of rebirth in which opposites are reconciled and after which the newly integrated person can be at peace with the world.[2]

Transposing Jungian psychology from the level of the individual to that of the social, Layard saw kinship as "an externalised form" of the self (1959: 102). Similarly, he regarded the voyage from male initiation through the *maki*

---

2. This all-too-brief précis of Jung's approach is heavily dependent on Fordham 1953 and Storr 1973.

to final rest in the Ambrym volcano as but a Malekulan process of individuation.

Thanks to the prescribed arrangement of intermarriage between moieties, which Layard called "circular connubium" (1956:364), the Vao kinship system could be depicted as a circle, an "externalised psychic mandala"—symbol of the basic order of the psyche as a whole (1959:102). And like the archetypal foundation of the psyche, Vao kinship rested on quaternity: the four kinship sections resembled the four basic functions of the self structured in pairs (102), while the four psychological functions—intuition, thinking, feeling, and sensation—corresponded internally with the overt behavior prescribed toward the members of the four sections (1944:131). Just as the permanent and creative tension between complementary opposites of the psyche was essential to one's existence, so the hostility evidenced between pairs of complementary opposites at any level of Vao social organization was "essential to the health and well-being of the race" (1942:593).

Layard discovered death and rebirth symbolism in all male *rites de passage* performed on Vao. Thus initiation into manhood was a rite of symbolic death and rebirth (1942:521); penile incision was a sacrifice performed on the body, conferring spiritual power that was located in the mutilated part (478). Killing pigs in the *maki* he also called sacrifice, "for the ultimate purpose of everything in life is sacrifice, which means transformation, the transformation of something 'natural' into that which is 'supernatural'" (1945:264). Sacrifice in the *maki* constituted the symbolic death and rebirth of the sacrificer, who was infused with the power and soul of the boar; each man passed through a succession of these rebirths as he entered new grades. Layard regarded the boar's specially cultivated tusks as symbolic of the *vagina dentata*, so that the tusked boar (a female symbol in male guise) represented both the devouring-mother archetype and man's own desire to be devoured by her (1952:294; 1955:30). The devouring mother and the man's self-devouring regressive passion—both symbolized by the tusked boar—were overcome ritually by the sacrificial act, out of which emerged the good mother in the form of the sacrificer's own more integrated personality (1952:294). Since the founding of civilization and the differentiation of man from nature were the result of the transformation of incestuous desire toward one's sister (1945), the boar, when sacrificed, "yields up the ghost" of this transformed desire (1956:382).

Vao Islanders repeatedly affirmed that they used to sacrifice men, not boars, in the *maki*. The sacrificer of a human victim, together with all the members of his clan who partook with him of the flesh, was thus ritually reborn, "becoming almost a god" (1942:623). Men, after death, proceeded to the Ambrym volcano, which symbolized the mother-child relationship, female sexuality, and male sexuality (1952:297). The volcano symbolized a totality, a womb to which the well-integrated personality returned, where the most earthly and the most spiritual symbolically unite (298). Thus, successful Vao men, after undergoing a series of symbolic deaths and rebirths, completed their life cycle as whole personalities, integrated in a totality.

The Explanatory Anomalies of Jungian Diffusionism

In the January 9, 1943, issue of the *New Statesman*, Tom Harrisson suggested that *Stone Men of Malekula* contained a "vivid, exact elaborate insight" and would surely take its place "among the foremost contemporary studies in social science." But it did not, and reading it forty years later, one can find many reasons to justify that failure. Layard's diffusionist explanations often create their own anomalies, giving the whole argument a somewhat contrived character.

Thus when Layard, after drawing parallels between the uses of labyrinths in both Malekula and the Near East, wished to argue that labyrinths have the same meaning in the two areas, he had to admit that the Malekulans have "lost the realization of the meaning" of their labyrinthine designs (1936: 140, 144). Similarly, after arguing that upright slit drums were "originally associated" with circular dancing grounds, Layard had to state that, while the Small Islands appear to have derived the upright slit drum from Malekula, "this influence was not strong enough to alter the whole shape of the dancing ground" (1942:317–18). When speaking of initiation, he noted that the operation of incision combined with a ten-day period of seclusion "occurs in the overtly patrilineal islands of Malekula, the Small Islands, Ambrym and South Raga (an island north of Ambrym)" (1942:474), but that the hoaxes initiates played on novices and the building of a special lodge in which the novices were secluded for thirty days were both items of culture that had been transmitted from northerly isles of Vanuatu to the southernmost of the Small Islands, from which they had proceeded further northward (499). Similarly, Layard showed that in every place where boys' penes were ritually incised, the right to perform the operation was bought from the mother's brother, and that "in most parts of the group except the Small Islands, North Malekula and South Raga, the mother's brother plays an important and often preeminent part in the rite" (500). But he was then forced to admit that "far from incision being originally a patrilineal institution, as would at first sight seem to be from its geographical distribution, it is in fact a matrilineal trait in which the function of the mother's brother has, in North Malekula and South Raga, been taken over by the boy's patrilineal kin, though the mother's brother continues to exact payment as in all childhood *rites de passage*" (502). Thus, in the Small Islands, when the mother's brother came to inspect the boy immediately after the operation, "the fury of the boy's patrilineal kinsmen at

the tribute they are . . . powerless to withhold vents itself in the severe beating he receives when he does so . . ." Layard went on to explain "the fact that
the beating of the boys' mothers' brothers is so much more severe on Atchin
than it is on Vao" as "clearly due to the much greater hold that patrilineal
institutions have gained there than on this island" (502). In short, to maintain his migrational-diffusionist hypothesis, Layard had to construct a series
of ad hoc explanations.

Layard's Jungianism, however, is even more open to criticism. He explicitly
insisted that the death and rebirth symbolism of the *maki* was "no arbitrary
interpretation made by the anthropologist" but rather "a fact of native thought"
(1952:291). He adduced two "facts" to support this. First, a reed enclosure was
placed around the sacrificial stone monument a few hours before sacrifice in
the *maki*, only to be torn down a few minutes before the sacrifice actually
occurred (1942:389, 423). This enclosure was called *hu ni-ar*, which Layard
translated in inverted commas (a rare practice for him) as "birth-enclosure"
(389). Special lodges in which women give birth were also called *hu ni-ar* (73),
as was the fence forming the triangular forecourt in front of a *ghamal* (the
men's house in a village, on the construction of which a special *maki* was performed) to hide its front dolmen from casual view (44). Layard noted that
ni-ar meant "reed-fence" and *hu-hu* meant "to suckle" (760, 764), but he gave
no meaning for *hu* alone. On this basis, *hu ni-ar* could well be translated rather
as "suckling enclosure," and one might instead regard the ascription of *hu ni-
ar* to the fence used in *maki* as an indigenous metaphor expressing similarity
between a sacrificer who draws in strength from his victim, a baby who draws
it in from its mother while at teat, and a *ghamal* which also draws it in from
a victim, so becoming prohibited to women. (It is interesting to note that on
Atchin, where the single large dolmen had been superseded by other forms
of stonework, the fence erected before these was called *ni-er merer*, which has
nothing to do with birth [389 n. 2].)

Second, Layard referred to the female nature of the dolmen upon which
boars were sacrificed in *ramben*, stating that it was simultaneously a womb
and a dolmen (368). Evidence that this symbolic equation may be an ethnographer's inference rather than "a fact of native thought" comes from his statement that "according to Dr. A. Capell" *na-vot*, the Vao word for dolmen, is
philologically derived from the Indonesian *batu*, meaning "to be born"—in this
case with the connotation of "rebirth" (367, 705). But, in a reply to a letter
of mine, Dr. Capell says that the word Layard read as "*batu*" was a misprint.
It should read "*bɔtu*," which in Proto-Austronesian means "appear, come into
sight." "If Layard read ideas of rebirth into that, it is his own concern!"

There is also a Proto-Austronesian wordbase *batu* meaning "stone" (Dahl
1973:36); thus, the Atchin word for "stone" is *bat* or *wat*, and the Vao word
is *vat*, *vet*, or *wet* (Layard 1942:761–66). The particular philological derivation

that Layard propounded was meant to support his idea of symbolic rebirth rather than vice versa. But, given that this derivation is only one of two plausible derivations, and given the degree of phonetic similarity between *vat* and *-vot*, it seems reasonable to assert that the philology of *na-vot* cannot be used to support a particular symbolic interpretation, since it is itself in doubt.

But even if we suppose that the dolmen had a female nature and did symbolize a womb, and that *hu ni-ar* does mean "birth enclosure," this still raises as many problems as it solves. For instance, if the dolmen did symbolize a womb through which one was reborn, then the stone platform used in *maki ru* should also be regarded as symbolizing a womb, since one undergoes ritual death and rebirth in performing a sacrifice in *maki ru* in the same way that one does in *ramben*—but Layard did not even make a suggestion about the sexual nature of the stone platform. Similarly, if *hu ni-ar* did symbolize a birth enclosure, why was it torn down *before* the sacrifice? And what death and rebirth were meant to be symbolically undergone behind the *hu ni-ar* of a *ghamal?* There is nothing to suggest that any such "rebirth" occurred—which implies that the fact that a fence was denoted as a *hu ni-ar* does not necessarily mean that a sacrifice behind it was symbolic of death and rebirth. Following this logic, that the fence was called a *hu ni-ar* during the performance of a *maki* cannot be used as an intellectual prop for supporting the statement that a *maki* sacrifice was symbolic of ritual death and rebirth.[3]

Layard also argued that the ceremony of initiation into manhood was one of ritual death and rebirth. While he admitted that much of the evidence regarding such symbolism in the Vao version of the ceremony was lacking, he promised that it would "be given in my more detailed account of initiation of Atchin" (1942:521). However, in his unpublished notes concerning initiation into manhood on Atchin, which, admittedly, do not appear to be final drafts, the only evidence I could find of ritual death and rebirth was the novices' seclusion in the initiation lodge for thirty days. Layard thought it "significant" that this was the common period of confinement for women who had given birth, for boys whose penes had been incised, and for men who killed pigs in the *maki* (521). But the common use of a thirty-day period in a number of ritual processes does not allow one to ascribe priority to the symbolism of any one of those processes. In pointing out the common use of a thirty-day period Layard may have been doing that, and nothing more. One might argue that he was simply repeating the Jungian formula: "basically ev-

---

3. It is also surprising that in an area of such great cultural diffusion as north and central Vanuatu the rebirth symbolism of graded society sacrifice appears peculiar to Small Island life. Beyond the Small Islands, it is only in north Ambrym and south Pentecost that anthropologists have found even a suggestion of rebirth symbolism in graded society ritual (Patterson 1981; Lane 1965), but analysis (which space does not permit to be included here) indicates that this material does not provide support for Layard's argument.

ery transition . . . signifies a kind of 'rebirth'" (Jacobi 1951:178). But this re-
definition of *rites de passage*, because universal, tells us nothing about Small
Island ceremonies in particular and would be an "arbitrary interpretation"—
something Layard wished to avoid.[4]

The detail of Layard's ethnography and the frequency of his arguments
preclude a more comprehensive analysis in the space of this article. One must
note, however, that in addition to the anomalies they separately created, there
are also various points in Layard's account where the diffusionism of Rivers
and the psychology of Jung pulled in different directions—as when he con-
fessed that he could not decide whether incision was a degraded form of circumcision, or circumcision an exaggerated form of incision (Layard 1942:490).
However, there are many places where the Jungian and diffusionist strands
seem deftly woven into the rich detail of life on Vao, and we can still appreciate how the reviewer for the *Listener* (November 19, 1942) could have found
the book "fascinating" and "enthralling."

Psychology and Social Structure in British Academic Anthropology

Nonetheless, the book seems to have been "politely ignored" by the community
of British social anthropologists (Allen 1981:1), and a consideration of some
possible reasons for this may tell us something about the way in which that
community was historically defined. As Edmund Leach has recently argued
(1984), that community was long a community of "outsiders" marginal to the
dominant British academic establishment: led by a Polish emigré and a lower-
middle-class Englishman who had endured two decades of colonial exile, it
included a number of colonials, South African Jews, and other "foreigners,"
along with educated English women who were outsiders by gender if not by
class. Layard, in contrast to most of the leading members of this group, was
(by ethnic, family, class, and educational background) relatively an "insider"
to that establishment. Paradoxically, this fact may have heightened his marginality vis-à-vis the emerging social anthropological community (although
others, notably Evans-Pritchard and Leach himself, were to overcome this
relative disadvantage). During the period in which Layard might have become a full-fledged member, this community was beginning to achieve a hard-
won, if still marginal, place within the British academic and intellectual es-

4. Layard's ideas about social groups also require reexamination. Dumont argues that what
he construed as "matrimoieties" should rather be called "alternate generations" (Dumont 1966).
If one pursues this argument, then Layard's dichotomy of *ni*-Vanuatu societies into "matrilineal"
and "patrilineal" collapses, as does his kinship mandala, and hence the quaternal foundation
of society.

tablishment—a process which inevitably involved the setting of many different intellectual and social conventions. In this context, Layard's multiple and uncompromising unconventionalities become a kind of contrapuntal commentary on the way in which the boundaries of the social anthropological community were defined.

In the first place, we must put Layard in a certain perspective, as one of a cohort of anthropologists who, after some academic training in English universities, went out before or during World War I to do ethnographic research in the more methodologically self-conscious mode that had emerged in the aftermath of the Torres Straits expedition, and which was at first articulated and exemplified by Rivers. That cohort was larger than we often recall: in addition to Radcliffe-Brown and Malinowski, it included Gerald Wheeler, A. M. Hocart, Diamond Jenness, Gunnar Landtman, Rafael Karsten, Barbara Freire-Marreco, and Marie Czaplička. And while sex and nationality account for the exclusion of some, it is still worth noting that only two were eventually successful in establishing themselves in English academic life (see Stocking 1983:83–84).

To have been a member of this group was to have been historically and biographically predisposed to academic marginality—the more so, if one spent the postwar years coping with personal psychological difficulties. The heritage of those difficulties was without doubt a further factor in Layard's particular marginality. Like Rivers, who figured in Sassoon's autobiography and in other literary works of the late 1920s (Sassoon 1936; Graves 1929), Layard was incorporated into British literature—but unlike Rivers, his literary apotheosis took place while he was still alive: by the early 1930s he had already figured in works by Isherwood and Auden, both pseudonymously and by name— as "loony Layard" in Auden's *Orators* (1932:88; see also Isherwood 1932, where Layard's suicide attempt is attributed to the character of "Edward Blake"). Decades later, Evans-Pritchard, who was his friend in Oxford until they quarreled in 1957, used unkindly to say, "Of course John Layard's mad. He put a bullet through his head and it made no difference. He must be mad" (J. Pitt-Rivers, personal communication). But psychological problems aside, Layard was by his own admission an unconventional and sometimes difficult personality—a rebel, "up against the social system" (n.d.a:302, 62). As A. S. Neill said to Layard in politely turning down his offer to help at Neill's Lane-inspired Summerhill school, he was "too much of an individualist" (Layard n.d.a:305). Similarly, veteran members of the Institute of Social Anthropology at Oxford remember that he could be "very difficult" to work with, too "possessive," often thinking up projects and then wanting to control them (G. Lienhardt, R. Needham, personal communications). Although he inspired discipleship in some, especially his patients, no anthropologist became his disciple (though several continued to visit him at his home in Oxford).

Being a difficult personality was not, however, a bar to discipleship in British social anthropology; and, in Layard's case, other factors were at work. One was of course his tie to diffusionism. When Bernard Deacon's Malekulan field notes were to be edited after his untimely death from blackwater fever, Layard was an obvious candidate for the job—despite his failure to find the six-section system which was Deacon's great discovery on Ambrym. But although Layard volunteered himself in 1927, Haddon and Radcliffe-Brown gave the job instead to Camilla Wedgwood, because they feared that Layard was "working in conjunction with Elliot Smith"—who had already entrusted him the task of "whipping Rivers' Ambrym material into shape" (Langham 1981:237). As it happened, Deacon had carried into the field copies of large portions of Layard's field notes without labeling them as such, which Wedgwood then attributed to Deacon. She compounded the insult by her "habit of inaccurately paraphrasing such material as Layard had then published about his Malekulan experience." In the event, Haddon was forced after all to include Layard in Deacon's posthumous publication, in a "Supplementary Preface" in which Layard detailed some of the inaccuracies (Langham 1981: 242).

Others, after early diffusionist beginnings, went on to become integrated into the social anthropological community (one thinks of Daryll Forde, who also attended the seminar at University College). But far from shedding his diffusionism, Layard compounded his theoretical heterodoxy by persisting in a second fading fashion: the psychological interests that for a time in the 1920s had seemed to mark the future direction of British anthropology (see Pear 1960; Stocking, in this volume). Not only Rivers, but also Seligman and Malinowski were influenced by psychoanalytic theory, and members of Malinowski's seminar read Freud and Jung and argued about their theories (Powdermaker 1967:39). But although several of the members of that seminar after 1930 (notably Fortes and Nadel) were in fact recruited from backgrounds in psychology, Fortes later recalled that by that time most of his colleagues were ambivalent toward, if not suspicious of, psychoanalysis (1977:130–32). By then, they were devoting their attention, not to psychology, but to Radcliffe-Brown's version of Durkheimian sociology; in the case of both Fortes and Nadel, psychological interests were put aside for social structural analysis, appearing only occasionally before reemerging late in their careers. If many anthropologists continued to interpret behavior in terms denoting psychological states, they did so without reference to an explicit, developed theory of personality and motivation. By 1951, Firth spoke for most British anthropologists when he described psychology as "a strange, rather diffuse territory" (487). In contrast, Layard had chosen to remain interested not only in psychological issues, but also in a psychological theory which, since Seligman's dabbling with the idea of "extravert" and "introvert" back in 1924, had come to seem to most anthropologists perhaps even more dubious than orthodox Freudian psycho-analysis.

The resistance to psychology was linked with the strong empiricist strain that was to characterize the British social anthropological tradition. Psychology, especially in its dynamic forms, came to be regarded as vaguely speculative. At a multidisciplinary conference held in London in 1936, Firth argued that anthropologists should keep their assumptions about human psychology to a minimum (Firth 1937:89), while Evans-Pritchard insisted that anthropologists, as practitioners of a "purely inductive science," subordinated theories to facts and not vice versa: "One of the main deterrents to our acting in closer collaboration with other branches of Social Science is that they have not cut adrift from philosophical speculation" (Evans-Pritchard 1937:66).

In the same conference Layard argued a very different thesis. He propounded the interdependency of apparent opposites: diffusion and function, self-preservation and sex, the collective and the personal unconscious, the individual and society, children and adults, the dolmen representing the female principle and the monolith representing the male—an all-embracing binary table that seems to catalogue the legacy of Layard's mentors. To him diffusionism and functionalism were valid only when taken in conjunction with one another, not when they were opposed (1937b). Throughout Layard's published work, we can see him playing with idea after idea (no matter what their intellectual source), setting them against the ethnography, and proffering hypotheses for further investigation. In contrast to the prevailing functionalist rationalism of social anthropologists, he was even willing to consider seriously the "possible efficacy of weather magic" (1942:576).

Layard's unfashionable joining together of opposing categories, his eclectic playfulness, and his willingness to conjecture were problematic even for non-anthropologists. Reviewing Layard's *Lady and the Hare*, John Wisdom, professor of philosophy at Cambridge, felt that "in some degree he spins the interpretations out of his 'inner consciousness'": "There is, I know, no harm in that if there is a check-up process—but is there?" (1953:191). If Layard's methodology disturbed nonanthropologists, it disturbed even more those concerned to establish an academic base for an intellectually and institutionally marginal inquiry. In the British academic and intellectual context, that process of disciplinary establishment seemed to be aided by insisting on boundaries, by marking off a well-delimited intellectual field, within which concepts could be clearly defined and methodologies honed, in order to make sense of a particular sphere of empirical phenomena.[5] And some went further, to insist on the utility of such knowledge in the administration of native popu-

5. The rhetorical aspect of this disciplinary definition is best exemplified by the implicit undeveloped psychology within British ethnography of that period, as mentioned above.

lations. There, especially, the Durkheimian tradition, with its narrowly focused but systematic analysis of kinship, politics, and social organization,
promised a rigor and an objectivity that contrasted dramatically with the con-
jectural hypotheses of diffusionism and dynamic psychology (whether in the
Freudian or the Jungian modes). In a period in which funding was limited,
and much of that which became available was justified in terms of practical
colonial purpose, this limitation of anthropological vision—or, from another
point of view, this acceptance of a set of blinkering conventions—became the
means by which British social anthropology defined its character and won
a certain status among more prestigious, well-established sciences (see Kuper
1983; Stocking 1985).

For Layard, who considered himself basically a rebel, "up against the social
system" (n.d.a:302), this establishment of disciplinary conventions was, given
his character, particularly uncongenial. And unlike the "foreign" outsiders who
"eventually assimilated into the life style and cultural conventions of Oxbridge
academics" (Leach 1984:11), he did not even regard anthropology as an academic study (Layard n.d.a:305). Even if he had wanted a university appointment, the analytic practice by which he supplemented his private means made
such a post unnecessary.

The response to Layard's major ethnographic opus is thus not surprising.
When he returned to anthropology in the 1930s after having been away from
it for fifteen years, people were not too sure how to assess him. If the little
that he had published seemed a mixture of good ethnography with unconventional psychological interpretation, the disciplinary conventions by which the
latter might have weighed heavily against him were not yet so clearly defined.
But by the time *Stone Men of Malekula* finally appeared, Layard had come
to be regarded as something of a "wild man," despite his obvious intellectual
gifts; furthermore, his major orienting assumptions were now clearly beyond
the conceptual pale. The book was, according to Firth, "an odd mix of Atchin
and Layard." British social anthropologists paid little attention to it; instead
they got on with their own work (Raymond Firth, Rosemary Firth, personal
communications).

John Layard died on November 26, 1974, in Oxford. At his funeral, Meyer
Fortes gave a memorial address—thus reaffirming Layard's connection to the
community of British social anthropologists. Social anthropology in Britain
is no longer a small face-to-face community in which one intellectual strategy is the dominant convention. The subject is now established, not only
at Oxford, Cambridge, and the University of London, but in departments
throughout Britain. And since the 1950s, new theoretical orientations and
methodologies have tended to come from abroad. If anthropology is now an
institutional collection of diverse approaches, in which no "school of thought"

has hegemony, and theoretical distinctiveness (if not contentiousness) is valued, then there may yet again be space for such an imaginative speculator as Layard. There may even be a place for Jungian psychology, especially if the attempt were made to compare psychologies, Western and non-Western, rather than to talk of one in terms of the other. Such a comparison might tell us as much about Jung as about more traditional exotica.

Acknowledgments

I am grateful to Edmund Leach, Rodney Needham, Bob Parkin, Anthony Storr, and George Stocking for their helpful comments and suggestions. Richard Layard kindly gave me access to his father's unpublished manuscript material. Raymond Firth and Margaret Gardiner generously gave their time to talk about their memories of Layard.

References Cited

Allen, M. R., ed. 1981. *Vanuatu: Politics, economics and ritual in island Melanesia.* Sydney.
Auden, W. H. 1932. *The orators.* London.
Bazeley, E. T. 1928. *Homer Lane and the Little Commonwealth.* London.
Blackwood, P. 1981. Rank, exchange and leadership in four Vanuatu societies. In Allen 1981:35–84.
Dahl, O. C. 1973. *Proto-Austronesian.* Lund, Sweden.
Dugdale, J. G., ed. 1937. *Further papers on the social sciences: Their relations in theory and teaching. Being the report of a conference held under the auspices of the Institute of Sociology at Westfield College, Hampstead, London, from the 25th to the 27th of September 1936.* London.
Dumont, L. 1966. Descent or intermarriage? A relational view of Australian section systems. *Southwest J. Anth.* 22:231–50.
Evans-Pritchard, E. E. 1937. Anthropology and social science. In Dugdale 1937:75–90.
Firth, R. 1937. Anthropology and the study of society. In Dugdale 1937:75–90.
———. 1951. Contemporary British social anthropology. *Am. Anth.* 53:474–89.
Fordham, M. 1953. *An introduction to Jung's psychology.* London.
Fortes, M. 1977. Custom and conscience in anthropological perspective. *Int. Rev. Psychoanal.* 4:127–54.
Gardiner, M. 1976. Auden: A memoir. *New Review* 3(28):9–16.
Graves, R. 1929. *Goodbye to all that.* London.
Isherwood, C. 1932. *The memorial: Portrait of a family.* London.
———. 1977. *Christopher and his kind: 1929–1939.* London.
Jacobi, J. 1951. *Complex/symbol/archetype in the psychology of C. G. Jung.* London.
Jung, C. G. 1940. Concerning rebirth. In *The archetypes and the collective unconscious, Collected works,* Vol. 9, pt. 1, ed. G. Adler & H. Read. London (1959).
Kuper, A. 1983. *Anthropology and anthropologists: The modern British school.* London.

Lane, H. 1928. *Talks to parents and teachers: Insights into the problems of childhood.* London.

Lane, R. B. 1965. The Melanesians of South Pentecost, New Hebrides. In *Gods, ghosts and men in Melanesia,* ed. P. Lawrence & M. Meggitt. Melbourne.

Langham, I. 1981. *The building of British social anthropology: W. H. R. Rivers and his Cambridge disciples in the development of kinship studies, 1898–1931.* Dordrecht.

Layard, J. W. 1928. Degree taking rites in South West Bay, Malekula. *J. Roy. Anth. Inst.* 58:139–228.

———. 1930a. Malekula: Flying tricksters, gods, ghosts, and epileptics. *J. Roy. Anth. Inst.* 60:501–24.

———. 1930b. Shamanism: An analysis based on comparison with the flying tricksters of Malekula. *J. Roy. Anth. Inst.* 60:525–50.

———. 1936. Maze dances and the ritual of the labyrinth in Malekula. *Folklore* 47: 123–70.

———. 1937a. Der Mythos der Totenfahrt auf Malekula. *Eranos-Jahrbuch* 5:241–91.

———. 1937b. Anthropology and the study of society. In Dugdale 1937:91–104.

———. 1942. *Stone men of Malekula.* London.

———. 1944. Primitive kinship as mirrored in the psychological structure of modern man. *Brit. J. Med. Psych.* 20:118–34.

———. 1945. The incest taboo and the virgin archetype. *Eranos-Jahrbuch* 12:253–307.

———. 1948. The making of man in Malekula. *Eranos-Jahrbuch* 16:209–83.

———. 1951. The pilgrimage to Oba: An Atchin sex-initiation rite. *South Seas Studies.* Basel.

———. 1952. The role of the sacrifice of tusked boars in Malekulan religion and social organisation. *Actes du IVe Congrès International des Sciences Anthropologiques et Ethnologiques, Vienne.* Vol. 2.

———. 1955. Boar sacrifice. *J. Analyt. Psych.* 1:7–33.

———. 1956. Identification with the sacrificial animal. *Eranos-Jahrbuch* 24:341–406.

———. 1959. Homo-eroticism in primitive society as a function of the self. *J. Analyt. Psych.* 4:101–15.

———. 1975. *The Welsh myth Cullwch and Olwen from the Mabinogion.* Boulder.

———. n.d.a. Study of a failure. (unpublished autobiography).

———. n.d.b. Transcript of conversation with G. Nameche.

Leach, E. R. 1984. Glimpses of the unmentionable in the history of British social anthropology. *Ann. Rev. Anth.* 13:1–23.

Mendelson, E. 1981. *Early Auden.* New York.

Patterson, M. 1981. Slings and arrows: Rituals of status acquisition in North Ambrym. In Allen 1981:189–236.

Pear, T. H. 1960. Some early relations between English ethnologists and psychologists. *J. Roy. Anth. Inst.* 90:227–37.

Powdermaker, H. 1967. *Stranger and friend: The way of an anthropologist.* London.

Prince, G. S. 1963. Jung's psychology in Britain. In *Contact with Jung: Essays on the influence of his work and personality,* ed. M. Fordham, 41–61. London.

Rivers, W. H. R. 1914. *The history of Melanesian society.* 2 vols. Cambridge.

———. 1923. *Conflict and dream.* London.

Sassoon, S. 1936. *Sherston's progress.* Garden City, N.Y.

Spieser, F. 1913. *Sudsee-Urwald Kannibalen.* Leipzig.

Stocking, G. W., Jr. 1983. The ethnographer's magic: Fieldwork in British anthropology from Tylor to Malinowski. *HOA* 1:70–120.

———. 1984. Radcliffe-Brown and British social anthropology. *HOA* 2:131–91.

———. 1985. Philanthropoids and vanishing cultures: Rockefeller funding and the end of the museum era in Anglo-American anthropology. *HOA* 3:112–45.

Storr, A. 1973. *Jung*. London.

Wisdom, J. 1953. *Philosophy and psychoanalysis*. Oxford.

ABRAM KARDINER AND THE NEO-FREUDIAN ALTERNATIVE IN CULTURE AND PERSONALITY

WILLIAM C. MANSON

Among historians of American anthropology of the interwar period, the significance of the psychocultural theorizing of Abram Kardiner (1891–1981) has remained persistently unappreciated. As a psychoanalyst with some anthropological training, Kardiner collaborated with anthropologists in a seminar at Columbia University for almost a decade, developing an innovative model of the culture-specific determinants of personality adaptation. Retrospectively, the appearance of his *The Individual and His Society* in 1939 seemed to many "the crystallizing event" in the emergence of neo-Freudian culture-and-personality research, and a determinative influence on the subsequent direction of the field (Gladwin 1961:158; see also Honigmann 1961:104–5; Kaplan 1961:235–36; La Barre 1961:16; Singer 1961:29). A notable exception was Margaret Mead (1959a), whose discussion of Ruth Benedict's participation in culture-and-personality studies in the 1930s omitted any reference to Kardiner's seminar. When Julian Steward (1959) called attention to this "surprising" omission, Mead (1959b) responded that Kardiner's contribution had lacked originality and influence (see also Mead 1959c). Shortly after the publication of *The Individual and His Society*, her estimation had been more favorable. Although she felt that it needed theoretical refinements, she had described the book as a "very real advance in a realistic integration" of psychoanalytic and cultural theory (Mead 1941:604).

William C. Manson is a doctoral candidate in the Department of Anthropology at Columbia University. His major previous publications include "Desire and Danger: A Reconsideration of Menstrual Taboos" (*Journal of Psychoanalytic Anthropology*, 1984) and "Sexual Cyclicity and Concealed Ovulation" (*Journal of Human Evolution*, 1986). His research interests include psychoanalytic anthropology, human sexuality, religion and ideological systems, and the history of anthropology.

Abram Kardiner lecturing in the 1950s. (Courtesy Mrs. Abram Kardiner.)

Student of Franz Boas and Sigmund Freud, collaborator with Ralph Linton and Sandor Rado, Abram Kardiner brought a synthesizing, interdisciplinary acumen to his interpretation of ethnographic data. A balanced assessment of the impact of his psychocultural synthesis on the maturation of psychoanalytically informed culture-and-personality research requires the delineation of his creative encounter with anthropology—within the wider context of neo-Freudian convergences with the social sciences between the two World Wars.

From Boas to Freud

In the years of World War I, Kardiner received training in both anthropology and psychoanalysis, two disciplines still relatively new to the American intellectual landscape. Under the organizational leadership of Franz Boas at Columbia University, American academic anthropology was scarcely two decades old; nonetheless, anthropology departments were already well established at several major universities (see Stocking 1974; 1976). In contrast, American psychoanalytic training was still largely embryonic, and until the second decade of the century the psychiatric community had no more than an eclectic familiarity with Freud's early classic works (Hale 1971). It was only after Freud's momentous visit to America in 1909 that fledgling professional organizations were established, and at the time the preeminent New York Psychoanalytic Society consisted of little more than a handful of physicians who irregularly gathered in the living room of A. A. Brill, its founder (Burnham 1967).

Young Abram Kardiner's contact with the two disciplines came well before that of most other major figures in the later culture-and-personality movement. Born to poor immigrant parents, Kardiner grew up in New York's Lower East Side, and the precarious insecurity of his early childhood was only worsened by his mother's death. After attending public schools, he graduated from the City College of New York in 1912, and enrolled in Cornell Medical School. However, at the end of 1912, devastated by the unhappy outcome of a love relationship, Kardiner dropped out of the medical program. A little more than a year later, he tried a new direction, enrolling in Columbia's doctoral program in anthropology. His training with Boas and Alexander Goldenweiser, Kardiner recalled a half century later, "made an enduring impression on me" (Kardiner 1965:280). Kardiner gained an inductive orientation toward discerning the loosely articulated congruences within cultural wholes—a methodological approach which he later adapted to the format of his seminar with anthropologists, and which radically distinguished his "psychoanalytic anthropology" from the more Frazerian "anecdotal" method of Géza Róheim. But despite his great respect for Boas, Kardiner reluctantly concluded that a career in anthropology was impractical, and decided to return to Cornell

Medical School. There he soon became both student and analysand of Horace W. Frink, an instructor in neurology and member of Brill's psychoanalytic circle who strongly encouraged Kardiner to specialize in psychiatry. When Frink returned from Vienna in 1920 after a didactic analysis with Freud, Kardiner, completing his internship and psychiatric residency, made arrangements to go the following year.

As analysand to Freud, Kardiner was impressed equally by his intuitive insight and by the fallibility of his analytic technique. Thus, although Freud ingeniously resolved Kardiner's childhood phobia of masks, he failed to discern the element of transference in the analysis (Kardiner 1977:58, 61, 98). Kardiner also noticed the remarkable absence in the six-month analysis of the libido theory which Freud had painstakingly refined in the decade before World War I, and had only recently submitted to a wholesale revision in *Beyond the Pleasure Principle* (1920) (Kardiner 1977:69).

While he was in Vienna, Kardiner also attended several lecture courses taught by other leading analysts, including Géza Róheim, who "inducted us into the relations of anthropology and psychoanalysis . . ." (Kardiner 1965: 111). Róheim, who had christened the field of "psychoanalytic anthropology" shortly after the appearance of Freud's *Totem and Taboo* in 1913 (Robinson 1969:81), hewed closely to psychoanalytic orthodoxy, later defending in highly polemical style the primal parricide, phylogenetic memory, and the universality of the Oedipus complex. However, Kardiner, already versed in Boas' unabating opposition to British cultural evolutionism, was less than enthusiastic about *Totem and Taboo*, which had just been sharply criticized by Alfred Kroeber (1920)—ironically, at the same time that Kroeber was engaged in a three-year stint as a practicing psychoanalyst.[1] Surprisingly, Kardiner's misgivings about the imaginative scenario for the origins of culture seem to have been encouraged by Freud himself:

> He regarded it as his privilege to say to me one day, when I was discussing his theory of primal parricide, "Oh, don't take that too seriously. That's something I dreamed up on a rainy Sunday afternoon." (Kardiner 1977:75)

Nonetheless, in the last two decades of his life, Freud had little more than a cursory acquaintance with the contemporary literature of cultural and social anthropology (Thompson 1950:135). "Freud preferred," Kroeber remarked, "to forage in Frazer rather than to read the intellectually sophisticated works of his own age-mate Boas" (1952:300). Freud's last major work, *Moses and*

---

1. Drawn to psychoanalysis during a midlife transition punctuated by personal conflict and professional restiveness with his Boasian inheritance, Kroeber for a time considered abandoning anthropology for his new analytic profession, and remained ambivalently fascinated with psychoanalysis for the remainder of his life (Kroeber 1970:102–16).

Monotheism (1939), reaffirmed the "primal horde" scenario—once again elicit-ing Kroeber's criticism (1939).

Despite his early reservations about Freud's excursion into anthropology, Kardiner's revisionist inclination remained dormant throughout the 1920s, awaiting the stimulus of his seminar on psychoanalysis and the social sciences.

"Culturalist" Psychoanalysis and Interdisciplinary Social Science

Shortly after his return to New York in 1922, Kardiner began several years of clinical study and treatment of hospitalized veterans of World War I suffer-ing from the so-called war neuroses. The libido theory, he came to realize, was inadequate in delineating how such patients, through regressive decom-pensation in response to trauma, exhibited immobilization of basic ego func-tions like speech. Using the concept of *reitschutz* (i.e., inhibitory defense against outer stimuli), which Freud had recently introduced in *Beyond the Pleasure Principle* (1920), Kardiner gradually refined a new etiological schema for the war neuroses, shifting the theoretical emphasis to the adaptive contraction of ego functions in reaction to inordinately stressful experience. His classic paper "The Bioanalysis of the Epileptic Reaction" (1932) synthesized his find-ings on traumatic stimuli and ego adaptation, laying the groundwork for his later formulations on the integrative constellations of ego structure in spe-cific cultures (see Kardiner 1941).

While American anthropologists of a "classical" Boasian persuasion were largely unreceptive to *Totem and Taboo* and to psychoanalysis in general throughout the 1920s (Kluckhohn 1957:67), the Boasian focus on the sym-bolic aspects of culture—language, religion, mythology—perhaps inevitably stimulated the exploration of Freudian theories of unconscious symbolism and psychic defenses, particularly by the "rebelling" Boasians Kroeber and Edward Sapir (Stocking 1974:17). And although Boas evidently viewed Kroeber's pre-occupation with psychoanalysis as "an unfortunate aberration to be borne patiently" (Kroeber 1970:109), he shared with Freud the dual heritage of the *Naturwissenschaften* and the *Geisteswissenschaften* intellectual traditions. Both inductive empiricist and phenomenological idealist, Boas conceived of cul-ture as an intricately coherent, cognitive mosaic which, once existing, orga-nizes and gives meaning to human experience (Stocking 1976:4). The empha-sis on the logico-meaningful congruence of unconscious cultural categories perhaps paralleled Freud's demonstration of meaningful connections between disparate psychic phenomena.

The investigation of interdisciplinary convergences, fostered in the 1920s by the establishment of the Social Science Research Council and the inception of new anthropology departments closely aligned with departments of sociology (Stocking 1976:10–11), was further facilitated by the organization of the interdisciplinary Hanover Conferences and the formation of the Institute of Human Relations at Yale. Harold Lasswell's *Psychopathology and Politics* (1930) pioneered the introduction of psychoanalytic concepts into political science (Jones 1974:25). By 1930 a small contingent of anthropologists was contemplating the theoretical assimilation of basic psychoanalytic formulations (see Kluckhohn 1944). This turn of events is generally credited to Sapir, whose wide-ranging intellectual interests in the social sciences and humanities stimulated the interdisciplinary explorations of both colleagues and students. Versed in Freudian theory as early as 1917, Sapir was increasingly drawn to its study after his first wife's emotional breakdown in the early 1920s. When he came from Ottawa to the University of Chicago shortly after his wife's death, Sapir sought the counsel of the analyst Harry Stack Sullivan (Perry 1982:242–43). Their meeting in 1926 evolved into a close personal friendship, and a remarkable interdisciplinary cross-fertilization. When he moved to Yale in 1931, Sapir initiated a "culture and personality" seminar, enlisting the active participation of Sullivan and the brilliant young social psychologist John Dollard, and influencing such students as Weston La Barre, Scudder Mekeel, John Whiting, and Irvin Child (La Barre 1961: 15).

The fruitful collaboration between Freudian psychology and the social sciences that had germinated in the exchange of ideas among Sapir, Sullivan, Dollard, and Lasswell was dramatically advanced by the influx of emigré scholars from Europe in the early 1930s. Notable among them were the psychoanalysts Karen Horney and Erich Fromm, prominent members of the Berlin analytic circle of the late 1920s who had worked closely with Wilhelm Reich, a pioneer in delineating the social determinants of character structure (Sharaf 1983). In America, their "culturalist" writings soon provided a powerful catalyst for psychoanalytically informed social science. The rise of authoritarian, fascist regimes in Europe, which seemed explicable neither by an exclusively materialist analysis nor by the aim-inhibited libidinal bonding between leader and follower delineated in Freud's *Group Psychology* (1921), was to be substantially illuminated by their psychoanalytic characterology (e.g., Fromm 1941; Reich 1946).

The establishment of formalized training programs in psychoanalysis coincided with the arrival of this first wave of emigré analysts. When a group of leading New York analysts including Kardiner founded the New York Psychoanalytic Institute in 1931, they invited noted Berlin analyst Sandor Rado to assume the position of educational director and to organize the training program according to the Berlin curriculum (Roazen 1975:383). A year later the renowned analyst Franz Alexander, also from Berlin, established the Chicago Institute for Psychoanalysis and enlisted Horney as associate director (Pollock 1978).

Despite his earlier training in anthropology, Kardiner later recalled that his initial involvement in a seminar on psychoanalytic perspectives on the social sciences was fortuitous: in 1932, Rado had responded to his suggestion for the inclusion of such a course in the Institute's curriculum by assigning Kardiner the task (Kardiner 1977:112). The beginning was hardly propitious: in 1933 only two students enrolled for Kardiner's course "The Application of Psychoanalysis to Problems in Mythology, Religion and Ethnology" (Kardiner 1965:282). Immersing himself in the works of Wallis Budge on Egyptian religion, Kardiner at first did little more than suggest that the "family constellation sagas" of specific cultures directly corresponded to actual features of social organization. Thus, in lieu of a patriarchal, monogamous Oedipus narrative, ancient Egyptian culture highlighted the saga of Osiris, whose marriage to Isis and murder by Set could be traced to brother-sister marriage and sibling rivalry as social structural features (see Kardiner 1956:60). The influence of Malinowski, particularly as mediated by the enthusiastic evaluation of the Trobriand materials regarding the Oedipus complex in Reich's *Der Einbruch der Sexualmoral* (1932), seems evident.

Several developments in 1934 gave a further impetus to the slowly emerging rapprochement between "culturalist" psychoanalysis and anthropology. Leaving the Chicago Institute, Horney came to New York, where she formed a neo-Freudian triumvirate with Sullivan and Fromm, and joined Kardiner and other nascent "culturalists" at the New York Institute. At the Hanover Conference that year, John Dollard's successful conversion of Margaret Mead to a modified Freudian theoretical orientation was something of a watershed for American anthropology (see Mead 1962:127–28). The same year saw Sapir's seminal paper "The Emergence of the Concept of Personality in a Study of Cultures," in which he argued that the reification of culture was only a "convenient fiction of thought," and stressed the panhuman, biopsychological bases of cultural adaptations (1934:413). However, it was in fact such a "reifying" work, Benedict's *Patterns of Culture* (1934), which galvanized anthropological interest in the interplay of "culture" and "personality." Grounded in the *Völksgeist* tradition (as exemplified by Dilthey, Nietzsche, and Spengler) and configurationist Gestalt psychology, Benedict elaborated the cultural-relativist and cultural-determinist tendencies in Boasian anthropology along lines that Sapir found questionable, depicting the passive enculturation of a personality essentially isomorphic with its magnified cultural counterpart. However, this did not preclude many of her Columbia students from recognizing the implicit psychiatric applications adumbrated in her work (see Henry 1936; Landes 1937; Opler 1938).

By the mid-1930s John Dollard's psychocultural perspective was manifested in his classic studies *Criteria for the Life History* (1935) and *Caste and Class in a Southern Town* (1937). At Yale, the Sapir-Dollard seminar was complemented by Clark Hull's seminars on psychoanalysis and learning theory, from which Dollard and Neal Miller derived the theoretical foundations for their later *Social Learning and Imitation* (1941). Influenced by the Freudian interests of Sapir, Scudder Mekeel published early papers on psychoanalytic approaches to culture (1935, 1937), and collaborated with the child analyst Erik H. Erikson in the late 1930s. Yet, despite these developments in New Haven and New York, and the increasing interest of American intellectuals in Freudian theory, anthropologists in the 1930s remained for the most part little interested (Du Bois 1961:xvii). Reviewing the indexes of the *American Anthropologist* and the leading anthropology texts of the decade, La Barre (1958) found virtually no listings for either Freud or psychoanalysis.

After mid-decade, however, Kardiner's seminar began to prosper. At the New York Psychoanalytic Institute he shared teaching duties with internationally known analysts such as Horney, Brill, Rado, and Zilboorg, who were joined at the end of the decade by the remarkable triumvirate of Hartmann, Kris, and Loewenstein. As the Institute increasingly drew students from a broad range of disciplines (Atkin 1962:27), Kardiner's seminar grew to a class of about a hundred, a number of whom were anthropologists (Fine 1979:107). In the spring of 1936, Kardiner began his collaborative efforts with Cora Du Bois, who had arranged to do postgraduate work with him under a National Academy of Sciences grant to study the uses of psychiatry in anthropology (Du Bois 1980:2). With a doctorate in anthropology from Berkeley and recent work in psychiatry and psychological assessment at Harvard (where Henry A. Murray had introduced the Thematic Apperception Test only the year before), Du Bois brought along an invaluable interdisciplinary training to her participation in Kardiner's seminar. The two of them collaborated in presenting a comprehensive critique of Freud's sociological and anthropological writings, which Du Bois elaborated the following year in her "Some Anthropological Perspectives on Psychoanalysis" (1937) (see also Kardiner 1939:372–408). The spring 1936 seminar also included Du Bois' presentation of ethnographic descriptions of Trobriand and Kwakiutl cultures for intensive discussion and analysis.

Although the seminar had so far produced no innovations in psychocultural theory, by the following spring the list of participating anthropologists was imposing. Coming down from Yale, Sapir attended, along with Dollard, who presented materials on the psychology of minority groups. Benedict, who had tentatively suggested folkloric elements of compensatory wish fulfillment in her *Zuni Mythology* (1935), joined Ruth Bunzel in providing field materials on Zuni socialization, religion, and mythology for Kardiner's seminar analysis (Modell 1983:258). Du Bois continued to present ethnographic synopses to the seminar (notably the Chukchee), but began to feel the need for new fieldwork to test the psychocultural concepts Kardiner was beginning to develop—although his published seminar analyses were still limited to the comparison of cultures in terms of the individual's "security system" (the constellation of ego-mediated impulse controls stabilized by guaranteed social acceptance and protection [see Kardiner 1936; 1937a; 1937b]).

Kardiner's theoretical framework was elaborated in the context of the increasing polarization in the New York analytic community between "orthodox" and "culturalist" factions—a polarization encouraged by Horney's wide-ranging critique of Freud's biologistic assumptions about individual development (see Horney 1939). Although he had delineated defensive processes of the ego as early as *The Interpretation of Dreams* (1900), Freud spent the better part of the next two decades refining his instinct and libido theories, returning to the study of the ego only in the 1920s (Loewenstein 1966: 473). Thus his well-known early paper "Character and Anal Eroticism" (1908) had traced character traits to fixations, sublimations, and reaction formations of pregenital libido. Róheim's early anthropological research had adhered to this framework, deriving cultural types from the outcome of instinctual and libidinal trends (see Róheim 1932). Similarly, other anthropologically oriented psychoanalysts had seen cross-cultural differences in "character" in terms of the impact of specific child-training practices on the libidinal investment of erogenous zones. After visiting a Dakota reservation with Mekeel in the summer of 1937, Erik Erikson suggested that the traditional practice of cradle boarding, often used to immobilize an enraged infant, produced a reservoir of unchannelized energy displaced in adulthood in warfare against external enemies (1939; see also 1945:326–27). Mead and Bateson's fieldwork in Bali in the late 1930s, implicitly grounded in the psychosexual characterology of Abraham, Róheim, and Erikson, also followed René Spitz's recent inferences about the object-relations matrix between mother and child (see Bateson & Mead 1942).

In contrast, Kardiner concurred with revisionists like Horney in rejecting the libido theory as empirically unverifiable. During his early years of collaboration with anthropologists, he had been simultaneously working with Rado in the development of an "adaptational psychodynamics" approach that shifted the theoretical focus of psychodynamics from the instincts and their vicissitudes to the adaptive maneuvers of the ego—the specific integrative formation of ego constellations in response to both organismic and cultural-environmental constraints (see Kardiner 1941:135–76; Rado 1956). Indeed, Kardiner's formulation in 1938 of "basic personality structure" stemmed directly from the theoretical orientation of this emerging "adaptational" school. Two decades later, in a rejoinder to Mead, Kardiner claimed precedence in the formulation of a psychocultural technique for deriving "the personality formation specific to each culture without the aid of the libido theory" (1959:1728).

Linton's Ethnography
and the Emergence of Basic Personality

Shortly after the end of Kardiner's spring 1937 seminar, Cora Du Bois completed extensive preparations for field research in Alor, an island in the Dutch East Indies. Her plan included the collection of detailed life histories and the administration of the Rorschach and other projective tests. But with her departure for the field that fall, another promising collaborator for Kardiner's seminar arrived, when Ralph Linton came to Columbia from the University of Wisconsin, as successor to Boas as chairman of the Anthropology Department. A former and unfavored student of Boas, Linton had left Columbia after World War I to earn his Ph.D. in anthropology at Harvard.[2] After two productive decades as an ethnographer, archeologist, museum anthropologist, and professor, Linton published *The Study of Man* (1936), a wide-ranging synthesis of the historical and functionalist approaches in anthropology which reflected his broad professional experience, fruitful interdisciplinary contacts at Wisconsin, and discussions with Radcliffe-Brown at Chicago. The psychologist Abraham Maslow, a frequent participant in Kardiner's seminar and a former student of Linton's, introduced the two men—a meeting which Kardiner much later called "a very lucky stroke" (1965:291).

In contrast to those Boasians who had worked only among American Indians, Linton had impressive field experience in diverse cultures—the Marquesans of Polynesia, the Tanala of Madagascar, and the Comanche—an asset that became invaluable for Kardiner's psychocultural analyses. Kardiner saw the beginning of their working relationship in the following spring as a turning point in his own theoretical work: "It was in this seminar in 1938 that I really began to find myself in new territory and realized the necessity for certain innovations in psychoanalytic theory" (1977:113). Meanwhile, Ruth Benedict, whose position as acting chairman of the Columbia department had been usurped by Linton's appointment, dropped out of the seminar and turned to the work of other neo-Freudians like Sullivan and Horney (Modell 1983:258).

2. Linton had one year of graduate work under Boas—who considered him a poor student—before serving in the Rainbow Division during World War I. Returning from France to resume his studies, Linton was still wearing his uniform when he came to Boas' office directly from Fort Dix. When Boas coldly told him that while he might register at Columbia, it was "doubtful that he could earn a doctoral degree there," Linton took the next train to Boston (Linton & Wagley 1971:12–14).

In an overcrowded seminar room at the Institute, Linton began by presenting a detailed account of fieldwork among the Tanala, delivering four lectures on the research he had conducted in 1926–27 under the auspices of Chicago's Field Museum of Natural History (see Linton 1933). In the seminar analysis that followed, Kardiner utilized for the first time his modified framework of ego psychology. It was an important precedent for culture-and-personality studies. At the same time that Roheim, Erikson, and Mead were deriving adult character from the libidinal investment of erogenous zones as mediated by child-rearing variables—an approach continued by Gorer (1943) and La Barre (1945) in their studies of Japanese obsessive-compulsive traits—Kardiner focused instead on the adaptive modalities of the ego in relation to impulse regulation. Linton had pointed out that although Tanala mothers freely nursed their infants on demand, they began stringent toilet training in the early months; after six months of age, an infant soiling his mother was severely punished. Such premature discipline, Kardiner suggested, formed the template for obligatory conscientiousness and obedience to authority in adulthood. Extrapolating from his concept of the "security system," he maintained that the concurrence of restrictive anal disciplines and the rewards of the breast initiated a basic ego constellation linking steadfast obedience with parental protection, a psychic adaptation later reinforced in the relation between father and son (see Kardiner 1939).

Later that spring Linton lectured on the Marquesan fieldwork in which he had collaborated with E. S. C. Handy in the early 1920s. The lectures highlighted certain features of Marquesan culture—periodic drought and the threat of famine, a highly skewed male-female sex ratio ostensibly derived from female infanticide, and the polyandrous household. He also gave a copy of Handy's *Marquesan Legends* (1930) to Kardiner, who was immediately intrigued by certain recurring motifs in the folklore. In his unpublished reminiscences Kardiner later suggested that his struggle to understand the Marquesan material had culminated in a radical insight:

> It was then that it first occurred to me to make this differentiation between what I called basic institutions and derived institutions—namely, that female infanticide was an institution that was decisive in creating a particular social patterning, but that the religion and the folklore . . . were derivatives of the kind of personality that was created by it. (1965:297)

This inference that supernatural belief systems derived from the personality integrated by parent-child relations was inspired by Freud's *The Future of an Illusion* (1928):

> While considering the methods used to control, govern, or placate the deity, Freud recognized that they were based on a prototype of real experience—that

of the child with his parents. . . . For the first time, Freud described here the origin of what may be called a *projective system*, that is to say, a system for structuring the outer world and one's relation to it in accordance with a pattern laid down in an earlier experience during ontogenesis. (Kardiner & Preble 1961:236)

This was the genesis of the highly influential "personality mediation" model (LeVine 1982:55–56) which was to be the mainspring for the psychocultural research of John W. M. Whiting and associates (see Whiting & Child 1953; Whiting & Whiting 1978).

In his seminar analysis Kardiner focused on the scarcity of women as a factor conditioning family structure and parent-child relations. In servicing the sexual needs of several husbands, the Marquesan woman developed erotic technique and attractiveness to the detriment of her maternal role. The virtual absence of breastfeeding, a practice viewed by Marquesan women as ruining the erotic shape of the breast, was merely the most salient aspect of maternal neglect. Kardiner then suggested that a constellation of frustrated dependency needs toward the mother was projected into Marquesan folklore. Thus, a frequent motif was the image of woman as a cannibalistic demon, threatening her children and stealing their food. Kardiner went on to point out that since Marquesan children were primarily cared for by the father and secondary husbands, who imposed no restrictive disciplines, the Oedipus complex was muted or nonexistent, and the parental imago was not inflated in its power for reward and punishment. The child's shifting reliance on several protectors was projectively recast in Marquesan religion: gods neither punished nor demanded self-renunciation, and should one deity prove ineffective in providing aid, another could be solicited (see Kardiner 1939).

Kardiner's interpretations were enthusiastically received by seminar participants, and his new collaborator was notably impressed. "As Linton himself repeatedly acknowledged, no one was more surprised than he himself at the astonishing meaningfulness that Kardiner made emerge from Linton's own classic fieldwork on the Marquesans and the Tanala" (La Barre 1961:16). Colleagues encouraged Kardiner to provide a systematic presentation of his psychocultural schema in book form, and shortly after the end of the spring term, he began writing. In a remarkably sustained burst of intellectual effort, Kardiner by the end of the summer had completed the 550-page manuscript (1965:298) of *The Individual and His Society: The Psychodynamics of Primitive Social Organization* (in which were included the two "ethnological reports" Linton had presented to the seminar).

In shifting from Freudian drive psychology and the vicissitudes of the libido, Kardiner emphasized "the relation between institutions and that part of the adaptive apparatus of the individual which is in direct contact with the institutions, that is, the ego" (1939:18). He designated the formative institutions structuring parent-child relations as *primary*: family organization, subsistence methods and sexual division of labor, regular patterns of child care or neglect, feeding and weaning regimens, anal training, and sexual taboos (including aim, object, or both). Creating basic problems of ego adaptation common to the society as a whole, the primary institutions shaped a configuration of related character adjustments Kardiner called *basic personality structure* (1939:126–34). And this culture-specific ego structure in turn integrated "projective systems" that were manifested in *secondary* institutions such as religion, myth, folklore, and ritual.

The success of Kardiner's seminar with Linton did not make the majority of his colleagues at the Institute any more receptive to his psychocultural theorizing. Bertram Lewin, the president of the Institute, had caustically responded to the Marquesan presentation, ridiculing Marquesan polyandry as comparable to the multiple liaisons of his Park Avenue patients (Rado 1973:200). To make matters worse, Kardiner was now arguing without equivocation that Freud's social theories were grounded in the outmoded biological theory of an earlier era: Lamarckian phylogenetic memory, Haeckelian recapitulation theory, instinctual dualism, and energy conservation-transformation (see Kardiner 1939:372–408). His critical modifications of psychoanalytic theory inevitably evoked negative evaluations from orthodox analysts at the Institute (e.g., Lorand 1941). Róheim (1940), whose Institute course "Psychoanalytic Interpretation of Culture" bore little resemblance to Kardiner's "Dynamic Sociology" seminar, claimed credit for some of Kardiner's formulations, although simultaneously criticizing him for emphasizing the socialization of restrictive disciplines rather than the universal "biological structure" of the human species, particularly the prolonged dependency of the child. The widening schism between the orthodox and revisionist factions had climaxed by the dramatic walkout of Horney and her allies in 1941 to form a new organization. Rado and Kardiner continued on at the Institute until 1944, when they established the Columbia Psychoanalytic Clinic (Klein 1956; Eckardt 1978). But already five years before that, Kardiner had accepted Linton's suggestion to move the seminar to Columbia's Department of Anthropology.

The Kardiner-Linton Seminar:
Comanche Permissiveness and Alorese Inconstancy

In the spring of 1939, Linton presented an account of his 1934 summer fieldwork on a Comanche reservation in Oklahoma for Kardiner's seminar analysis. Traditionally bound on cradle boards, Comanche infants nonetheless received consistent maternal care and were nursed on demand. Neither weaning nor sphincter control was prematurely imposed, and children's sex play, with the exception of the brother-sister taboo, was freely permitted. This rather tenuous impulse repression, Kardiner suggested, restricted intrapsychic conflict and compensatory fantasy, and the relatively unimpeded ego development was further bolstered by the socialization emphasis on the child's increasing mastery of the outer world. Kardiner suggested that the resulting ego structure, relatively free of conflicts, was reflected in the paucity of elaborated projective systems among the Comanche. And with the absence of any psychodynamic constellation linking self-renunciatory obedience with parental protection, Comanche ritual, unlike other Plains cultures, was devoid of masochistic privations or ingratiation as means of soliciting supernatural aid (see Kardiner et al. 1945).

Kardiner and Linton's seminar on the "Psychological Analysis of Primitive Cultures" proved extremely popular among anthropology graduate students at Columbia. As in previous years, eminent anthropologists were invited to discuss their fieldwork. Although Mead, recently returned from Bali, declined to participate in the seminar (Kardiner 1965:306), Clyde Kluckhohn, in New York for the fall, agreed to present his Navajo research for Kardiner's interpretation. And although she never presented her Pueblo or Canadian Blackfoot materials, Esther Goldfrank was a regular participant for several years (Goldfrank 1978:111–12).

When Cora Du Bois returned from Alor that year, Kardiner immediately recognized the outstanding potential of her field materials for psychocultural analysis. Linton's fieldwork, impressive as it was, had been carried on in more traditional terms, and had lacked the life histories and personality-assessment materials needed to test Kardiner's predictions about basic personality structure. Du Bois' Alorese work, however, had been explicitly focused on psychological issues. Her material included an extensive account of the life cycle and personality development, eight highly detailed autobiographies, and various projective test results including Rorschach, Porteus maze, word association, and children's drawings. Eager to devote the fall 1939 and spring 1940 semesters to the study of Alorese personality, Kardiner hurried through a cursory and unconvincing analysis of Kluckhohn's Navajo presentation (Kardiner 1965: 320–21). (Even so, five years later Kluckhohn acknowledged the Kardiner-Linton Seminar as unquestionably "the outstanding integration" of anthropology and psychiatry [1944:611].)

In a series of presentations Du Bois demonstrated how both Alorese parent-child relations, and their consequent *modal personality* (a more statistical term she preferred to Kardiner's "basic personality structure"), were structured by the subsistence economy and the sexual division of labor. Away tending and harvesting her gardens the entire day, the Alorese mother typically left her infant with family members unable to nurse him. When the child learned to walk, his deprivations were increased by irregular weaning, as well as the lack of regular provision for food when the mother was away. This frustration of hunger and dependency needs created more tensions than sources of discharge, which resulted first in temper tantrums, and later in theft and running away.

In his seminar analysis, Kardiner suggested that the intermittent maternal presence encouraged a tenuous attachment to the mother and an ambivalent maternal imago, as both a frustrating and gratifying object. Gender relations in adulthood were also strongly ambivalent, men seeking an industrious mother-provider who could never be found, and women resentful of their maternal and economic burdens. These early constellations of Alorese parent-child relations were projectively refashioned in religion and folklore. Just as the poor frustration-reward balance reduced the parental imago as a source of beneficence and aid, so the ancestors were not solicited for good fortune, but appealed to only in times of emergency. Motifs of parental deceit and desertion commonly recurred in the folklore. One striking tale, for example, recounted how a boy named Pada was sent by his mother to fill a water tube in a stream, only to discover that she had secretly made a hole in the tube. When he finally returned, he found that his parents had left the village, deserting him (see Du Bois 1944; Kardiner 1944; Kardiner et al. 1945).

To cross-check the validity of Kardiner's conclusions about Alorese basic personality as manifested in the life histories, the psychiatrist and Rorschach expert Emil Oberholzer was requested to undertake a "blind" analysis of the protocols. His synopsis of Alorese personality traits remarkably paralleled Kardiner's, presenting "many striking correspondences" (Barnouw 1973:155).

In later semesters, participants who presented their field materials included Carl Withers (on a small Missouri town he called "Plainville"), Charles Wagley (on the Tapirapé of Brazil), Marian Smith (on the Sikh), Francis L. K. Hsu (on the pseudonymous "West Town," a village in western Hunan, China), and Ernestine Friedl and Victor Barnouw (on the Wisconsin Ojibwa). Although Kardiner's subsequent interpretations were generally well received, none of these presentations yielded the definitive psychocultural analyses he had achieved when working with Linton and Du Bois.

The Wartime Shift to "National Character"

Despite the initially favorable reception of The Individual and His Society by a few anthropologists, a combination of circumstances limited its immediate impact on developing culture and personality theory. Its publication by a university press, which Kardiner was obliged to subsidize, did not facilitate wide distribution; and, shortly after the first printing was exhausted, the plates were destroyed (Kardiner 1965:299–300). More significantly, the fact that the book was a genuine attempt at psychocultural synthesis seems to have made it more difficult for members of both the synthesized disciplines to appreciate. Boasian anthropologists, who emphasized the ideational components of culture, could readily follow theories regarding "patterns," "configurations," and "ethos," but they balked at unfamiliar psychodynamic constructs. Neo-Freudian analysts, despite their avowedly "culturalist" orientation, proved to be surprisingly uninformed about anthropological theory and comparative ethnography; Fromm's well-known concept of "social character" (1941), for example, was delineated within the exclusive confines of Western history and culture. Orthodox psychoanalysts steadfastly ignored Kardiner's interdisciplinary theorizing; as Kardiner later remarked with chagrin,

> . . . I have had to work completely alone, without benefit of discussion with my fellow psychiatrists. Their avoidance of the problems connected with this work has been due largely to the fact that they regarded it as "sociology," and hence not worthy of attention. (Kardiner 1945:xix)

Anthropologists with psychoanalytic training were still anomalous in 1940; thus, the praise of Kardiner's work by Devereux (1940; 1945)—and, more begrudgingly, by Róheim (1947)—fell largely on deaf ears. Mead acknowledged Kardiner's work as "an important theoretical emancipation" from the classical psychoanalytic anthropology of Roheim (1941:604), but she was little more cognizant of the recent innovations of ego psychology (A. Freud, Hartmann) and adaptational psychodynamics (Rado, Kardiner) than other culture-and-personality theorists at the time.

Perhaps most important, the appearance of *The Individual and His Society* just before World War II was less than opportune. With the curtailment of fieldwork possibilities for the duration of the war, Benedict and Mead spearheaded a shift from small-scale tribal societies to the "study of culture at a distance"—more specifically, to the "national character" of the major European and Asian nations involved in the conflict (see Mead & Métraux 1953). Despite a selective application of Freudian concepts (e.g., Gorer 1943; La Barre 1945), the seminal "national character" studies of this period continued in the *Völksgeist* tradition revitalized by Benedict's widely read *Patterns of Culture*. If culture was indeed "personality writ large," then the collective psyche of an entire nation—its distinctive configuration of temperament, values, *Weltanschauung*—could be illuminated from the analysis of its literary, artistic, and religious creations. Mead's *And Keep Your Powder Dry* (1942) was soon followed by Benedict's *The Chrysanthemum and the Sword* (1946) and Geoffrey Gorer's *The American People* (1948). Gregory Bateson, who had earlier described the complementary ethoses of Iatmul males and females in *Naven* (1936), elaborated his concept of recurrent polarities in interpersonal relations (e.g., dominance-submission) as related to the distinctive national character of each nation (Bateson 1942).

When it was published in 1944, Du Bois' *The People of Alor*, which included Kardiner's analyses, was uniformly commended as a pioneering psychocultural synthesis of field observation, life histories, and projective testing (see Hallowell 1945; Henry 1945; Powdermaker 1945). The second volume produced by the seminar, *The Psychological Frontiers of Society* (Kardiner et al. 1945), included the ethnographic accounts and analyses of Alor, Comanche, and "Plainville"—as well as substantial refinements of Kardiner's categorizations in his psychocultural model. However, the inclusion of the Plainville analysis, which drew broad inferences about Euro-American basic personality from this rural community of 275 inhabitants, subjected Kardiner to the same criticisms about personality uniformity in complex societies that were to be accorded to Mead, Benedict, Gorer, and their colleagues for their national-character studies. Anticipating such objections, Linton (1945) complemented his affirmation of the basic-personality concept with an elaboration of his own formulation of "status personality" (see also Linton 1949).

As a result of Linton's departure in 1946 to accept a Sterling professorship at Yale, and the appointment of Julian Steward to succeed him as chairman of the Columbia Anthropology Department, Kardiner's seminar continued in a less favorable theoretical climate. When Benedict initiated Columbia's Research in Contemporary Cultures project in 1947, enlisting Mead, Gorer, Erikson, and many others in interdisciplinary studies of national character, Kardiner's opposition to the project was unwavering. Without a psychodynamic technique for tracing intrapsychic integrative processes, he argued, the researchers would be unable to distinguish the enduring character constellations formed during ontogenesis from more superficial, transient attitudes (see Kardiner 1949:64). His eroding position in the Anthropology Department was not strengthened by his negative assessment of the Benedict project, and in 1947 he transferred his seminar to the Department of Sociology.

Gorer and Rickman's ill-fated *The People of Great Russia* (1949), one of the main products of the Contemporary Cultures project, precipitated the eventual demise of simplified Freudian causal schemes relating adult personality to the instinctual canalization of specific child-rearing practices. Despite Mead's (1954) attempted defense of Gorer's research, his "inductive leap" from the alleged practice of infant swaddling to adult "manic-depressive" personality was widely criticized (Inkeles & Levinson 1954:997). Karl A. Wittfogel's dismissal of such studies as "diaperology" (Goldfrank 1983:6) merely distilled the growing criticism of anthropological "national character" research (see Orlansky 1949; Lindesmith & Strauss 1950). In this context, Kardiner's work tended to suffer a certain guilt by mis-association. Nonetheless, although its genetic and integrative features were sometimes neglected, his basic-personality concept proved more enduring than the ambiguous notion of national character.

Kardiner's Legacy to Psychological Anthropology

Twenty years after the appearance of *The Individual and His Society*, Kaplan suggested that Kardiner's concept of basic personality structure was "perhaps the most influential conception in the culture and personality field" (1961: 235–36). Du Bois' related concept of modal personality was widely adopted by culture-and-personality researchers as a statistical construct for their analyses of Rorschach protocols (e.g., Wallace 1952). Her innovative research design, collecting life histories and Rorschach test results to be independently analyzed by psychiatrists, set a methodological precedent for later interdisciplinary field studies, perhaps most notably Gladwin and Sarason's *Truk: Man in Paradise* (1953).

More adequate testing of hypotheses about culture-personality interactions was further facilitated by the Cross-Cultural Survey (later HRAF) which George Peter Murdock had initiated at Yale with support from the U.S. Navy during World War II. John W. M. Whiting, whose classic *Becoming a Kwoma* (1941) had applied Hull's behaviorist learning theory to the enculturation process, later incorporated both Hullian theory and Murdock's methodology into a modified version of Kardiner's psychocultural model. Using a revised terminology, Whiting and Child's landmark *Child Training and Personality* (1953) nonetheless adhered to Kardiner's scheme of personality as "mediator" between formative and derivative cultural institutions (LeVine 1982:56), and tested various hypotheses on the relation between child-training variables and "projective systems." Discussing the theoretical continuity between Kardiner and Whiting, Marvin Harris argued that "in essence, Whiting has carried the work of Kardiner's seminar into its cross-cultural phase and produced the first statistically valid proofs of the feasibility of explaining the details of ideological patterns through a modified version of Kardiner's causal chain" (1968: 450). Although Whiting's cross-cultural method and his schematic recasting of Kardiner's "primary" and "secondary" institutions were not uniformly accepted by other culture and personality researchers, his recognition of the utility of Kardiner's "projective systems" was widely shared among psychologically oriented anthropologists (Devereux & La Barre 1961:392). John J. Honigmann, for example, followed Kardiner's delineation of projective systems, and demonstrated a meaningful congruence between parent-child relations and folklore among the Kaska Indians (1949:307–10). Melford Spiro stated that it was through Kardiner's work that he "became convinced of the importance of 'projective systems' for the understanding of those aspects of culture that are not 'reality' based" (1978:337; see also Spiro & D'Andrade 1958). Victor Barnouw, whose fieldwork in the 1940s among the Wisconsin Chippewa was an assignment for the Kardiner-Linton seminar, has similarly testified to the impact of Kardiner's approach (1978; 1981). In *The Making of Psychological Anthropology*, George Spindler emphasized the importance of Kardiner's theoretical schema for the whole postwar generation of culture-and-personality workers:

> . . . this model was a major breakthrough in the attempt to integrate psycho-cultural systems with one explanatory model. It promised to bring it all together. It is impossible now to recapture the great excitement that this grand model generated. . . . It was a daring conception and we have not seen its like since. Today this model is still somewhere in the thinking of most of us. (1978a:23)

The demonstrable impact of Kardiner's psychocultural synthesis on leading culture-and-personality researchers of the postwar period refutes Mead's claim that his only original contribution—which neither she nor Benedict "found useful"—was "his theory of primary and secondary institutions" (1959b: 1514). Although Mead later suggested that "an enormous amount of time is wasted in arguing out claims and counter-claims of priority, originality, and magnitude of contribution" (1962:116), her own depreciation of the significance of Kardiner's work has plainly necessitated some revisionist compensation in the history of the culture-and-personality field. Despite the gradual demise of "national character" studies in the early 1950s, a young generation of psychologically informed anthropologists incorporated Kardiner's formulations of basic personality, projective systems, and personality mediation into the various syntheses of neo-Freudian theory, behaviorist learning models, and cross-cultural methodology which came to comprise the field of "psychological anthropology" (see Hsu 1961).

Acknowledgments

I wish to thank George W. Stocking and Robert F. Murphy for helpful suggestions on previous versions of this essay, and the staff of the Oral History Research Office of Columbia University for assistance in locating materials.

References Cited

Atkin, S. 1962. The fruition of an idea. In *Fruition of an idea: Fifty years of psychoanalysis in New York*, ed. M. Wangh, 23–29. New York.
Barnouw, V. 1973. *Culture and personality*. Rev. ed. Homewood, Ill.
———. 1978. An interpretation of Wisconsin Ojibwa culture and personality: A review. In Spindler 1978b:62–86.

————. 1981. Ruth Benedict. In *Masters: Portraits of great teachers*, ed. J. Epstein, 165–77. New York.

Bateson, G. 1936. *Naven*. Cambridge.

————. 1942. Some systematic approaches to the study of culture and personality. *Character & Personality* 11:76–82.

Bateson, G., & M. Mead. 1942. *Balinese character: A photographic analysis*. New York.

Benedict, R. 1934. *Patterns of culture*. Boston (1959).

————. 1935. *Zuni mythology*. New York.

————. 1946. *The chrysanthemum and the sword: Patterns of Japanese culture*. Boston.

Burnham, J. 1967. Psychoanalysis and American medicine: 1894–1918. *Psych. Issues* 5(4), Monograph 20.

Devereux, G. 1940. Review of Kardiner 1939. *Character & Personality* 8:253–56.

————. 1945. The logical foundations of culture and personality studies. *Trans. N.Y. Acad. Scis.* 7:110–30.

Devereux, G., & W. La Barre. 1961. Art and mythology. In *Studying personality cross-culturally*, ed. B. Kaplan, 361–403. Evanston, Ill.

Dollard, J. 1935. *Criteria for the life history*. New Haven.

————. 1937. *Caste and class in a Southern town*. New Haven.

Du Bois, C. 1937. Some anthropological perspectives on psychoanalysis. *Psychoanal. Rev.* 24:246–73.

————. 1944. *The people of Alor: A social-psychological study of an East Indian island*. Minneapolis.

————. 1961. Two decades later. In *The people of Alor* (reprint of Du Bois 1944), xvi–xxx. New York.

————. 1980. Some anthropological hindsights. *Ann. Rev. Anth.* 9:1–13.

Eckardt, M. H. 1978. Organizational schisms in American psychoanalysis. In *American psychoanalysis: Origins and development*, ed. J. Quen & E. Carlson, 141–61. New York.

Erikson, E. H. 1939. Observations on Sioux education. *J. Psych.* 7:101–56.

————. 1945. Childhood and tradition in two American Indian tribes. *Psychoanal. Study Child* 1:319–50.

Fine, R. 1979. *A history of psychoanalysis*. New York.

Freud, S. 1900. *The interpretation of dreams*. New York (1937).

————. 1908. Character and anal eroticism. *Collected papers* II, 45. London (1924).

————. 1913. *Totem and taboo*. London (1950).

————. 1920. *Beyond the pleasure principle*. London (1950).

————. 1921. *Group psychology and the analysis of the ego*. New York (1965).

————. 1928. *The future of an illusion*. New York (1957).

————. 1939. *Moses and monotheism*. New York (1955).

Fromm, E. 1941. *Escape from freedom*. New York.

Gladwin, T. 1961. Oceania. In Hsu 1961:135–71.

Gladwin, T., & S. Sarason. 1953. *Truk: Man in paradise*. New York.

Goldfrank, E. S. 1978. *Notes on an undirected life: As one anthropologist tells it*. Flushing, N.Y.

————. 1983. Another view: Margaret and me. *Ethnohistory* 30:1–14.

Gorer, G. 1943. Themes in Japanese culture. *Trans. N.Y. Acad. Scis.* 5:106–24.

————. 1948. *The American people.* New York.

Gorer, G., & J. Rickman. 1949. *The people of Great Russia.* London.

Hale, N. G. 1971. *Freud and the Americans.* New York.

Hallowell, A. I. 1945. Review of Du Bois 1944. *Am. J. Soc.* 50:322.

Handy, E. S. C. 1930. *Marquesan legends.* Honolulu.

Harris, M. 1968. *The rise of anthropological theory.* New York.

Henry, J. 1936. The personality of the Kaingang Indians. *Character & Personality* 5:113–23.

————. 1945. Review of Du Bois 1944. *Am. J. Orthopsychiatry* 15:372–73.

Honigmann, J. 1949. *Culture and ethos in Kaska society.* New Haven.

————. 1961. North America. In Hsu 1961:93–134.

Horney, K. 1939. *New ways in psychoanalysis.* New York.

Hsu, F. L. K., ed. 1961. *Psychological anthropology: Approaches to culture and personality.* Homewood, Ill.

Inkeles, A., & D. Levinson. 1954. National character: The study of modal personality and sociocultural systems. In *Handbook of social psychology*, ed. G. Lindzey, II, 977–1020. Reading, Mass.

Jones, R. A. 1974. Freud and American sociology, 1909–1949. *J. Hist. Behav. Scis.* 10(1):21–39.

Kaplan, B. 1961. Cross-cultural use of projective techniques. In Hsu 1961:235–54.

Kardiner, A. 1932. The bio-analysis of the epileptic reaction. *Psychoanal. Quart.* 1:375–483.

————. 1936. The role of economic security in the adaptation of the individual. *Family* 17:187–97.

————. 1937a. Influence of culture on behavior. *Social Work Today* 4(5):11–14, 4(6):13–16.

————. 1937b. Security, cultural restraints, intrasocial dependencies, and hostilities. *Family* 18:183–96.

————. 1939. *The individual and his society: The psychodynamics of primitive social organization.* New York.

————. 1941. *The traumatic neuroses of war.* New York.

————. 1944. Some personality determinants in Alorese culture. In Du Bois 1944:176–90.

————. 1945. Preface. In Kardiner et al. 1945:xv–xxi.

————. 1949. Psychodynamics and the social sciences. In Sargent & Smith 1949:59–73.

————. 1956. Adaptational theory: The cross-cultural point of view. In Rado & Daniels 1956:59–68.

————. 1959. Psychosocial synthesis. *Science* 130:1728.

————. 1965. The reminiscences of Abram Kardiner. Unpublished manuscript. Oral History Research Office. Columbia University.

————. 1977. *My analysis with Freud: Reminiscences.* New York.

Kardiner, A., & E. Preble. 1961. *They studied man.* Cleveland.

Kardiner, A., R. Linton, C. Du Bois, & J. West. 1945. *The psychological frontiers of society.* New York.

Klein, H. 1956. The Columbia Psychoanalytic Clinic: A development in psychoanalytic training. In Rado & Daniels 1956: 4–14.

Kluckhohn, C. 1944. The influence of psychiatry on anthropology in America during the past one hundred years. In *One hundred years of American psychiatry*, ed. J. K. Hall, 589–617. New York.

———. 1957. The impact of Freud on anthropology. In *Freud and contemporary culture*, ed. I. Galdston, 66–72. New York.

Kroeber, A. L. 1920. *Totem and taboo*: An ethnologic psychoanalysis. Am. Anth. 22: 48–55.

———. 1939. *Totem and taboo* in retrospect. Am. J. Soc. 45:446–51.

———. 1952. *The nature of culture*. Chicago.

Kroeber, T. 1970. *Alfred Kroeber: A personal configuration*. Berkeley.

La Barre, W. 1945. Some observations on character structure in the Orient: The Japanese. *Psychiatry* 8:319–42.

———. 1958. The influence of Freud on anthropology. Am. Imago 15:275–328.

———. 1961. Psychoanalysis in anthropology. In *Psychoanalysis and social process*, ed. J. Masserman, 10–20. New York.

Landes, R. 1937. The personality of Ojibwa. *Character & Personality* 6:51–60.

Lasswell, H. 1930. *Psychopathology and politics*. New York.

LeVine, R. A. 1982. *Culture, behavior and personality*. 2d ed. Chicago.

Lindesmith, A. R., & A. L. Strauss. 1950. A critique of culture-and-personality writings. Am. Soc. Rev. 15:587–600.

Linton, A., & C. Wagley. 1971. *Ralph Linton*. New York.

Linton, R. 1933. *The Tanala: A hill tribe of Madagascar*. Chicago.

———. 1936. *The study of man*. New York.

———. 1945. *The cultural background of personality*. New York.

———. 1949. Problems of status personality. In Sargent & Smith 1949: 163–73.

Loewenstein, R. 1966. Heinz Hartmann: Psychology of the ego. In *Psychoanalytic pioneers*, ed. F. Alexander et al., 469–83. New York.

Lorand, S. 1941. Review of Kardiner 1939. Am. J. Orthopsychiatry 11:605–6.

Mead, M. 1941. Review of Kardiner 1939. Am. J. Orthopsychiatry 11:603–5.

———. 1942. *And keep your powder dry*. New York.

———. 1954. The swaddling hypothesis: Its reception. Am. Anth. 56:395–409.

———, ed. 1959a. *An anthropologist at work: Writings of Ruth Benedict*. Boston.

———. 1959b. Reply to Steward. *Science* 129:1514.

———. 1959c. Reply to Kardiner. *Science* 130:1728.

———. 1962. Retrospect and prospect. In *Anthropology and human behavior*, ed. T. Gladwin & W. Sturtevant, 115–49. Washington, D.C.

Mead, M., & R. Métraux, eds. 1953. *The study of culture at a distance*. Chicago.

Mekeel, S. 1935. Clinic and culture. J. Abnorm. Soc. Psych. 30:292–300.

———. 1937. A psychoanalytic approach to culture. J. Soc. Philos. 2:232–36.

Miller, N., & J. Dollard. 1941. *Social learning and imitation*. New Haven.

Modell, J. S. 1983. *Ruth Benedict: Patterns of a life*. Philadelphia.

Opler, M. E. 1938. Personality and culture. *Psychiatry* 1:217–20.

Orlansky, H. 1949. Infant care and personality. Psych. Bul. 46:1–48.

Perry, H. S. 1982. *Psychiatrist of America: The life of Harry Stack Sullivan.* Cambridge, Mass.

Pollock, G. 1978. The Chicago Institute for Psychoanalysis from 1932 to the present. In *American psychoanalysis: Origins and development,* ed. J. Quen & E. Carlson, 109–26. New York.

Powdermaker, H. 1945. Review of Du Bois 1944. *Am. Anth.* 47:155.

Rado, S. 1956. Adaptational psychodynamics: A basic science. In Rado & Daniels 1956:15–30.

————. 1973. Psychoanalytic movement: Sandor Rado. Unpublished transcript. Oral History Research Office. Columbia University.

Rado, S., & G. Daniels, eds. 1956. *Changing concepts of psychoanalytic medicine.* New York.

Reich, W. 1932. *Der Einbruch der Sexualmoral.* Berlin.

————. 1946. *The mass psychology of fascism.* 3d ed. New York.

Roazen, P. 1975. *Freud and his followers.* New York.

Robinson, P. 1969. *The Freudian left.* New York.

Róheim, G. 1932. Psycho-analysis of primitive cultural types. *Int. J. Psycho-Anal.* 13:1–224.

————. 1940. Society and the individual. *Psychoanal. Quart.* 9:526–45.

————. 1947. Introduction: Psychoanalysis and anthropology. *Psychoanal. & Soc. Scis.* 1:9–33.

Sargent, S. S., & M. Smith, eds. 1949. *Culture and personality.* New York.

Sapir, E. 1934. The emergence of the concept of personality in a study of cultures. *J. Soc. Psych.* 5:408–15.

Sharaf, M. 1983. *Fury on earth: A biography of Wilhelm Reich.* New York.

Singer, M. 1961. A survey of culture and personality theory and research. In *Studying personality cross-culturally,* ed. B. Kaplan, 9–90. Evanston, Ill.

Spindler, G. 1978a. Introduction to part I. In Spindler 1978b:7–38.

————, ed. 1978b. *The making of psychological anthropology.* Berkeley.

Spiro, M. 1978. Culture and human nature. In Spindler 1978b:330–60.

Spiro, M., & R. D'Andrade. 1958. A cross-cultural study of some supernatural beliefs. *Am. Anth.* 60:456–66.

Steward, J. 1959. Review of Mead 1959a. *Science* 129:322–23.

Stocking, G. W., Jr., ed. 1974. *The shaping of American anthropology, 1883–1911: A Franz Boas reader.* New York.

————. 1976. Ideas and institutions in American anthropology: Thoughts toward a history of the interwar years. In *Selected papers from the* American Anthropologist, *1921–1945,* ed. Stocking, 1–44. Washington, D.C.

Thompson, C. 1950. *Psychoanalysis: Evolution and development.* New York.

Wallace, A. F. C. 1952. *The modal personality of the Tuscarora Indians.* Washington, D.C.

Whiting, J. W. M. 1941. *Becoming a Kwoma: Teaching and learning in a New Guinea tribe.* New Haven.

Whiting, J. W. M., & I. Child. 1953. *Child training and personality.* New Haven.

Whiting, J. W. M., & B. B. Whiting. 1978. A strategy for psychocultural research. In Spindler 1978b:41–61.

MELVILLE HERSKOVITS AND THE SEARCH FOR AFRO-AMERICAN CULTURE

WALTER JACKSON

In the years immediately following World War I, Franz Boas and his students faced a delicate task as they analyzed race and ethnicity in the United States. In a period of intense racism and nativism, Boas used two conflicting strategies to oppose popular beliefs that immigrants and blacks were genetically inferior and "unassimilable" to American culture: one, universalist/assimilationist, the other, particularist/pluralist. His universalist strategy denied the importance of "race" as a category for understanding the mental and emotional characteristics of individuals, and insisted that modern technology was creating a uniform culture in America to which immigrants and blacks were rapidly assimilating. Looking beyond cultural assimilation, he even predicted the eventual physical absorption of immigrant groups and blacks into the American population (see Stocking 1978).

In contrast to this universalist strategy, another strain of Boasian thought emphasized the importance of understanding each culture on its own terms and appreciating the unique contribution of each culture to human civilization. Nineteenth-century romantic nationalism had led to a renewed interest in traditions and folklore in most European countries, and part of the mission of Boasian anthropology was to give to groups that did not enjoy a sense of antiquity the equivalent of a classical past by collecting texts of myths and folklore and by preserving artifacts (Stocking 1977).

Boas never confronted the contradiction between his universalism and his commitment to respect minority cultures; but it would become a central issue for Melville Herskovits, the only Boas student to conduct major investiga-

---

Walter A. Jackson is Assistant Professor of History at North Carolina State University. He is the author of "The Making of a Social Science Classic: Gunnar Myrdal's *An American Dilemma*" (*Perspectives in American History*, 1986).

Melville Herskovits holding a West African religious artifact at Northwestern University, ca. 1935. (Courtesy Northwestern University Archives.)

tions of both African and Afro-American cultures. Herskovits felt this tension between the universal and the particular as he analyzed the relationship between Afro-American and white American culture, studied the historical diffusion of African culture to the New World, and developed a theory of cultural relativism. His ethnographic studies of various Afro-American peoples also reflected tensions in American anthropology during the interwar years between the "scientific" and "historical" methods, between trait analysis and cultural integration, and between social criticism and applied anthropology (Stocking 1976:13–37).

Herskovits is best known to students of Afro-American culture for his book *The Myth of the Negro Past* (1941), in which he argued that blacks in the United States had retained African cultural elements in their music and art, social structure and family life, religion and speech patterns. This position ran counter to the prevailing view in American social science from the 1930s to the 1960s, which was that slavery had stripped blacks of any significant remnants of African culture. During this period, advocates of integration often linked the fight for civil rights to a claim that blacks were as "American" as any other group, fearing that an emphasis upon the Negro's African past would give ammunition to segregationists. Many social scientists argued that black assimilation to white American cultural norms was a necessary part of the struggle for political equality and economic opportunity (Myrdal 1944:928–29). Indeed, the universalist strain of Boasian thought had contributed powerfully to this liberal, assimilationist position.

Ironically, Herskovits, too, had begun his study of Afro-American culture with the view that black culture was much like white culture. In an early article in *Survey Graphic* magazine, he argued that there was "not a trace" of African culture in Harlem and that Harlem was a quintessentially "American" community (1925b). Why, then, did Herskovits' views change so drastically in the late 1920s and 1930s? Why did he embrace this unusual position stressing the retention of African cultural patterns by blacks in the United States? In pursuing these questions, we shall consider not only Herskovits' theory of culture, but also his feelings about ethnic identity, his encounter with the Harlem Renaissance, and his role as a critic of biological racism and as a spokesman for black culture.

Boasian Assimilationism and the "Nordic Nonsense"

Most white American scholars of the early twentieth century portrayed Africa as a land of primitive savagery (Tillinghast 1902; Dowd 1907–14). If they discussed African survivals among Afro-Americans at all, it was generally in the course of arguing that these characteristics unfitted blacks for citizenship.

These racist claims were challenged by a number of pioneer black scholars (Smith 1980). The historian George Washington Williams had offered a more detailed discussion of the African heritage as early as 1883 (Franklin 1985). The Tuskegee sociologist Monroe N. Work, who had become interested in Africa as a graduate student of W. I. Thomas at Chicago, published several articles on African history and culture during the first two decades of the century (McMurry 1985). W. E. B. Du Bois considered the vitality of African influences on Afro-American life in *The Negro* (1915). Carter G. Woodson's Association for the Study of Negro Life and History, founded in 1915, fostered research on the African background of black American culture (Goggin 1983).

Almost alone among white social scientists, Franz Boas had already by that time sought to encourage research on African and Afro-American cultures as part of his wide-ranging attack on nineteenth-century racist assumptions. In 1906 he wrote Andrew Carnegie urging the establishment of an "African Institute" which would study African cultures, measure the anatomy of the Negro, and make "statistical inquiries of the Negro race in this country" (FB/AC 11/30/06, in Stocking 1974:316–18; see also BP: FB/B. T. Washington 11/8/08)). That same year, Boas was invited by Du Bois to deliver the commencement address at Atlanta University, where he spoke of the great kingdoms of West African history, the military power of the Zulu, and the delicate craftsmanship of African art (Boas 1906). Although he believed that African culture had been lost by blacks in America, he stressed the importance of educating black Americans about African culture as a way of increasing race pride and countering the "strong feeling of despondency among the best classes of the Negro." Nevertheless, this interest in using anthropology to foster race pride coexisted with an assumption that miscegenation offered the ultimate solution to racial conflict: "Thus it would seem that man being what he is, the Negro problem will not disappear in America until the Negro blood has been so much diluted that it will no longer be recognized, just as anti-Semitism will not disappear until the last vestige of the Jew has disappeared" (Boas 1921).

Herskovits encountered these issues as a graduate student and postdoctoral fellow at Columbia in the early 1920s. Like several others of his Boasian generation, he wrote a trait-distribution dissertation, "The Cattle Complex in East Africa." But after receiving his Ph.D. in 1923, he was unable to secure funding to undertake fieldwork in Africa. Instead, Boas succeeded in obtaining for him a three-year National Research Council fellowship, for a project in physical anthropology on the effects of race crossing on the bodily form of American Negroes. Boas had long wished to disprove the theory that the mulatto was an unstable type that inherits "all the bad traits of both parental races" (Stocking 1974:317). So Herskovits set about measuring and gathering genealogies from three populations of Afro-Americans: residents of Harlem, Howard University students, and a rural community in West Virginia.

Herskovits' research came at a time of intensified racism and nativism in the United States. In the aftermath of World War I, race riots had broken out in more than twenty American cities. A revived Ku Klux Klan became a politically powerful force in many areas of the North and West as well as in the South. Popular magazines carried articles using IQ test scores and other "scientific" measurements to argue the inferiority of non-Nordic peoples. In 1924 Congress passed an immigration law that imposed quotas based on national origin which drastically reduced immigration from southern and eastern Europe (Higham 1963).

Boas wrote many articles attacking scientific racism in this period. When he was too busy to do them, he delegated these tasks to Herskovits, who quickly became a leading opponent of what Boas called "The Nordic Nonsense" (Herskovits 1924a&b; 1925a&c; 1926a). Charles S. Johnson, the editor of *Opportunity*, wrote him, "I expect the work that you are doing to push that pretentious pile of pseudo-science about race out of the field. So far as I know, now, you have more of the facts for your judgments than any of the others . . ." (HP: CJ/MH 7/29/26).

This young man who threw himself so enthusiastically into the fight against scientific racism was the son of a small-town dry-goods merchant from the Midwest. Born of a Hungarian-Jewish father and a German-Jewish mother, Herskovits for a time considered becoming a rabbi. But although he attended the University of Cincinnati and studied Hebrew and theology at Hebrew Union College in Cincinnati, he found he could not believe in a personal God, and rejected other beliefs of Reform Judaism. A friend who was a rabbinical student urged him to "interpret these traditions to suit your own beliefs" and to "pray to the Social Force and call that God in your mind" (Herskovits 1927a:114). But Herskovits remained unconvinced—and the experience of World War I, during which he served in the Army medical corps, made belief even more difficult. Returning to finish college at the University of Chicago, he majored in history, and then went to New York to the New School for Social Research, where a sparkling array of academic marginals inspired others of his generation who sought rather to understand social forces than pray to the Social Force. There, like Ruth Benedict, he came under the influence of the brilliant Boasian nomad Alexander Goldenweiser, who helped him find an intellectual home in Boas' seminar at Columbia.

Herskovits' circle of friends in New York included Benedict, A. I. Hallowell, the sociologist Malcolm Willey, and Margaret Mead—who later described him as "a bouncing, cheerful, unsquelchable extrovert, writing with gusto, and a fair pride in what he produced" (Simpson 1973:3). Among them he found his future wife, Frances Shapiro, a New Yorker with literary ambitions who had spent a few months in Paris as an expatriated but unpublished writer. In this circle, Herskovits discussed music, avant-garde art, literature, feminism, and politics—reveling in its cosmopolitan ambiance, and sharing its generational revolt against Babbittry. His early unpublished writings include an assault on the *Saturday Evening Post* ideal of the businessman and the "Philosophy of the Plutocracy," and his first published piece was a letter to the editor of the *Freeman* in which he attacked Warren G. Harding and predicted "four more years of staunch, unerring stupidity" (1920). When he first read the Lynds' *Middletown* (1929), Herskovits reacted to it, not as a methodologically innovative work of social science, but as an indictment of bourgeois culture: "a stunning piece of work—much more effective than, for instance, '*Main Street*'" (HP: MH/M. Willey 1/29/29).

As he attempted to apply Boasian cultural analysis to issues of the day, Herskovits realized that the concept of "cultural pattern" had both radical and conservative implications. On the one hand, if culture patterns were "unconscious in their development and capricious in the extreme," it meant that repressive attempts to achieve "social control" over immigrants were unlikely to succeed. Herskovits and Willey glimpsed liberating possibilities as "the concepts of 'good' and 'bad' which we apply in cultural judgments fade before the broadness of vision which is consequent upon an application of the workings of the cultural pattern" (Herskovits & Willey 1923b:197–98). On the other hand, Herskovits acknowledged that William Graham Sumner's "doctrine of the folkways and mores" was "just about the same thing that we call social pattern" (HP: MH/H. Odum 7/5/27). Although he wore an I.W.W. button around Columbia and took an active interest in labor issues, he became discouraged rather early by the conservatism of American workers, who he and Willey argued identified unconsciously with their bosses. Like his teachers Boas and Thorstein Veblen, Herskovits tended to explain economic behavior in cultural terms: culture patterns become established through historical processes and are difficult to alter, even when it is in the interest of the group concerned to change. Similarly, in an unpublished essay on feminism, Herskovits argued that enacting equal-rights legislation would not change the "mores" of society, and that feminists should "attack the huge imponderable of the pattern of the civilization in which we live, rather than keep to the more spectacular but less productive attack on the legislative bodies" ("Toward Masculine Equality," n.d.). Although Herskovits remained politically liberal throughout his life, he retained a quiet pessimism about the ease with which state intervention could alter fundamental social attitudes.

He was very optimistic, however, in the 1920s about the power of American cultural patterns to overcome ethnic particularism. Seeking to refute the racists' claim that immigrants and blacks were incapable of assimilating American culture, he argued that assimilation was, in fact, occurring and that it was an inevitable social process. Although Herskovits had known Horace Kallen at the New School, he rejected Kallen's theory of cultural pluralism, and embraced a thoroughgoing assimilationism as the best answer to the "Nordic Nonsense" (Kallen 1924). And like Goldenweiser (1924:133), he also attacked chauvinistic attitudes within his own ethnic group. In a debunking article rejected by the *Menorah Journal* and published in the *Modern Quarterly*, he ridiculed the myth that Jews enjoyed hereditary advantages in intellect or character, arguing that they possessed no common language, culture, or religion, and that their only common experience was a sense of being vaguely different from those around them. As for himself, he insisted that "neither in training, in tradition, in religious beliefs, nor in culture am I what might be termed a person any more Jewish than any other American born and raised in a typical Middle Western milieu." Jewish identity, Herskovits argued, was a matter of personal and very subjective choice: "A Jew is a person who calls himself a Jew, or who is called Jewish by others" (1927a). In an even more provocative piece, published in the *American Hebrew*, Herskovits chided a Jewish audience about prejudice against blacks and other outsiders: "I do not know of any class of people who are quite as proud, quite as snobbish, as the Jews. . . . [U]ntil we have an attitude of mind that is attuned to tolerance and good will, we will get the prejudices that we deserve." He did observe, however, that "in our radical intellectual circles, Jews or non-Jews, tolerance and good-will toward all persons of whatever type of background are characteristic features" (1926a:624).

It was this cosmopolitan and assimilationist vision that Herskovits brought to the struggle against scientific racism in the 1920s. Although it sustained him for a time, it began to pose problems as he encountered the Harlem Renaissance and the desire of black intellectuals to develop a distinctive cultural tradition with roots in the African past and in Afro-American folklore.

In Cultural Dialogue with the "New Negro"

Not long after he began work on his physical anthropology project, Herskovits met Alain Locke, the philosopher and cultural critic at Howard University, with whom he discussed the Boasian approach to cultural anthropology, focusing on the observation of "traits" and "culture-patterns," (see Herskovits 1925d). In April 1924, Locke asked Herskovits to contribute an article to a special "Harlem" issue of *Survey Graphic* magazine, on the topic "Has the Negro a Unique Social Pattern?" Although Locke sought "an analysis of the Negro's peculiar social pattern, and an estimate of its capacity in social survival and culture building" (HP:AL/MH 4/24/24), the article Herskovits submitted took precisely the opposite approach. Applying a small-town model of community, Herskovits argued that Harlem was an American community like any other, boasting YMCAs, businessmen's associations, Greek-letter fraternities and sororities, gossipy newspapers, and inhabitants who were hardworking, churchgoing, and sexually puritanical. Herskovits was particularly eager to debunk the notion, then popular among black intellectuals such as James Weldon Johnson, that blacks possessed a "distinctive, inborn cultural genius" that manifested itself in African and Afro-American art and music. An integral part of his critique was a rigid insistence upon the discontinuity between African and Afro-American culture. Arguing that there was "not a trace" of African culture in Harlem, Herskovits concluded the piece with a ringing affirmation of the assimilative power of American culture:

> That [Negroes] have absorbed the culture of America is too obvious, almost, to be mentioned. They have absorbed it as all great racial and social groups in this country have absorbed it. And they face much the same problems as these groups face. The social ostracism to which they are subjected is only different in extent from that to which the Jew is subjected. The fierce reaction of race-pride is quite the same in both groups. But, whether in Negro or in Jew, the protest avails nothing, apparently. All racial and social elements in our population who live here long enough become acculturated, Americanized in the truest sense of the word, eventually. They learn our culture and react according to its patterns, against which all the protestations of the possession of, or of hot desire for, a peculiar culture mean nothing.

Black culture and white culture, Herskovits wrote, "were the same pattern, only a different shade!" (1925b:678).

This pointed reference to Locke's request for a study of the Negro's "peculiar social pattern" did not go unanswered. In an "editorial note" published along with Herskovits' article, Locke wrote that while "looked at in its externals, Negro life, as reflected in Harlem, registers a ready—almost feverishly rapid—assimilation of American patterns, what Mr. Herskovits calls 'complete acculturation,'" looked at "internally perhaps it is another matter." Echoing Kallen's cultural-pluralist view, Locke asked, "Does democracy require uniformity? If so it threatens to be safe, but dull. . . . Old folkways may not persist, but they may leave a mental trace, subtly recorded in emotional temper and coloring social reactions" (1925a:676; Herskovits 1925e).

The "Harlem" issue of *Survey Graphic* appeared in revised form as a book entitled *The New Negro*—the most important manifesto of the Harlem Renaissance (Locke 1925b; see also Huggins 1971:56–60). In his introductory essay, Locke observed that while the political goals of the "New Negro" were "none other than the ideals of American institutions and democracy," his "inner objectives" included the development of "self respect" and "race pride." Harlem had become the cultural capital of the "New Negro," the center of a great "race-welding," the "home of the Negro's 'Zionism'"; black Americans were the "advance-guard of the African peoples in their contact with Twentieth Century civilization"; Pan-African congresses and the Garvey movement were harbingers of growing "race consciousness" among both African and Afro-American peoples. Furthermore, blacks had brought a number of "gifts" to American culture, including folk art and music. "The South has unconsciously absorbed the gift of [the Negro's] folk-temperament"—gaining "humor, sentiment, imagination and tropic nonchalance from a humble, unacknowledged source" (1925b:3–16).

Other contributors to *The New Negro* celebrated African art and culture, and discussed their significance for Afro-Americans. Folklorist Arthur Huff Fauset noted the African origin of "Br'er Rabbit" and other Afro-American animal tales. African themes and imagery appeared in the poetry of Claude McKay, Countee Cullen, and Langston Hughes, and several of Aaron Douglas' drawings depicted African subjects. W. E. B. Du Bois surveyed the Pan-African movement and its importance for black Americans. Most significantly, Arthur Schomburg argued that a major cause of bigotry was "that depreciation of Africa which has sprung up from ignorance of her true role and position in human history and the early development of culture": "The Negro has been a man without a history because he has been considered a man without worthy culture." Schomburg believed, however, that the scientific study of African history, culture, and art would allow Negroes to feel "pride and self-respect" (1925:237).

Herskovits was truly the odd man out in this anthology: one of only three white authors, he was the most starkly assimilationist. Nevertheless, he continued his dialogue with black intellectuals. He and Locke remained friends, exchanging books and articles about African art and culture, visiting art collections, and attending Roland Hayes and Paul Robeson concerts. Locke, together with the biologist Ernest Just, arranged for Herskovits to conduct his physical anthropology measurements and to teach at Howard in the spring of 1925 (HP: AL/MH n.d., filed 1/25; MH/AL 1/19/25; MH/AL 4/19/27; MH/AL 11/2/27). At Howard, Herskovits also developed a friendship with Abram Harris, a young economist. As he became more aware of the range of opinion among Afro-American intellectuals, he could not ignore the desire of many blacks to give expression to a sense of cultural uniqueness and to feel a closer relationship to African culture. In an article entitled "Negro Art: African and American," Herskovits observed that "the New Negro . . . has been awakened to the beauty which was produced by his slave ancestry" (1926b:291–98). Noting James Weldon Johnson's claims that there were many African remnants in American Negro songs, he called for further research in this field. The following year, in an article on "Acculturation and the American Negro," he directed attention to "the change at present occurring

in the attitude of intellectual negroes who are interested in artistic movements"
(1927b:218; see also Herskovits 1930:7).

His growing acquaintance with Afro-American intellectuals also made Herskovits aware of their antagonism to the conservatism and materialism of the
black bourgeoisie, a sentiment that paralleled his own aversion to Babbittry
among whites (Locke 1925c; Wolters 1975:89; HP: A. Harris/MH 10/22/27).
He began to ask himself, if YMCAs and businessmen's associations were really all there was to Harlem, what would inspire Afro-Americans to fight for
their rights? His environmentalist theory forced him to deny the claims of
those blacks who argued for an innate Negro spiritual or artistic genius. But
what was he able to offer to them as an alternative source of inspiration, since
he himself held deep reservations about the American dream as professed by
whites in the 1920s?

Herskovits' experiences during these years also confirmed his view that self-
confidence was a key issue for black Americans. He was appalled by the color
prejudice he found among Howard students toward darker-skinned Negroes
(1927b:219–20; 1928b:60). The opposite side of the same coin was the "inferiority complex" of blacks and Jews, which led members of minority groups
to make exaggerated claims for their groups' achievements (HP: MH/H. Kallen
3/27/25). Herskovits believed that the best response he could offer to these
problems was to attempt to achieve "scientific" accuracy in both cultural and
physical anthropology. If he could give Afro-Americans a detailed account
of their history and culture, this knowledge might serve as a basis for race
pride. In a letter to Herbert Seligmann of the N.A.A.C.P., Herskovits emphasized that a change in psychological attitude on the part of blacks was crucial
to the progress of the race:

> As a more or less detached observer of Negro life in this country and of the
> friction between Negroes and Whites, it has been forced upon me that one of
> the reasons the Negro is under the handicap of as much discrimination as he
> is, is because he has never learned to fight back. Though my association with
> Negroes in this country has been in the course of Anthropological research,
> I have again and again encountered situations in which only the refusal to
> undergo an embarrassing situation rather than give up a right was the cause
> of a Negro's being deprived of that right.
>
> It is only the N.A.A.C.P. who have realized the fact I have pointed out above,
> and it is undoubtedly due to their willingness to endure unpleasant situations
> and fight for a right rather than weakly give it up that has resulted, in large
> measure, in making the general white population not quite as ruthless in over-
> riding the Negroes. It is to be hoped that the N.A.A.C.P. will continue with
> as much fervor in the future as in the past to insist that the Negro be regarded
> as the full-fledged and adult human being he is. (HP: MH/HS 10/22/28)

Although he endorsed the work of the N.A.A.C.P., Herskovits was reluctant to join any political organizations, because "the more detached I am in my work, the more effective my results will be and the more they will be trusted by all persons concerned" (MH/HS 10/8/28).

Herskovits' role changed gradually during the middle and late twenties, from speculative, freewheeling advocacy, using social science to make points about a wide range of social issues, to a Boasian restraint, stating the conclusions of "science" about race and culture. Increasingly science, rather than journalistic debunking or cultural radicalism, gave Herskovits a sense of personal autonomy and critical distance from American society. Although he later practiced a kind of implicit social criticism of his own society through his ethnographic writings about other cultures, he contended that the most effective response to the "racial hysteria" of the 1920s was the cultivation of a "detached point of view and a willingness to suspend judgment pending definite information" (1924b:166–68). That such a stance involved a partial denial of his own feisty temperament and passionate concern for justice did not diminish the sincerity with which he attempted to hold to the "coldly analytic approach." By the end of the decade, Herskovits had developed an ability to take criticisms from all quarters, and a conviction that he was pursuing his scientific investigations with scant regard to current political fashions.

His exchanges with Locke and other black intellectuals coincided with the emergence of theoretical problems in Herskovits' research that undermined certain of his initial assumptions. By the fall of 1925, he realized that the data from his study of racial crossing indicated that Negroes were not being absorbed into the general white population as Boas had hoped: more racial mixture had occurred in the nineteenth century than in the twentieth. American Negroes, he concluded, were forming a new racial "type" that was a mixture of African, American Indian, and Caucasian ancestry—and were likely to remain physically distinctive for a long time (HP: MH/Miss Davis 9/23/25; Herskovits 1928a:30–33). As Herskovits pondered this prospect, he began to focus his attention on Afro-American culture and the historical process of acculturation of Africans in the Americas.

Researching African Cultural Survivals in the New World

With his study of race crossing nearing completion, Herskovits wrote a grant application in January 1926 that mapped out much of his life's work. Entitled "Plan for Research on the Problem of the Negro," it proposed an ambitious five-year project entailing research on the physical makeup and culture of blacks in both West Africa and the southern United States. Herskovits defined his research topic as nothing less than the "fundamental problem of the American Negro." He sought to discover from what African peoples the New World Negroes derived, what changes in bodily form had occurred, and whether there were any temperamental similarities between African and American Negroes. He planned also to study African cultural survivals among Afro-Americans, an issue on which his views were to undergo a dramatic reversal during the next two years (HP: MH/National Research Council 1/27/26).

Herskovits proposed first to visit the West African collections in the major European ethnological museums, to conduct fieldwork in Liberia for eighteen months, and to take anthropometric measurements of various peoples in the Ivory Coast and Gold Coast. While fresh from Africa, he would then study the culture and physical characteristics of blacks in the Carolina Sea Islands and in other isolated parts of the American South. After that, he hoped to pursue fieldwork in the West Indies, Brazil, and Surinam. Applying Boasian methodology to the study of the historical diffusion of culture traits, Herskovits intended to look at the persistence of African names such as "Countee" among American blacks, similarities between West African and Afro-American art, and "remnants" of African witchcraft, folklore, and religion in the New World. He also hoped to find out whether there were any connections between African songs and American Negro spirituals.

The proposal was submitted both to the biologically oriented National Research Council and to the Inter-Racial Relations Committee of the Social Science Research Council. Although funding on this scale was generally beyond the reach of young scholars, Herskovits lobbied energetically with members of both organizations for over a year on behalf of the project. Eventually it was endorsed by the S.S.R.C., but it failed to win support from the Laura Spelman Rockefeller Memorial (HP: S. M. Harrison/MH 12/11/26; MH/W. Alexander 10/29/28). Undaunted by this setback, Herskovits pressed on with his research; but he became increasingly frustrated by the foundations' tendency to give priority to sociological work on the contemporary "Negro problem" at the expense of his more "fundamental" investigations.

As he charted a new direction for his research, Herskovits began corresponding in 1926 with the German ethnomusicologist Erich von Hornbostel concerning African influences on Afro-American music and dance. Although Hornbostel had published an article arguing that American Negro spirituals were primarily derived from European musical forms, he had noted one African characteristic: "the form consisting of the leading lines sung by a single voice, alternating with a refrain sung by the chorus,"—a form which was "comparatively scarce in European folksongs." He also suggested that the slaves had selected from the range of European folk tunes those reminding them of African rhythmical devices (1926:751). Herskovits regarded Hornbostel's article as "one of the best studies in the processes of acculturation I've come across," but he objected to Hornbostel's claim that similarities in motor behavior in African and Afro-American dances could be explained as an innate racial characteristic, since most American Negroes were of mixed ancestry. Suggesting that human beings were "very fundamentally conditioned (this in the sense of the word as used by the behavioristic psychologists) by the manner of behavior of the people among whom they happen to be born," Herskovits wondered if it was not possible that "this element of motor behavior might not be a cultural remnant brought to America by the African slaves, which their descendants retained even after the songs themselves were fundamentally changed according to the European pattern?" (HP: MH/E. M. Von Hornbostel 6/10/27).

Herskovits made it clear that his views were not the result of abstract speculation. He had had the opportunity to observe the motor behavior and gestures of his research assistant, Zora Neale Hurston, who was then an anthropology graduate student at Columbia. Although she was "more White than Negro in her ancestry," her "manner of speech, her expressions,—in short, her motor behavior"—were "what would be termed typically Negro." Herskovits had noted Hurston's motor behavior while she was singing spirituals, and he suggested that these movements had been "carried over as a behavior pattern handed down thru imitation and example from the original African slaves who were brought here" (HP: MH/E. M. von Hornbostel 6/10/27).

Despite this discussion of African "remnants" in his private correspondence, Herskovits continued for another two years to maintain in his published work that Negroes in the United States had accepted the culture patterns of white Americans and retained little of their ancestral culture. In his study of physical anthropology, *The American Negro*, Herskovits included a chapter "White Values for Colored Americans," which essentially repeated the arguments of his essay in *The New Negro*: Harlem was "to all intents and purposes an American community peopled by individuals who have an additional amount of pigmentation in their skins," (1928a:57–58). The idea of Negro acculturation to white values was too central to the argument of *The American Negro* to be abandoned without major evidence to the contrary. In a review of Newbell Niles Puckett's *Folk Beliefs of the Southern Negro*, Herskovits accepted with some reservations the African origin of Southern Negro conjuring practices, but he doubted that there were any African elements in American Negro religion (1928b).

After he failed to obtain a grant to go to Africa, Herskovits was offered an opportunity to study the "Bush Negroes" of Surinam, a group descended from runaway slaves who had maintained a culture remarkably free of white domination since the seventeenth century. The fieldwork was financed by Elsie Clews Parsons, an anthropologist of independent means who had written books and articles on Afro-American folklore. Herskovits and his wife made two trips to Surinam, in the summers of 1928 and 1929 co-authoring

Rebel Destiny (1934), a popular account of their experiences with the Saramaccan people, and *Suriname Folklore* (1936), a more scholarly volume.

Herskovits had gone to Surinam with two purposes in mind: to discover
the cultural origin of the American Negro by correlating traits of Bush Negro
culture with traits of various West African cultures, and to study the fusion
of European, American Indian, and African elements in Bush Negro culture
(HP: MH/E. M. von Hornbostel 5/23/28). Once in the field, however, he
was genuinely startled by the large number of West African words and place
names he found among the Saramacca, and by similarities between Saramaccan and West African music, folklore, religion, and art (HP: MH/Boas
10/22/28; MH/C. G. Seligman 10/29/28; MH/D. Westermann 9/27/28).
When he returned from his first trip, he wrote excitedly to Ralph Linton that
"the civilization of the Bush Negroes is much more African than anyone has
dreamed" (HP: MH/RL 10/1/28). Similarly, a letter to W. E. B. Du Bois proclaimed that "Our trip to Suriname exceeded all my expectations. It is a rich
culture there and a going concern that is almost completely African" (HP:
MH/Du Bois 10/29/28).

In *Rebel Destiny* the Herskovitses provided an engaging, if slightly romantic, account of their visit to the Saramacca, along with some indirect social
criticism of white American culture. They greatly admired the pride and dignity of the Saramacca, who had defeated white attempts at reenslavement
and maintained for 300 years what they believed to be an essentially African
civilization. "Today when a Bush Negro drinks with a white man," they noted,
"his toast is 'Free'" (vii). The Saramacca were clever, practical people who took
a "trickster's" delight in outwitting the white man. The book's novelistic format allowed scope to develop in some depth the personalities of several
Saramaccans and to give a sense of how each of these individuals functioned
in the culture: Apanto, the sorcerer; Sedefo, their guide and paddler; Bayo,
the playboy; and that most memorable figure, Moana Yankuso, the headman, who proved to be a formidable critic of the white man's culture. Fearing
that another world war would deprive the Saramacca of needed trade down
river, he addressed a letter, through a missionary, to the League of Nations,
counseling the white leaders to keep the peace (253).

Rebel Destiny offers glimpses of Melville Herskovits' cultural relativism. In
an era when many writers attributed practices such as spirit possession and
polygamy to innate racial temperament, the Herskovitses took pains to explain that these behavior patterns were part of an ordered, coherent, disciplined culture that made sense to its members and provided some benefits
that white American culture did not. They devoted a great deal of attention
to how they were perceived by the Saramacca, and explained how the Saramacca summoned their *obia*, or magic, to confront and control the visitors:
at every turn, their research was shaped by the limits of permissible behavior

in Saramacca culture—which allowed no one "to impart to a stranger . . . more than half of what he knew" (30). Even so, the Herskovitses were able to overcome some of the suspicions of their hosts by playing recordings of West African songs and showing photographs of West African art. After returning to the United States, Melville Herskovits wrote headman Yankuso, "When we return [sic] to Africa we shall tell the people there of their children in the Saramacca country and I am sure they will be as glad to hear of you as you were to hear of them" (HP: MH/M. Jankoeso 10/7/29).

Surinam was for Herskovits a key that unlocked the historical problem of which West African cultures furnished the slaves to America, and the "leads" he found there pointed him toward Dahomey. After he and Frances Herskovits finally succeeded in getting to Africa in 1931 for fieldwork in Dahomey, he became the only social scientist who had studied at first hand both African and Afro-American cultures (1937c). But the Saramaccan people had also offered a vision of how the ancestors of North American blacks had lived in the seventeenth century, and a model for blacks in the United States of pride in the African past. Herskovits now began to see himself as an interpreter of Africa to Afro-Americans.

Herskovits' basic position on "Africanisms" in the Americas was defined by 1930 in an article, "The Negro in the New World," in which he developed a scale of the "intensity of Africanisms"—ranging from the Bush Negroes at one end to urban blacks in the northern United States at the other. He also outlined some of the issues that he would investigate for the next fifteen years, including the questions of how various New World Negro peoples had adapted African cultural traits to their societies and of how "tenacious" African cultural forms were when they came into contact with more technologically advanced societies. Emphasizing how little was known about New World Negro groups, Herskovits pointed out the need for more research in physical anthropology, linguistics, the family, and especially the expressive elements of culture. "Certainly it is in folklore, religion, and music that much of the attack must be centered"—"for it is principally here, certainly as far as the Negroes of the United States and most of the West Indies are concerned, that possible African cultural survivals are to be salvaged." Although Herskovits was cautious in making claims about the persistence of African cultural elements among blacks in the northern United States, he did suggest that vestiges of African culture remained in Harlem. Closely paraphrasing Locke's editorial note from the Survey Graphic issue, he asked, "What do the Africans do that the inhabitants of the Negro quarter of New York city also do? May we find perhaps, on close examination that there are some subtle elements left of what was ancestrally possessed? May not the remnant, if present, consist of some slight intonation, some quirk of pronunciation, some temperamental predisposition?" (1930:6).

From Trait Analysis to the Psychology of Acculturation

During the 1930s Herskovits rapidly established his reputation as a major scholar of Afro-American and African peoples. As he pursued his investigation of African influences on Afro-American cultures, he moved toward a more holistic, integrative theory of culture, experimented with various methodologies for analyzing the relationship between personality and culture, and developed an approach to the study of acculturation. Although he participated in scholarly debates about these questions, Herskovits remained relatively isolated from the major centers of American anthropology. When he began teaching at Northwestern in 1927, he was the only anthropologist in a rather undistinguished sociology department. As one of the first Jewish faculty members at a conservative Midwestern university, he faced cultural and political, as well as intellectual, isolation. But although he complained to Boas that "the row that has to be howed [sic] at Northwestern is a pretty hard one," he declined an offer from Wisconsin after the Northwestern trustees finally approved a separate department of anthropology in 1938 (BP: MH/FB 4/28/38). Because of these institutional difficulties, Herskovits got a late start training graduate students in Afro-American anthropology, and much of his own fieldwork had to be done during summers because of his teaching obligations. Furthermore, his relations with the anthropologists at the University of Chicago were rather chilly, and he had to combat an attitude within the discipline that Afro-American anthropology was less prestigious or significant than work on other groups. Herskovits had a strong sense of purpose about his Afro-American research, but his pronouncements about the field often had an embattled quality. If his detractors found him dogmatic and unyielding, an explanation may lie in his institutional isolation as well as in his combative personality.

Although Herskovits was primarily concerned with cultural diffusion in his dissertation and his early work, he had become interested in functionalism as early as 1927, when he suggested that Malinowski's criticisms of Boasian methods rested on a "lack of understanding of the interest which the American school has in the interrelation of the aspects of cultural elements within the cultures studied . . ." (Herskovits & Willey 1927:274). In contrast, he insisted that the historical and psychological approach of the Boasians was compatible with functionalism (HP: MH/H. Odum 7/5/27). In 1933, when Herskovits brought Malinowski to Northwestern for a lecture series, he still hoped for a rapprochement between functionalism and Boasian anthropology —suggesting to Boas that Malinowski

> has come to a point where he agrees that our point of view and approach is
> much closer to his than he had realized. I know that he is looking forward with
> great eagerness to spending some time with you at Columbia and I think that

he will be much more than ready to meet you on the basis of common interests. I was impressed by the extent to which he had become mellowed since he was here in 1926, and to which his point of view in general theoretical matters had broadened. I only hope you will enjoy him as much as we did. (BP: MH/FB 4/10/33)

By the mid-1930s, however, Herskovits had concluded that Malinowski was dogmatically "anti-historical" and that his culture theory did not adequately explain cultural change. In his own book *Acculturation* he warned that the study of acculturation "must not strain too much to integrate all aspects [of a culture] with each other lest confusion also result," and argued that "the less the sense of history, the more sterile the results" (1938:25). In 1936 he wrote Robert Lowie, "I hope that eventually the ferociousness of the anti-historical position of the functionalists . . . will be diminished and we can direct our energies toward finding out about culture instead of quarreling as to the way we should go about the job" (HP: MH/RL 12/11/36).

During this same period Herskovits also devoted much attention to the relationship between personality and culture. In 1927 he had criticized Alfred Kroeber and William Fielding Ogburn for "cultural determinism," arguing that they were inclined to "objectify culture" and treat the individual as a "secondary factor" (Herskovits & Willey 1927:274). As we have seen, the Herskovitses discussed in narrative form the personalities of several Saramaccans in *Rebel Destiny*, and shortly thereafter Herskovits experimented briefly with psychoanalysis in "Freudian Mechanisms in Primitive Negro Psychology" (1934a). But he quickly returned to more mainstream Boasian approaches to the problem.

Although the concept of cultural pattern remained central to Herskovits' work, he held that cultures have unique *combinations* of patterns, rather than one *dominant* pattern. Thus while he praised Benedict's *Patterns of Culture*, he also questioned whether "any classifications of entire cultures [according to one pattern] are tenable," and pointed out that her study did not discuss "aberrant types" (1934b). And in a letter to Robert Redfield, he was even more dubious:

As to "Patterns of Culture," for all its charm of presentation and the excellence of its opening and closing chapters, I feel its theoretical contribution is not altogether a happy one. I am afraid of the application of psychological concepts to great masses of cultural data, and I am convinced that this is only possible through the distortion of the data, however honest the presentation. The term "culture pattern" was, I believe, one of the most valuable in currency among anthropologists; the twist it has been given makes it essential that your committee rescue it from the pseudo-psychological meaning it has for a number of people who only know it through this book. (HP: MH/RR 4/19/38)

To explain what elements of a particular culture were most tenacious in interaction with another culture, Herskovits developed instead the concept of "cultural focus": "that element in the psychology of the inhabitants which gives to an area its peculiar characteristics—the manner in which one phase of culture dominates the interest of a given people at a given time." In an attempt to explain how West Africans had adapted to life in the New World under slavery, Herskovits argued that "pecuniary motivation" was the "underlying psychological drive" in West African culture—noting that West Africa, with a high density of population, had a "more complex" economic life and a greater "degree of specialization" than other parts of Africa (1935a:215, 221). Although Herskovits retained the concept of "cultural focus," in his later work he contended that religion was "focal" for West Africans while economic relations were "focal" for the slaveowners. The largest number of African survivals were therefore in practices concerning the supernatural (1941:136; 1945:59).

In 1935, Herskovits was still judicious in making claims about the retention of African cultural patterns by blacks in the United States. Thus, among Negroes in the large cities it was "practically impossible to discern Africanisms in any aspect of outward manner except in certain phases of motor behavior." Noting the preference of many Negroes for lighter skin colors and hair-straightening devices, Herskovits concluded that "certainly, as far as the psychology of the Negroes of the United States is concerned, the sanctions of the white population are the accepted sanctions of Negroes; white behavior patterns are not only automatically adhered to but consciously striven for" (1935a:253).

That same year, however, Herskovits was more provocative in an article in the *New Republic*, "What Has Africa Given America?" (1935b). Asserting that the slaves came from areas of West Africa where "high and complex civilizations" existed, he argued that the slaves brought with them cultural traits that they passed on to their masters. Thus he argued that African music influenced Negro work songs, love songs, "songs of derision," jazz, and religious singing in "shouting" churches, that Southern speech had been influenced by West African pronunciation and intonation, that certain African idioms had entered American speech, that Southern manners were influenced by African codes of politeness, and that Southern cuisine owed some of its distinctive qualities to African cooking. Finally, Herskovits suggested that the behavior of both whites and blacks in "hysterical sects" might be influenced by African forms of worship that involved spirit possession.

The field materials Herskovits collected in 1934 in Haiti were to provide further evidence of the continuity of African spirit possession among Afro-Americans, and to force Herskovits to consider further the relationship of personality and culture in the process of acculturation. Seeking to refute racist interpretations of Haitians as emotional people who lived in a savage state without the benefits of white civilization, he provided descriptions of intricately structured traditions, both religious and secular, and attempted to explain the meaning of these traditions according to the logic of Haitian culture. Nevertheless, he saw Haitian culture not as a stable, functionally interdependent whole, but as an unstable, partial "amalgam" of African and French elements. Probing the inner conflicts of the Haitians, he sought to interpret these tensions in historical perspective. In an era when the study of slavery in the United States was dominated by the work of the conservative historian Ulrich B. Phillips (1929) Herskovits attacked the concept of the "slave psychology" attributed by earlier writers to Negroes in the Americas, and argued that the slaves reacted to their condition with a "constantly active discontent." Slaves resisted through open revolt, sabotage, the practice of the *vodun* cult, and *marronage*. The maroon communities in the mountains had kept alive African traditions and had given hope to those still in bondage. Even when revolt proved impossible, slaves resisted psychologically by maintaining their African traditions (1937a:56–61; see also Mintz 1964).

Herskovits noted that Haitian peasants of the twentieth century combined an adherence to Roman Catholicism with the practice of *vodun* (1937a:78–79, 278–81). But he insisted that the two traditions had "never been completely merged," and that the Haitian was pulled in two directions at once: his "outwardly smoothly functioning life is full of inner conflict." Offering the concept of "socialized ambivalence" to explain the Haitian peasant's "rapid shifts in attitude from one emotional tone to another," he suggested that perhaps this "socialized ambivalence underlies much of the political and economic instability of Haiti . . ." (295). Spirit possession of the *vodun* cult proved to be a fascinating problem in the relationship between personality and culture. Rejecting genetic explanations of this widespread phenomenon, Herskovits took a cultural-relativist view that "in terms of the patterns of Haitian religion, possession is not abnormal, but normal. . . ." He argued that "to consider all possession as something which falls within the range of psychopathology is to approach it handicapped by a fundamental misconception" (147–48).

After having done fieldwork in Dahomey and Haiti, Herskovits became even more certain of the importance of African influences on New World Negro societies. Historical studies of the acculturation process therefore held the key to understanding contemporary Afro-American culture in the United States as well as in Latin America and the Caribbean. In his short book *Acculturation*, Herskovits spelled out some of the methodological premises that he had developed in his research on Afro-Americans. Defining "acculturation" as "continuous contact over a long time in which a people are exposed to a culture different from their own" (1938:15), he defended trait analysis as a necessary step in making generalizations. However, he argued that the ethnographer must get at "attitudes, points of view, and those psychological mechanisms which underlie these outer forms . . ." (59). To understand the life of a people, the ethnographer must organize his data in a way that reveals "the patterning of their conduct, or, in psychological terms, those consensuses of individual behavior patterns that permit the student of culture to differentiate one civilization from another" (21).

Herskovits' psychological approach to the study of Afro-American culture thus resulted in a complex and innovative interpretation of Haitian culture and of the historical process of acculturation. Concepts such as "cultural focus" and "syncretism," and the cultural-relativist interpretation of spirit possession, allowed him to treat Afro-American slaves as actors who shaped a large part of their culture and resisted the world view of their masters. This psychological approach would lead to problems, however, when applied to blacks in the contemporary United States. Herskovits displayed a curious naiveté about the relationship between culture and power, and assumed that political power would follow from greater cultural awareness and race pride. This assumption, together with his aversion to policy-oriented research, led him to a position in *The Myth of the Negro Past* (1941) that put him at odds with most other students of Afro-American life.

Applied Anthropology, the Myrdal Study, and the Myth of the Negro Past

Ever since his days as a critic of the "Nordic Nonsense," Herskovits had resolutely maintained that the anthropologist should pursue scientific studies of race and culture and avoid involvement with government-sponsored social engineering. A corollary principle was that, while the anthropologist might support reform movements in his role as citizen, he should not allow these movements to define the goals of his scientific research. During the 1930s, Herskovits adhered to these views in a global context in which "applied anthropology" in British colonies in Africa, Nazi anthropology, and social-problem-oriented research on race relations in the United States all seemed to threaten the independence of social science. Yet Herskovits' own work was informed by a strong desire to impart to blacks in the United States pride in the African past, and by a belief that a better understanding of Afro-American culture by whites would help to lessen racial prejudice. This tension between Herskovits' view of the role of the anthropologist in society and the liberal purpose that propelled his research affected his relations with other scholars and helped to shape *The Myth of the Negro Past*.

In a review of Mead's *Growing Up in New Guinea*, Herskovits praised her ethnographic work, but gently reproved his friend for her "applied anthro-

pology." He did not think that Mead's drawing "lessons for our own civilization" invalidated the whole book, however, and he suggested that "whether
one likes one's science to stay within the confines of its own boundaries or
to be applied to the problems of the day is a matter of personal preference"
(1931). The "applied anthropology" of Malinowski was a different matter,
however. Herskovits believed that the systematic use of anthropology to aid
the British government in administering its African colonies jeopardized the
independence of the discipline and threatened to distort the anthropologist's
understanding of the cultures under investigation. In his *Acculturation* book,
Herskovits observed that a "basic justification of ethnological research is that
it gives a broad background against which to judge our own rules of behavior,
and a more inclusive view of human cultures than can be attained by any
other social discipline." He argued that anthropologists who study the contact between their own and "native" cultures ran the risk of "narrowing" their
perspective: "The uncritical tendency to see native cultures everywhere forced
out of existence by the overwhelming drive of European techniques; the feeling that these 'simpler' folk must inevitably accept the sanctions of their more
efficient rulers as they do some of the outward modes of life of those under
whose control they live; all these reflect a type of ethnocentrism that should
be absent from the scientific studies of an anthropologist" (1938:32). In private communications, Herskovits criticized anthropologists who "go off half-
cocked under the pressure of social conditions," and condemned Malinowski's "prescriptions for running the lives of the East Africans" (HP: MH/T. W.
Todd 3/17/36).

Herskovits' opposition to applied anthropology rested on a fundamental
conviction about the role of anthropology as a science, and on a perception
of the discipline as an international community of scholars who placed their
devotion to scientific truth ahead of policy concerns. Herskovits carried the
banner of Boasian anthropology to an international congress in Copenhagen
in 1938, where he debated Eugen Fischer, whom he called the "führer" of the
German delegation. Ironically, Herskovits had admired Fischer's early work
in physical anthropology, and had once sought to have one of Fischer's books
tran[.]'ated into English. But he was appalled that Fischer had become a leading ˙ lazi anthropologist, and he wrote to Boas with great pride after having
disputed Fischer's claim that "*geistiger*" characteristics were inherited genetically (BP: MH/FB 8/10/38).

Applied work in the social sciences also posed dangers in the United States.
Herskovits sharply criticized American philanthropic foundations for steer-
ing social science investigations of blacks toward practical concerns at the expense of historical and cultural studies. At the end of *Life in a Haitian Valley*,
he condemned "current attempts to solve the 'Negro problem' in the United
States" with "simple solutions, rapid in their operation . . ." (1937a:301). Her-

skovits lambasted the colonial mindset that led several of the foundations to sponsor visits to the United States by British colonial officers who studied the theory and practice of "Negro education" in the South and met with white officials of segregated school systems (HP: MH/C. G. Seligman 5/18/38; CCA: C. Dollard memo 9/1/38). When the Julius Rosenwald Fund brought over Bertram Shrieke, a Dutch colonial administrator, to study American minorities, Herskovits panned Shrieke's book in a review in the *Nation* (1936), and criticized the Rosenwald Fund for sponsoring only "practical" studies of race relations (HP: MH/E. C. Parsons 2/12/36). The Phelps-Stokes Fund, under the leadership of Thomas Jesse Jones, came in for especially strong censure for its "missionary spirit and the conviction that they knew all the answers" (CCA: memo "SHS & M. Herskovits" 6/4/48).

Herskovits' frustration at the foundations' tendency to give priority to practical research on the "Negro problem" led to some antagonism toward rival scholars. When he accepted an invitation from Charles S. Johnson to lecture in a summer program Johnson directed at Swarthmore College's Institute of Race Relations, he confided to Boas, who was on the board of the Institute, his estimate of Johnson as "a 'professional' Negro of the worst sort—very much in with the powers that be, highly innocuous especially when it comes to wasting perfectly good funds that might be used for adequate research" (HP: MH/FB 4/10/33; see also Meier 1977:259–69). Herskovits' animus against "melioristic" and "philanthropic" approaches to the study of blacks led him to resign from the advisory board of the *Encyclopedia of the Negro*, a projected multivolume reference work under the editorship of W. E. B. Du Bois and the white reformer Anson Phelps-Stokes (HP: MH/Du Bois n.d.). Although he respected Du Bois as an intellectual and political figure, he felt that Du Bois had been "much too close to the firing-line to have the necessary detachment for the job," and he wrote to other scholars on the board, urging them to resign (HP: MH/E. C. Parsons 8/23/36; MH/D. Young 7/8/36; MH/C. G. Seligman 5/18/38). Du Bois abandoned the project in 1941 because he could not obtain enough support from foundations (Goggin 1983:358).

Herskovits was a tough reviewer and a vigorous critic of much of the social science literature on race relations in the late 1930s. He believed that the work of Franklin Frazier suffered from a failure to comprehend the tenacity of African cultural patterns in contact with white American culture (Herskovits 1940). He scored Du Bois for "Negro chauvinism" in a review of *Black Folk, Then and Now* (1939). He regarded Lloyd Warner's "caste-and-class" approach as "an extremely dangerous concept," and thought that, while "the Negro is not a caste, . . . I fear if we talk about it enough, people will get the idea and he may become one" (HP: MH/K. Wolff 1/6/45). The student of contemporary race relations whose work Herskovits admired most was his good friend Donald Young, sociologist and author of *American Minority Peoples* (1932; HP:

MH/Redfield 3/19/38). Herskovits also served as patron of the circle of young scholars at Howard University, consisting of Abram Harris, Ralph Bunche, and Sterling Brown—"the only group known to me among the Negroes able to approach the tragedy of the racial situation in this country with the objectivity that comes from seeing it as the result of the play of historic forces rather than as an expression of personal spite and a desire to hold down a minority people" (HP: MH/H. A. Moe 1/6/37; MH/D. Young 10/7/35).

This opposition to social engineering and skepticism about much of the research on contemporary race relations left Herskovits in a somewhat isolated position in the late 1930s and during World War II. Although he was willing to write popular articles on the anthropological view of race, his conception of the scientist's role caused him to remain aloof from political reform movements at a time when most of the younger black scholars and many of the young white social scientists embraced an activist position. Herskovits was never very specific about the policy implications of his views concerning the distinctiveness of Afro-American culture in the United States. But he did repudiate the use of his African survivals thesis to support segregation or to support the Communist program of the early 1930s for the creation of an "autonomous Black Republic in the South" (1937a:303). Herskovits endorsed civil rights and desegregation, but he never advanced a coherent theory of cultural pluralism or speculated on how divergent cultures would coexist once legal barriers had fallen. While in Britain in 1937, he gave a radio talk on the B.B.C. in which he praised the interracial unionism of the C.I.O. and the Southern Tenant Farmers' Union as the most heartening developments in American race relations during the 1930s (1937b). When he returned to America, however, he did not write about strategies for social change. Like most of Boas' students, he considered programmatic thinking to be outside the scope of anthropology.

After completing *Life in a Haitian Valley*, Herskovits planned to spend several years studying Afro-Americans in various countries before writing a major interpretive book on the "New World Negro" (HP: MH/R. Pattee 9/7/38). Coincidentally, his application to the Carnegie Corporation for support for this research arrived just as the Corporation was considering the sponsorship of a major study of American blacks (CCA: MH/F. Keppel 4/8/36). Carnegie President Frederick Keppel briefly considered Herskovits for the job of director of the study, but he consulted John Merriam of the Carnegie Institution of Washington, who was skeptical about Herskovits' research, and Robert Crane of the Social Science Research Council, who reported that Herskovits was hard to work with (CCA: Keppel memo 7/15/37).

Keppel then conceived the idea of inviting a foreigner to head the study, and he considered selecting a man with colonial experience. Keppel discussed this idea with Herskovits, hinting that he might be invited to serve on an advisory committee of American scholars who would work with this European visitor. However, Herskovits emphatically objected to appointing a colonial administrator, arguing that the conclusions of such an observer would inevitably be discounted by black Americans. If the Carnegie Corporation should decide to invite a European, they should instead consider choosing someone from Switzerland or the Scandinavian countries (HP: MH/D. Young 1/2/37; CCA: Keppel memo 12/4/36).

Herskovits secretly collaborated with his friend Donald Young, who was then an official of the Social Science Research Council, in drawing up a memo proposing a large research project, nominally headed by the European visitor, that would fund independent investigations by American scholars of various aspects of Afro-American life. The purpose of its proposed advisory committee, he wrote Young, would be to "tell this European what was to be seen and give him the necessary documentation for this report. . . ." He added, "I really think it is our chance to do what we've been wanting to do, and sketch in, with far greater support than we dreamed would be possible, the outlines of the longtime research we've planned" (HP: MH/DY 1/2/37). In his role as an S.S.R.C. official, Young presented the memo to Keppel, who liked the idea of a large, collaborative research project involving both a European observer and American scholars.

After a long search, Keppel appointed the Swedish economist Gunnar Myrdal, who arrived in the United States in the fall of 1938. A man with considerable experience on parliamentary committees and royal commissions, Myrdal took firm control of the study and steered it in the direction of liberal social engineering. He did, however, hire a number of American social scientists to write reports on different aspects of American race relations. Though skeptical of Herskovits' thesis regarding "Africanisms," he regarded Herskovits as an important scholar in the field, and invited him to write a study of African cultural influences on blacks in the United States. But he insisted that all of his collaborators complete their studies within a year, so that he could read their manuscripts before writing his own book. Herskovits was reluctant to undertake such an important project under these constraints, and would have preferred to have done fieldwork in a Southern black community. But he realized that "because of its importance in determining the Foundation grant [sic] for future research in the field of Negro studies, it had absolutely to be made a first order of business . . ." (HP: MH/L. Parrish 7/26/40). With some misgivings, Herskovits thus climbed aboard what turned out to be the most influential social-engineering project concerning race relations in American history. He finished *The Myth of the Negro Past* within a year, and it was published in 1941 as part of the Carnegie Corporation's "The Negro in America" series (see Jackson 1986).

The result of this prodigious labor was a provocative book of very uneven quality. Herskovits declared that "the myth of the Negro past is one of the principal supports of race prejudice in this country." Among the elements of the myth were the ideas that blacks were naturally childlike, that the cultures of Africa were "savage and relatively low in the scale of human civilization," and that Afro-Americans had lost their African traditions under slavery (1941:1–2). Herskovits' central point was really the observation that Arthur Schomburg had made in *The New Negro*: "The Negro has been a man without a history because he had been considered a man without a worthy culture" (1925:237).

Herskovits sharply criticized scholars who denied the existence of African survivals among blacks in the United States, including in his indictment such prominent figures as Robert Park, E. Franklin Frazier, Hortense Powdermaker, and Guy B. Johnson. Acknowledging that many writers had minimized the significance of African survivals because they did not want white Americans to perceive the Negro as "the bearer of an inferior tradition" (1941:27), he insisted that the eradication of misunderstandings about African and Afro-American cultures was necessary to "endow" blacks with "confidence," and that it would contribute to a "lessening of interracial tensions" (1941:32).

In a survey of African cultures, Herskovits emphasized the "resilience" in West African cultures and their "tenacity" in contact with European and Euro-American cultures. He stressed the complexity and stability of West African states, the variety of agricultural practices, the intricate rituals of religion, and the beauty of African art. He then made his case for the retention of African traditions by arguing that most of the slaves came from the "culture area" of West Africa and the Congo, that the major ethnic groups were close enough in language and culture to allow communication among the slaves and synthesis of similar traditions, and that the slaves from the dominant cultural groups may have imposed their culture on slaves from the other groups (1941: 52–53, 78, 295).

In discussing "Africanisms" in the United States, Herskovits pointed to trait similarities between African and Afro-American cultures, but he also analyzed acculturation, syncretism, and the "reinterpretation" of traditions. Considering the issue of acculturation under slavery, Herskovits observed that differences among various New World societies in retention of African customs could be explained by "climate and topography; the organization and operation of the plantations; the numerical ratios of Negroes to whites; and the extent to which contacts between Negroes and whites in a given area took place in a rural or urban setting" (1941:111). African religious practices had the best chance of surviving, because they were of central importance to the slaves and were relatively unimportant to the masters (1941:136–37).

Herskovits went far beyond his earlier work in identifying a vast number of "Africanisms" in contemporary Afro-American life in the United States, including motor behavior, family patterns, economic cooperation, naming practices, and funerals. In discussing religious life, Herskovits drew upon his work in Dahomey and Haiti to argue that the spiritual life of the West African had been "reinterpreted" by black Americans (1941:214). Pointing to specific characteristics such as possession, the role of the preacher, and the preference of blacks for baptism by total immersion as evidence of "Africanisms," he maintained that because "religion is vital, meaningful, and understandable to the Negroes of this country, . . . it is not removed from life, but has been deeply integrated into the daily round" (1941:207). All of this added up to a strong cultural heritage for Afro-Americans, comparable to the traditions of various European ethnic groups in the United States (1941:299).

Particularism and Universalism in Boasian Anthropology and Black Consciousness

Between 1925 and 1941, Herskovits' thinking on the continuity of African culture among Afro-Americans had thus changed quite drastically: instead of emphasizing the assimilative power of the dominant culture, he emphasized the survival power of the dominated culture. But paradoxically, he remained as much the "odd man out" among the predominantly white social scientists who provided background studies for *An American Dilemma* as he had been among the black intellectuals who contributed to *The New Negro*. And the reviews of *The Myth of the Negro Past* were a rather mixed and somewhat ambivalent lot—whether the authors were black or white social scientists.

Two black scholars were extremely laudatory. Not surprisingly, W. E. B. Du Bois, who had always been deeply interested in the African background of black American culture, found the book "epoch-making": "no one hereafter writing on the cultural accomplishments of the American Negro can afford to be ignorant of its content and conclusions" (1942). And the leading black historian, Carter G. Woodson, who had criticized Herskovits' early work on the physical anthropology of the American Negro, now praised his scientific objectivity and his "courage" in questioning conventional stereotypes about the Afro-American past (1942). But other black reviewers were dubious. The sociologist E. Franklin Frazier feared that Herskovits' thesis would have dangerous implications: "when Professor Herskovits says that the Negro problem is psychological—that African patterns of thought prevent the complete acculturation of the Negro—as well as economic and sociological, is he not saying that even more fundamental barriers exist between blacks and whites than are generally recognized?" (1942).

Even more striking was the review by Alain Locke, who felt that since *The New Negro* Herskovits had learned the lessons of the Harlem Renaissance much too well. Locke—who had always balanced his interest in African traditions with an insistence that Afro-Americans were contributing to American culture and a demand for full political participation in American institutions —was skeptical of Herskovits' claim that "a knowledge of [the Negro's] cultural background will lessen prejudice and rehabilitate the Negro considerably in American public opinion . . .":

> ". . . a reformist zeal overemphasizes the thesis of African survivals, transforming it from a profitable working hypothesis into a dogmatic obsession, claiming arbitrary interpretations of customs and folkways which in all common-sense could easily have alternative or even compound explanations. Instead of suggesting the African mores and dispositions as conducive factors along with other more immediate environmental ones, the whole force of the explanation, in many instances, pivots on Africanisms and their sturdy, stubborn survival. The extreme logic of such a position might . . . lead to the very opposite of Dr. Herskovits' liberal conclusions, and damn the Negro as more basically peculiar and unassimilable than he actually is or has proved himself to be." (Locke 1942)

Guy B. Johnson, a white Southern sociologist, echoed Frazier's and Locke's concerns in the *American Sociological Review*. Although Herskovits faulted educators and health officials for ignoring the "practical implications of African-rooted customs," he had not himself made any "concrete suggestion as to how the knowledge of Africanisms is to be applied." In this context, "One immensely practical problem [was] how to prevent this book . . . from becoming the handmaiden of those who are looking for new justifications for the segregation and differential treatment of Negroes!" (Johnson 1942).

But the most interesting reaction came from Ruth Benedict—who, along with Herskovits himself, is perhaps the Boasian anthropologist most closely associated with the elaboration of the idea of "cultural relativism." Benedict had previously resonated to the romantic relativism and implied social criticism of *Rebel Destiny*, writing with admiration of the Bush Negroes as "a society which against all odds has made possible for its people ordered lives of dignity and honor" (1934). But the Boasian idea of cultural determinism had always had a dual aspect, and in the context of World War II, Benedict no longer emphasized cultural pluralism but rather cultural plasticity. In *Race: Science and Politics*—a popular book designed to combat racist attitudes—she took an assimilationist stance regarding blacks in the United States, and minimized the cultural differences between black and white Americans. Accepting Frazier's argument that slavery had "stripped" blacks of their African culture and that slaves had quickly acquired the culture of white Southerners, she turned it to antiracist ends: such "radical and rapid changes in mental and emotional behavior give the lie to the racists' contention that these patterns are eternal and are biologically perpetuated" (1940:132–33). She con-

cluded her book by advocating social engineering designed to improve hous-
ing, health, welfare, and labor conditions for both blacks and whites (255–
56).

In this context, it is less surprising to find Benedict asserting that Herskovits had overstated the importance of his findings about African influences
on black culture. Condemning the "extremely polemic tone" of *The Myth of
the Negro Past*, she wrote:

> The author feels that all investigations of American Negro life and all pro-
> grams for the betterment of interracial relations are hamstrung for want of an
> appreciation of the Negro's African heritage. Actually his present volume on
> historical perspectives seems rather a footnote to the valuable studies of Ameri-
> can Negro communities that have been appearing in recent years. . . . It does
> not alter the importance of their emphasis on contemporary conditions; much
> less does it supersede them. . . . The studies of Negro life and arts which Dr.
> Herskovits quarrels with most vigorously are still those which throw most light
> on the interracial problems of our day and of our continent. (1942)

It is ironic that, shortly after American entry into the war against Nazi
Germany and a few months before Boas' death, two of his most prominent
students disagreed publicly on how to combat prejudice, with each appealing
to a different strain of Boasian thought. Benedict now edged away from cultural relativism, in order to advocate a universalist, assimilationist approach
to race relations in the United States; Herskovits adhered to historical particularism, in order to recover underlying cultural patterns, in the hope of
encouraging black pride and white respect for Afro-American culture. Herskovits' unique interpretation of Afro-American culture reflected the tensions
within Boasian culturalism. On the one hand, his psychological approach to
acculturation allowed him to argue that slaves, resisting the world view of
their masters, had synthesized African traditions and reinterpreted them in
America—thus according to blacks a significant amount of power in shaping
their culture under the most adverse circumstances. On the other hand, his
emphasis on the significance of African-derived cultural patterns among
twentieth-century American blacks led him to argue that unconscious cultural patterns were a major determinant of the behavior of an ethnic group
in a modern society—an interpretation that took little account of economic
and political power in a society undergoing rapid social change due to economic depression, urbanization, and wartime mobilization.

Herskovits had long recognized the susceptibility of the Boasian culture
concept to both radical and conservative uses. While Benedict was prepared
to recommend ambitious programs of social engineering, hopeful that a more
democratic, tolerant, and free society would emerge from the war, Herskovits
was inclined to emphasize the "tenacity" of cultural patterns and the difficulty

of predicting cultural change. A strong supporter of civil rights and desegregation, he was nevertheless more pessimistic than Benedict or Myrdal about
achieving rapid changes in the fundamental character of American race relations. Herskovits' uncompromising opposition to applied anthropology led
him to overlook the policy implications of his arguments, and to fail to grasp
the connection between his research and the political issues of his day. He
may have, paradoxically, fallen victim to the error against which he warned
Malinowski: the loss of perspective in studying the interaction of another
culture with one's own.

While admitting that he was something of a "lone wolf" on the subject
of "Africanisms" (HP: Shavelson interview, 1944), Herskovits held his ground
in the face of critical reviews. He believed that he had confronted his own
ethnocentrism in the 1920s, abandoned his assimilationist assumptions when
the evidence no longer supported them, pursued his investigation of blacks
in the Americas according to rigorous Boasian methods, and resisted tempta-
tions to tailor his findings to changing political fashions. Above all, he thought
that his field experience in Dahomey, Surinam, Haiti, and Trinidad gave him
a broad perspective on West African and Afro-American cultures that no one
else had, enabling him to see African characteristics in black American culture that other observers missed.

Herskovits' interpretation of Afro-American culture offered an intellectually compelling alternative to the assimilationist perspective of Myrdal and
Frazier. But by 1942, assimilationism had already started on a long upswing
in both the social scientific and the sociopolitical realms, and for the next
two decades Herskovits had remarkably few followers among scholars writing
about blacks in the United States. During those years he turned his primary
attention to African studies—the foundations having finally become willing
to support research in that area. With funding from the Carnegie Corporation, he started the first African Studies program in the United States at Northwestern in 1947 and remained a major figure in the field until his death in
1963 (Greenberg 1971:71). He also sought support for research on Afro-
Americans, but the foundations were not inclined to launch any large projects on black Americans in the wake of the Myrdal study (HP: MH/R. Evans
4/9/45; see also Jackson 1986). Although Herskovits continued to publish
in the field, and trained a number of graduate students in Afro-American
anthropology, most of them worked on Caribbean or Latin American topics.
He lacked the resources to institutionalize an interdisciplinary research tradition of Afro-American studies, publish a journal, or train a significant number of students of black culture in the United States.

But just as particularism and universalism were both tendencies in Boasian anthropology, so were they also in black consciousness. With the re-
emergence of black nationalism in the late 1960s, there was a reawakening

of interest in African traditions among Afro-Americans and a reexamination by scholars of the whole issue of African influences. Anthropologists turned to Herskovits' writings as a starting point for investigations of Afro-American culture (Whitten & Szwed 1970). Historians found in his emphasis on slave resistance and the reinterpretation of African traditions a way of discovering the world of early Afro-Americans (Blassingame 1972; Levine 1977; Raboteau 1978). By the end of the 1970s it was rare to find an anthropologist or historian who would argue that slavery had "stripped" blacks of African culture. Through a complex process of political and intellectual change Herskovits' work received its greatest recognition in the years after his death. Although the political consequences of Afro-American research remain problematic, few scholarly observers would now consider Afro-Americans a people without a past.

References Cited

Benedict, R. 1934. Review of Herskovits & Herskovits 1934. *N.Y. Herald Trib.* 6/10.
———. 1940. *Race: Science and politics.* New York.
———. 1942. Cultural continuities. *N.Y. Herald Trib.* 1/18.
Blassingame, J. 1972. *The slave community: Plantation life in the antebellum south.* New York.
Boas, F. 1906. The outlook for the American Negro. In Stocking 1974:310–16.
———. 1921. The Negro in America. *Yale Quart. Rev.* 10:395.
BP. See under Manuscript Sources.
CCA. See under Manuscript Sources.
Dowd, J. 1907–14. *The Negro races.* 2 vols. New York.
Du Bois, W. 1915. *The Negro.* New York.
———. 1939. *Black folk, then and now.* New York.
———. 1942. Review of Herskovits 1941. *Annals Am. Acad. Pol. & Soc. Sci.* 222:226–27.
Frazier, E. 1942. The Negro's cultural past. *Nation* 154:195–96.
Franklin, J. 1985. *George Washington Williams: A biography.* Chicago.
Goggin, J. 1983. Carter G. Woodson and the movement to promote black history. Doct. diss. Univ. Rochester.
Goldenweiser, A. 1924. Race and culture in the modern world. *Soc. Forces* 3:127–36.
Greenberg, J. 1971. Melville J. Herskovits. *Biog. Mems. Natl. Acad. Scis.* 42:65–75.
Higham, J. 1963. *Strangers in the land: Patterns of American nativism, 1860–1925.* New Brunswick, N.J.
Herskovits, M. 1920. Médiocrité jusqu'à la fin! *Freeman* 2:30.
———. 1924a. What is a race? *Am. Mercury* 2:207–10.
———. 1924b. The racial hysteria. *Opportunity* 2:166–68.
———. 1925a. Brains and the immigrant. *Nation* 120:139–41.
———. 1925b. The dilemma of social pattern. *Survey Graphic* 6:677–78.
———. 1925c. The color line. *Am. Mercury* 6:204–8.
———. 1925d. Social pattern: A methodological study. *Soc. Forces* 4:57–69.
———. 1925e. The Negro's Americanism. In Locke 1925b:353–60.

————. 1926a. It is better to receive: How far are we willing to be tolerant ourselves? *Am. Hebrew* 118:624.

————. 1926b. Negro art: African and American. *Soc. Forces* 5:291–98.

————. 1927a. When is a Jew a Jew? *Mod. Quart.* 4:109–17.

————. 1927b. Acculturation and the American Negro. *Southwest. Pol. & Soc. Sci. Quart.* 8:211–24.

————. 1928a. *The American Negro: A study of racial crossing.* New York.

————. 1928b. Review of N. N. Puckett, *Folk beliefs of the Southern Negro. J. Am. Folk-Lore* 70:310–12.

————. 1930. The Negro in the New World: The statement of a problem. In Herskovits 1966:1–12.

————. 1931. Primitive childhood. *Nation* 132 (3422):131–32.

————. 1934a. Freudian mechanisms in primitive Negro psychology. In Herskovits 1966:135–45.

————. 1934b. Review of R. Benedict, *Patterns of culture. N.Y. Herald Trib.* 10/28.

————. 1935a. Social history of the Negro. In *Handbook of social psychology,* ed. C. Murchison. Worcester, Mass.

————. 1935b. What has Africa given America? *New Republic* 84 (1083):92–94.

————. 1936. Through alien eyes. *Nation* 142 (3704):850–51.

————. 1937a. *Life in a Haitian valley.* New York.

————. 1937b. The Negro in the United States. *Listener* 17 (442):1290–91.

————. 1937c. *Dahomey: An ancient West African kingdom.* 2 vols. New York.

————. 1938. *Acculturation: The study of culture contact.* New York.

————. 1939. Review of Du Bois 1939. *New Republic* 90 (1289):55–56.

————. 1940. Review of E. F. Frazier, *The Negro family in the United States. Nation* 150 (4):104–5.

————. 1941. *The myth of the Negro past.* New York.

————. 1945. Problem, method and theory in Afroamerican studies. In Herskovits 1966.

————. 1966. *The New World Negro.* Bloomington.

Herskovits, M., & F. Herskovits. 1934. *Rebel destiny: Among the Bush Negroes of Dutch Guiana.* New York.

————. 1936. *Suriname folklore.* Columbia Univ. Conts. Anth. No. 27. New York.

Herskovits, M., & M. Willey. 1923a. Servitude and progress. *Soc. Forces* 1:228–34.

————. 1923b. The cultural approach to sociology. *Am. J. Soc.* 24:188–99.

————. 1927. Psychology and culture. *Psych. Bul.* 24:253–83.

Higham, J. 1963. *Strangers in the land: Patterns of American nativism, 1860–1925.* New Brunswick, N.J.

Hornbostel, E. 1926. American Negro songs. *Int. Rev. Missions* 15:748–53.

HP. See under Manuscript Sources.

Huggins, N. 1971. *Harlem Renaissance.* New York.

Jackson, W. 1986. The making of a social science classic: Gunnar Myrdal's *An American dilemma. Perspectives Am. Hist.* 2:43–61.

Johnson, G. 1942. Review of Herskovits 1941. *Am. Soc. Rev.* 7:289–90.

Kallen, H. 1924. *Culture and democracy in the United States: Studies in the group psychology of the American peoples.* New York.

Levine, L. 1977. *Black culture and black consciousness: Afro-American folk thought from slavery to freedom.* New York.

Locke, A. 1925a. Editorial note to Herskovits, The dilemma of social pattern. *Survey Graphic* 6:676.

———, ed. 1925b. *The new Negro.* New York.

———. 1925c. Negro education bids for par. *Survey* 54:570.

———. 1942. Who and what is "Negro"? *Opportunity* 20:83–84.

Lynd, R. S. & H. M. Lynd. 1929. *Middletown: A study in American culture.* New York.

McMurry, L. 1985. *Recorder of the black experience: A biography of Monroe Nathan Work.* Baton Rouge.

Meier, A. 1977. Black sociologists in white America. *Soc. Forces* 56:259–69.

Mintz, S. 1964. Melville J. Herskovits and Caribbean studies: A retrospective tribute. *Carib. Studies* 4:42–51.

Myrdal, G. 1944. *An American dilemma.* New York.

Phillips, U. 1929. *Life and labor in the Old South.* Boston.

Raboteau, A. 1978. *Slave religion: The "invisible institution" in the antebellum South.* New York.

Schomburg, A. 1925. The Negro digs up his past. In Locke 1925b:231–37.

Simpson, G. 1973. *Melville J. Herskovits.* New York.

Smith, J. 1980. A different view of slavery: Black historians attack the proslavery argument, 1890–1920. *J. Negro Hist.* 65:298–311.

Stocking, G. W., Jr. 1968. *Race, culture, and evolution: Essays in the history of anthropology.* New York.

———, ed. 1974. *The shaping of American anthropology, 1883–1911: A Franz Boas reader.* New York.

———. 1976. Ideas and institutions in American anthropology: Thoughts toward a history of the interwar years. In *Selected papers from the American Anthropologist, 1921–1945*, ed. Stocking, 1–44. Washington, D.C.

———. 1977. The aims of Boasian ethnography: Creating the materials for traditional humanistic scholarship. *Hist. Anth. Newsl.* 4(2):4–5.

———. 1978. Anthropology as *Kulturkampf*: Science and politics in the career of Franz Boas. In *Anthropology and the public*, ed. W. Goldschmidt, 33–50. Washington, D.C.

Tillinghast, J. 1902. *The Negro in Africa and America.* Pubs. Am. Ec. Assn. 3(2):6–101.

Whitten, N., & J. Szwed, eds. 1970. *Afro-American anthropology.* New York.

Wolters, R. 1975. *The new Negro on campus: Black college rebellions of the 1920s.* Princeton.

Woodson, C. 1942. Review of Herskovits 1941. *J. Negro Hist.* 27:115–18.

Young, D. 1932. *American minority peoples: A study in racial and cultural conflicts in the United States.* New York.

Manuscript Sources

BP   Franz Boas Papers, American Philosophical Society, Philadelphia.
CCA   Carnegie Corporation Archives, New York.
HP   Melville J. Herskovits Papers, Northwestern University Library, Evanston, Ill.

VIGOROUS MALE AND ASPIRING FEMALE

Poetry, Personality, and Culture in Edward Sapir and Ruth Benedict

RICHARD HANDLER

Edward Sapir and Ruth Benedict have been placed together in the history of American anthropology—as theorists of cultural patterning, as ancestors of Culture and Personality, as humanists and poets. Yet neither Sapir nor Benedict agreed or felt comfortable with the ideas that the other held concerning cultural "integrity" and the relationship of individuals to cultures. For Sapir, Benedict's conception of culture as personality writ large was but another example of the reification he had first criticized in his comment on Kroeber's superorganic (1917a). Thus in his Yale seminar on the "Psychology of Culture" he mentioned Benedict's *Patterns of Culture* as typical of what he called "the AS-IF psychology." "A culture," he remarked, "cannot be paranoid," and he criticized both Benedict and Margaret Mead for their "failure to distinguish between the As-if psychology of a culture and the actual psychology of the people participating in the culture." Culture, he said, "has in itself no psychology" (SSLN: 4/19/37). For her part, Benedict was troubled by certain implications of Sapir's notion of a "genuine culture" (Sapir 1924a). She formulated her critique, as she was writing *Patterns of Culture*, in a letter to Mead:

> I understood him to say that centrifugal cultures (ones with many uncoordinated elements) were spurious, and centripetal ones (well-coordinated) genuine. Then he remarks that genuine cultures are poised, satisfactory, etc., etc.,

Richard Handler is Assistant Professor of Anthropology at the University of Virginia. He is an editor of one of the volumes in the forthcoming *Collected Works of Edward Sapir* (The Hague: Mouton). His other research interests include the cultural politics of nationalism, and the anthropological interpretation of the works of Jane Austen.

spurious ones muddled, unsatisfactory, etc. Therefore I remarked that homo-
geneous cultures could be built on basic ideas far from gracious . . . and that
the fact that a society indulged in pretentiousness and hypocrisy might be because it had a most well-coordinated culture which expressed itself in that form.
(10/16/32, in Mead 1959:325)

The present essay examines some of the intellectual and personal issues
that motivated this mutual conceptual discomfort. It takes as its point of entry the aesthetic philosophy of the "new" poets whom Sapir and Benedict
both emulated. I have tried to capture the central values of that poetic culture
by explicating the notion of hardness, a metaphor that Ezra Pound used to
convey his theory of the relationship between self-expression and poetic form
—or, one might say, between personality and culture writ small. Focusing on
the poetic aspirations of Sapir and Benedict—their striving for hard personality and genuine culture—will give us a sense of the broader experiences out
of which their anthropological discourse emerged. Moreover, "hardness," with
its obvious sexual implications, takes us to questions of sexuality and gender
roles, two issues that became major sources of disagreement between Sapir
and Benedict, both personally and professionally. Ultimately I will relate their
contrasting theories of culture and personality—Sapir's concern for genuine
culture, Benedict's for cultural tolerance—to their profoundly different approaches to what Sapir called, in the title of a 1928 essay, "the sex problem
in America."

Hardness: Passion and Intellect

Historians like T. J. Jackson Lears and Warren Susman have written persua-
sively on what Susman has called "the transition . . . from a culture of character to a culture of personality" that occurred at the turn of the twentieth
century (1984:275). The argument goes back at least to Weber, who pointed
out that the worldly success of ascetic Protestants often led to moral laxity
among their descendants, who found themselves possessed of great wealth
but lacking in spiritual fortitude (1905:155–76). In Lears's version (1981; 1983),
the modernization of American society—involving the replacement of Puritan morality and a frontier economy oriented to production by a liberalized
Protestantism and an urbanizing, mass-market consumer economy—led to a
"crisis of cultural authority" whose symptoms, among the bourgeoisie, were
feelings of "weightlessness" and "unreality" leading to "neurasthenic" mental
breakdowns. Lears argues that the demise of Puritanism left a secular culture
still obsessed with an individualistic work ethic, but without the transcen-
dental referent that had earlier validated the suffering and striving of individuals. In such a cultural void, the hard work to which people were driven

came to seem meaningless, and people's lives, weightless and unreal. The cultural response was a new "therapeutic" morality of personal health and self-development, in which the secular self became an ultimate value, an end in itself which people systematically cultivated in order to achieve fuller lives and truer experiences. As Susman puts it, the earlier concern with "building character" gave way to the desire to "develop personality."

Much of Lears's analysis concerns the "anti-modernistic" reaction against weightlessness—people's search for "reality" and "real experience" in the past, the primitive, the natural, the exotic. And it is here that these historians' interpretations help us to place the yearnings of Sapir, Benedict, and the poets of their generation—for the characteristic quest of the new poets was for the real, the authentic, vital, and genuine. "I go about this London hunting for the real"—so wrote Ezra Pound to Harriet Monroe in the early days of *Poetry* magazine, when Pound, as Monroe's foreign correspondent, had taken on the task of purveying real poetry, "the good work . . . obscured, hidden in the bad" (10/22/12, in 1971:12). Pound's equation of the real with the artistically valid is characteristic, and he came to formulate that equation in the aesthetic of what he called hardness, an aesthetic that tempted both Sapir and Benedict.

For Pound and the imagist poets, hardness pertained first of all to style, both personal and poetic—or, better, the personal in the poetic. The crucial notion was that sincere self-expression—considered the essence of Art—depended (in poetry) upon an absolutely original use of language, because the individual's unique experience could not be conveyed through conventional language, encumbered as it is with dead metaphors and cliché. Thus among the "principles" of imagism we find:

1. Direct treatment of the "thing" whether subjective or objective.
2. To use absolutely no word that does not contribute to the presentation.
   (Pound 1918:3)

This is not a prescription for realism: the "thing" can be "subjective or objective"—"of external nature, or of emotion" (Pound 1918:11). In other words, the "thing" is any experience the poet has, and his task is to translate that unique experience "directly," via an absolutely original use of language. T. E. Hulme, advocating "dry, hard, classical verse," puts the matter in these terms:

> The great aim is accurate, precise and definite description. The first thing is to recognise how extraordinarily difficult this is. It is no mere matter of carefulness; you have to use language, and language is by its very nature a communal thing; that is, it expresses never the exact thing but a compromise—that which is common to you, me and everybody. But each man sees a little differently, and to get out clearly and exactly what he does see, he must have a terrific struggle with language . . . (1924:132–33)

Since "communal" language is inadequate to express individual experience, the poet is enjoined to create his own language by avoiding past usages, dead metaphors—all "decorations and trappings," "flaccid" styles, or "slither"—that do not and cannot contribute to the presentation because they belong to the language of past, of someone else's, experience (Pound 1914a:217; 1918:3, 12).

This emphasis on the poet's experience—on his direct intuitions of reality, as Croce phrased it (1902:30)—suggests the significance of another key element in the aesthetics of the new poetry: sincerity. In Pound's view, conventional language meant conventional thought, impersonal, unoriginal, insincere: "most men think only husks and shells of the thoughts that have been already lived over by others" (1914b:371). By contrast, the poet sees in an original fashion—"intuits reality directly"—and expresses what he sees originally; the poet is "sincere." This was explained to readers of *Poetry* by the imagist poet Richard Aldington, translating and quoting Edouard Dujardin, a symbolist poet and critic:

> An artist's first problem is sincerity . . . the bad writer . . . is the man who is not "sincere.". . . All artists believe they say what they think; in reality they only repeat and re-arrange what others have thought before them. Result: an approximation, insufficient, factitious and generally false expression. (1920:166–67)

When writers fall back on convention they abandon the attempt to intuit reality directly, adopting instead the experiences, thoughts, and expressions of others; in other words, their experiences and their poetry become "unreal." And the lure of convention plays at all levels of poetic language: metaphor, diction, rhyme, meter. Thus, for example, the *vers libristes* battled to escape conventional metric schemes which, they thought, corrupted poets by extracting loyalty to traditional form at the expense of personal intuition. The temptation when using traditional forms was, as Pound phrased it, to "put in what you want to say and then fill up the remaining vacuums with slush." For Pound, "technique" was "the test of a man's sincerity" (1918:7, 9).

Hardness, then, in the aesthetics of the new poetry, referred both to technique and to the artist's vision; it suggested that real art depended on the discovery of a personal reality, a reality penetrated, understood, embraced, and expressed by the self standing alone. Such a conception accorded well with the mystique of the artist in the wider culture, preoccupied as it was with the search for real experience; it also helps to explain the spate of would-be poets who emerged during and after World War I as poetry became, unbelievably, "popular." Ever the elitist, Pound inveighed against "my *bête noire* —the charlatans," those "turning out shams" instead of real art:

> I know there are a lovely lot who want to express their own personalities. . . . Only they mostly won't take the trouble to find out what is their own personality.

Pound also complained about the "many habile poseurs . . . who only want to be 'prominent'" (Oct./1912, in Monroe 1938:263; March/1913, in 1971:15). Similarly, Monroe wrote a *Poetry* editorial on "Those We Refuse," in which she pictured the magazine's office as flooded with "intimate self-revelations" expressed in "comically-pathetically bad verse," though she admitted that "Even the editors, hardened as they are, sometimes 'fall for it' . . . [for] some poem whose softness makes our readers marvel" (1920a:322).

Like other contributors to *Poetry*, Sapir and Benedict found the aesthetic of hardness compelling as a model for the artist's personality and work. For both, hardness combined passion and intellect—represented, that is, an emotional, personal commitment to aesthetic craftsmanship and intellectual striving. Sapir analyzed such issues in his theoretical and critical writings on literature, music, and culture, where he examined the relationship between technique and vision—the artist's creative appropriation of traditional forms to express a personal conception. "Culture, Genuine and Spurious" presented these ideas in their broadest application, as a theory of culture; here Sapir defined the "genuine" culture as one sufficiently rich in aesthetic resources to stimulate (rather than hinder) creative personalities to express themselves and, thereby, to develop the cultural tradition still further. In his essays on poetry Sapir explicitly formulated these ideas in terms of the aesthetic of hardness. Summarizing a discussion of the creative stimulus to be derived from "technical struggles," from the demands of traditional formal devices such as rhyme, Sapir wrote: "it is precisely the passionate temperament cutting into itself with the cold steel of the intellect that is best adapted to the heuristic employment of rhyme" (1920:497–98). Sapir also expressed such ideas, in more obviously self-referential fashion, in his poetry:

BLUE FLAME AND YELLOW

I strove for a blue flame
That would rise like a point of steel,
Cleaving the vast night
Up to the starry wheel.

I burned with a yellow flame,
I was edged with a curl of smoke,
I went out under the stars,
Leaves of the world oak.

(SUP: 3/15/19)

Images of flame and steel were congenial to Benedict, too, who aspired, in diary entries rather than critical essays, to a hardness combining passion and intellect. On October 25, 1912, she wrote of her "aspirations" and "longing" for "understanding," "expression," "service," and "friendship," a list which runs from intellect to passion (Mead 1959:122). In January 1917 she listed the "big things of life" as "love, friendship, beauty, clear thinking, honest personality," and on August 15, 1919, she praised "hard thinking" as well as "art values" (Mead 1959:139–40, 143). But it was to Walter Pater that she turned for a philosophy that captured these disparate goals in one image. In December 1915 she relived her discovery of Pater's philosophy of art for art's sake, a discovery she dated to her freshman winter at Vassar in 1906:

> And it is Pater's message that comes back to me as the cry of my deepest necessity: "to burn with this hard gem-like flame"—to gain from experience "this fruit of a quickened, multiplied consciousness," to summon "the services of philosophy of religion, of culture as well, to startle us into a sharp and eager observation." (Mead 1959:135)

Benedict quoted accurately (though not word for word) from the "Conclusion" to The Renaissance. There Pater adumbrated what Hugh Kenner has called "an aesthetic of glimpses" (1971:69). Pater wrote of a once-unified reality dissolving under the pressure of "modern thought," with the result that "what is real in our life fines itself down" to a succession of fleeting, disconnected, private experiences. In the face of such chaos and isolation, Pater urged his readers to a passionate, aesthetic savoring of each momentary experience:

> How may we see in them all that is to be seen in them by the finest senses? How shall we pass most swiftly from point to point, and be present always at the focus where the greatest number of vital forces unite in their purest energy? (1873:194–95)

To succeed in the endeavor was "To burn always with this hard, gemlike flame." And, he continued, "our failure is to form habits," in other words, to surrender to conventional interpretations of experience, to become insincere. Like Pater, Benedict feared insincerity, and much worse, a loss or absence of selfhood. Again and again in her diaries she echoes Pater as she urges herself on to a "superb enthusiasm for life," an "enthusiasm for one's own personality," or, attributing to Mary Wollstonecraft what she felt to be lacking in herself, "a passionately intellectual attitude toward living" (Mead 1959: 123, 491).

The Vigorous Male and Aspiring Female

Personality imaged as a hard, gemlike flame is the self standing alone, creating and mastering reality with its passion, intelligence, and art. But in a culture that associates hardness with masculinity and softness with femininity, to conceive the essence of human personality in terms of hardness poses a particular problem to women: the generically human belongs preeminently to the other sex. The problem was implicit in the "new" poetry which, in rejecting the softness of Victorian art, also rejected a conception of culture as a feminine domain, the domain of "sweetness and light," as Matthew Arnold termed it in *Culture and Anarchy* (1868). Monroe broached the issue in a comment entitled "Men or Women?" in which she responded to a Philadelphia newspaper editorial lamenting a perceived demise of "the vigorous male note" in poetry. Monroe remarked that the magazine received some three thousand "real or alleged poems" each month, adding that "*Poetry* receives more publishable verse, and less hopelessly bad verse, from the 'vigorous male' than from the aspiring female." And she concluded by encouraging female aspirations in the arts, calling for a "feminine note . . . as authentic, . . . as vigorous and beautiful, as the masculine" (1920b:148).

Monroe's pairing of masculine vigor and feminine aspiration reminds us that Sapir and Benedict were differently situated as each undertook the quest for poetry, personality, and culture. As Benedict put it in an undated journal entry, "The issue . . . is fine free living . . . for men as for women. But owing to artificial actual conditions their problems are strikingly different" (Mead 1959:146). In their private lives each had to confront "the sex problem in America," a problem that included not only sexuality, but marriage, family, and sex roles—the relations of men to women in the wider society. Sapir faced such problems with a professional identity at least minimally secured; as his poetry and letters show, his dilemma was to make room for other aspects of life—familial, romantic, artistic—during the course of the productive scientific career he expected of himself. By contrast, Benedict, without a secure identity during much of her early adulthood, was torn between "feminine" and "masculine" aspirations: marriage and motherhood, on the one hand, and the desire for work and for intellectual and moral purpose, on the other.

The "sex problem," then, was posed more sharply for Benedict than for Sapir: his dilemma was one of accommodation; hers involved a fundamental choice. We can read this contrast in their literary endeavors, and it is reflected as well in their approaches to the study of culture and personality. It will be convenient to analyze their poetry, and its relationship to their theories of culture and personality, in terms of two questions: why did they write poetry, and what did they write about?

Publishing personality

Though both Sapir and Benedict were skeptical of the value of their own poetry, both very much desired to publish it, and we should distinguish that desire from other (though not incompatible) reasons for writing poetry. Among the latter we must recognize self expression as a response to loneliness, as well as the cultural definition of poetry as an appropriate medium in which to discuss the personal agonies associated with love, sexuality, death, and fate. For Sapir, writing poetry also provided an alternative method to work out his developing culture theory, with its concern for the dialectic between traditional discipline and individual creativity (Handler 1983). Modell has made a similar point about Benedict:

> Absorption in anthropology . . . led her back to poetry. Ruth Benedict entered a discipline just developing a concern for individual creativeness within cultural constraints. . . . She was encouraged at once to learn scientific procedures and to have confidence in her own voice. (1983:129)

Yet one might turn to poetry without attaching importance to publication. What, then, is the cultural significance of publication?

An answer is suggested by Arthur Symons' account of the symbolist Mallarmé, an account influential at the time when Sapir and Benedict were writing poetry. According to Symons, Mallarmé considered "publication . . . unnecessary, a mere way of convincing the public that one exists" (1919:193). The remark recalls Pound's irate dismissal of the "lovely lot who want to express their own personalities . . . [without taking] the trouble to find out what is their own personality." Beyond Pound, there lies a critique of egalitarian mass societies that begins with Tocqueville and goes through Riesman (1950) to Lears (1983)—the idea that anonymous and indistinguishable individuals must struggle to raise themselves above the crowd, to forge a personal identity, yet must construct their "unique" identity out of symbols readily comprehensible to the mass public. The result, as Pound's remark suggests, is that people seek personality in and of itself rather than develop, in the pursuit of other goals, personal qualities which, after the fact, might constitute personality.

Certainly for Benedict, publication (whether of poetry or of prose) was a way of convincing the public, and herself, that she existed (see Modell 1983: 107–9). In her earliest journal entry, written at the age of twenty-five, Benedict tells of an identity crisis that suggests Susman's transition from "character" to "personality":

> I tried, oh very hard, to believe that our own characters are the justification of it all. . . . But the boredom had gone too deep; I had no flicker of interest in my character. What was my character anyway? My real *me* was a creature I dared not look upon. . . . (Oct./1912, in Mead 1959:119)

Thereafter, the quest for personality was a major theme of her journals, as it was of her biography of Mary Wollstonecraft, who, as Benedict saw it, "never flinched before the hazard of shaping forth a personality" (Mead 1959:494). Benedict prodded herself to "self-development" via a "culture of . . . aspirations," seeking the "*Me* . . . of untold worth" that she found in poets like Whitman, and promising to "manage" herself and avoid "floundering" (122–23, 128). She described her "striving toward the dignity of rich personality" as a "consummate duty" (134)—an attitude that suggests Lears's interpretation of the "therapeutic world view" of modern culture, that is, the Puritan concern with personal salvation transmuted into a purely secular, though religiously obsessive, pursuit of self-cultivation, guided by therapists instead of clerics (1981: 52–58). Sapir remarked on this aspect of Benedict's quest for personality. Commenting on a poem entitled "Our Task Is Laughter," he saw her "banking a little too heavily on the philosophy of prescription and therapeutic protest. . . . It seems hard to have to say, 'Our *task* is laughter'" (12/12/24, in Mead 1959:166).

Seeking personality, Benedict had to work her way through the issues raised by feminism. She never renounced love, marriage, or the desire for children as high ideals for women, but came to reject the social arrangements that made it impossible for women to fulfill those ideals without sacrificing the "achievement of a four-square personality" (Mead 1959:147). Shortly after her marriage she told herself that "it is wisdom in motherhood as in wifehood to have one's own individual world of effort and creation" (136). And she rejected such conventionally feminine efforts as teaching and social work, remarking that "the world has need of my vision as well as of Charity Committees" (135)—a comment that recalls Pound's equation of committees (for awarding prizes to artists) with "mediocrity" and "the least common denominator," that is, with the abandonment of creative personality (1914a:223).

All of which brought Benedict to writing. As a child she had received familial encouragement for her writing, and later, during her struggle for personality, she could tell herself that "my best, my thing 'that in all my years I tend to do' is surely writing" (Mead 1959:144). But writing without recognition was not sufficient: "more and more I know that I want publication" (135). Writing became a duty for her in her therapeutic quest for personality: she chided herself to "work at writing with sufficient slavishness" (136) and longed "to prove myself by writing" (142). At first she worked at her biographies of famous women (a project rejected by Houghton Mifflin in 1919); later, at poetry and anthropological writing.

Benedict was a careful writer who revised her work extensively (Modell 1983:18, 76–77). She described "the process of verse," in a 1929 letter to Mead, in terms of "incubation, gestation" (Mead 1959:94), metaphors that suggest composition over extended lengths of time; and it is clear that she expected to work meticulously at poetry. Since her poetry expressed a private self she feared showing to others, the quest for recognition through publication aroused no little anxiety—a dilemma solved by writing poetry under a pseudonym. By the time she felt enough confidence in her voice and the self it represented to abandon her pseudonym, she had begun to achieve success as an anthropologist. According to Mead, after *Patterns of Culture* Benedict was unwilling "to trade on her success in one field to bolster up a much more minor success in another" (1959:93). One publicly validated professional identity was enough for her, and she gave up poetry.

For Sapir, by contrast, public recognition as a poet seems to have been a sign of intellectual vigor, of Renaissance virtuosity. He began writing poetry in 1917 (9/29/27, in Mead 1959:185), at a time when American intellectuals were engaged in a search for "a real national culture," as Mead put it in a letter to Benedict (8/30/24, 285). "Culture, Genuine and Spurious" was intended as a contribution to that search, and Sapir's poetry and literary criticism represented further modes of participation. Moreover, the practice of art was congenial to Sapir—a "cosmographical" scientist for whom the human realities studied by anthropologists were above all aesthetic phenomena (see Handler 1986; Silverstein 1986).

Beyond Sapir's desire to participate in the general intellectual culture of his time lay the possibility of another career. He flirted with the idea of leaving anthropology for music, but he knew that his music was not of professional quality—so also, his poetry (9/29/16, in Lowie 1965:21). Despite Sapir's refusal to delude himself, however, the publication of poetry and criticism gave him, one feels, a sense of alternative career possibilities at a time when he felt frustrated by his inability to land a university position. The other intellectually dominant figure among the prewar generation of Franz Boas' students, A. L. Kroeber—whose reifying view of culture Sapir had attacked at an early point (1917a)—was later to explain Sapir's personalistic theory of culture as "wish-fulfilment expression set against the backdrop of a partly regretted career" (1952:148); but the remark more justly applied to Sapir's poetic aspirations. From the security of his professorship at the University of California, Kroeber lectured Sapir about building a professional reputation: "If I had half your philological wits I'd have five times your place and influence in the philological world" (7/24/17, in Golla 1984:245). For his part, Sapir sometimes expressed a sense of guilt in the face of his inability to live up to his own expectations for scholarly productivity: "[Paul] Radin [a brilliant Boasian intellectual bohemian who never did find secure academic status] may have sinned in starting too many things and leaving them unfinished, but I have sinned so much more that I am inclined to be charitable" (11/21/18, 281). Poetry must have served at once as an escape from such anxieties and, when practiced in place of scientific work, as a stimulus to them.

Whatever the relationship between Sapir's professional ambivalence and his poetic aspirations, he wrote over five hundred poems, and he wrote them quickly. Seeing his work in print excited him with the "feeling of being a poet" (5/14/25, 9/29/27, in Mead 1959:179, 185), but he habitually submitted what he called "half-baked stuff" for publication (1/18/19, in Golla 1984:296). As

Edward Sapir, ca. 1920. (Courtesy Philip Sapir.)

he admitted to Monroe, "Yes, you are right about my not working hard enough at my verses. I *do* let things go before I should" (PMP: 10/28/18). Perhaps Sapir expected the same degree of virtuosity in poetry that he possessed in linguistics. Lacking it, he accepted Monroe's sometimes drastic editing in exchange for the possibility of publication:

> I think it would be well to omit stanza 3 of "Charon." I am not quite so certain of both stanzas 4 and 5 of "She went to sleep below," but am inclined to think stanza 4 should come out. Stanza 5 seems somehow to place the sun image that follows, but if you feel that it too should come out, please remove it. (PMP: 3/7/25)

It is hard to imagine Sapir brooking such interference in his linguistic work! Thus when Boas suggested that Sapir send him a preliminary outline of his Paiute grammar, Sapir reacted indignantly:

> The precise method that you suggest for the preparation of the manuscript by July 1st is in the highest degree irksome to me. . . . My own habit is always, in both scientific and literary attempts, to prepare the ground thoroughly beforehand and write out the final manuscript once and for all. In fact, I think that I have never in the course of my whole life written a second or revised version of anything. (ANMM: 3/28/17)

It is equally hard to imagine Benedict reacting in such fashion to editorial criticism. Daring and vigorous, Sapir expected to be able to "dash off" publishable writings in half a dozen genres (2/7/25, in Mead 1959:171). Benedict's aspirations were more modest: she was contented by the possession of but one voice, coherent and publicly acclaimed.

Poetries of passion and despair

Modell has described Benedict's poetry as combining "an English metaphysical tradition" with biblical and Greek mythology and "her own perceptions of landscape" in an "eccentric yoking of image to abstraction" (1983: 135–37). Sapir, too, saw Benedict's poetic originality to lie in the seriousness of her themes and the relationship of her work to English religious poetry. "Your great merit," he wrote her, "is that you are finely in the tradition, even Puritan tradition, but with a notable access of modernity" (12/12/24, in Mead 1959:166). Or, as he told Monroe, "I know of no one who has anything like her high and passionate seriousness. She knows how to use difficult words well, her imagery is bold, and her thought is never banal. Above all, every line of her work is sincere" (PMP: 3/23/25).

Religious imagery is central in Benedict's poetry, but she used it without religious conviction. As she explained in an autobiographical fragment written for Mead, her religion was a culture, not a faith: "I was brought up in

Ruth Benedict, ca. 1925. (Courtesy Vassar College Library.)

the midst of the church. . . . Nevertheless my religious life had nothing to do with institutional Christianity nor with church creeds. . . . For me, the gospels described a way of life . . ." (Mead 1959:107). Thus her poetry used religious imagery to speak of the impossibility of belief, the hollowness of high ideals, or the futility of striving. Only rarely did she write of the believability of ideals and dreams, and even then her attitude was ambivalent. In "Sight," for example, she mocked those who would confine their "dreaming" within "four walls," yet equated dreaming with "tortured promises" (170). Such imagery accords well with Benedict's quest for personality and career, for something "real" to believe in.

Aside from metaphysical despair, the dominant theme of Benedict's poetry is passion—suppressed or uncontrollable, sated or unfulfilled, but above all, passion confined to the self, passion without reply. As Modell has pointed out, most of Benedict's poetry was written during a time when she was withdrawing from a sexually barren and failing marriage, yet before she had secured the professional identity that would sustain her after 1930: "In the guise of Anne Singleton, Ruth Benedict expressed a self that included 'ripeness' and 'ecstasy' along with high moral purpose, a self that Stanley Benedict no longer recognized and Edward Sapir would be permitted to know" (1983: 129). To express that private, passionate self, Benedict used religious and naturalistic imagery, as, for example, in "She Speaks to the Sea" (Mead 1959:487):

> For I am smitten to my knees with longing,
> Desolate utterly, scourged by your surface-touch,
> Of white-lipped wave and unquiet azure hands.

In other poems Benedict wrote of the autumnal beauty of barrenness, and the deathlike quiescence following the consummation of passion.

Modell has written that "Benedict's poetry reveals a repetitiveness in concept and vocabulary" (1983:140). It is also stylistically narrow, most of it written in the sonnet or similar lyric forms. Sapir urged Benedict to experiment with other forms: "Have you ever thought of dramatizing your theme and treating it in . . . narrative blank verse? . . . I am very eager to see you get away for a while from the sonnet form, for I want an ampler field for your spirit" (1/26/25, in Mead 1959:171). Yet Benedict had not gained enough control of her voice to distance herself from it, to allow herself to experiment outside the narrow range of techniques she found intuitively congenial. In Benedict's confessional poetry, there is little to separate the poet's persona from the poet herself. As Modell puts it, "at its best the poetry of Anne Singleton displayed a classical purity and disciplined cadence," but at its worst "confession lay close to the surface and control tightened into hysteria" (1983:140).

It is with respect to stylistic and technical choices that Sapir's poetry can be most usefully compared with Benedict's. Sapir not only wrote theoretical papers (1917b; 1920) on the relationship between technique and conception, he actively experimented with a wide range of poetic forms. His poetry includes sonnets and other short, rhymed forms, blank verse, free verse, and dramatic and narrative verse; he wrote short poems of two lines as well as longer pieces of several pages. More important, Sapir tried on different voices in his poetry, characteristically distancing himself from his subject, *writing about* personalities and states of mind rather than expressing them as the immediate product of his own soul. If Benedict's poetry is confessional, Sapir's is observational—though he himself is often the object observed.

Sapir's penchant for psychological observation was mentioned by Kroeber, who reminisced about Sapir's "intense interest in people and seeing what made their wheels go around." According to Kroeber, Sapir "was likely to take a close friend and watch him, dissect him, try to draw him out . . . just from sheer interest in individuals, in personalities" (1959:136). That attitude suggests why Sapir was particularly drawn to the poetry of Edwin Arlington Robinson. Sapir wrote Monroe that "I am left with an impression of overwhelming mastery, a strength at once fine and careless, in Edwin Arlington Robinson. He has the real stuff—for psychology" (PMP: 9/20/18). Elsewhere Sapir analyzed Robinson's "real stuff" in some detail:

> One of the most striking features in his poems is the use of "Skeleton Plots." It is as though he had a specific plot in mind, made vivid the psychology, then rubbed out the plot and kept the psychology, giving the reader the opportunity to build up one of several possible explanations. (SN: 28–29)

Like Benedict, Sapir used poetry to talk about love and passion. Most of Sapir's poetry was written between 1917 and 1925, the years when he was preoccupied with the tragedy of his first wife's physical and mental collapse, leading to her death in 1924. Sapir's poems explore the sentiments and experiences shared "Twixt a Man and a Wife," as the title of an unpublished poem puts it, projecting and analyzing feelings that run "from love to kindred hate" (SUP: 9/30/18). In these poems Sapir rehearses the romantic relationship backward and forward, reminiscing about first love, imagining the death of love or unsuccessful love, creating heartbroken characters who indulge in their own reminiscences, and occasionally narrating psychological confrontations in the manner of Robinson. Though some of Sapir's poems seem to be direct expressions of immediate feeling, he more frequently uses poetry to stand aside, even from his closest relationships:

SHE HAS GONE OUT

She has gone out for a walk in the twilight snow
With our little daughter by her side,

And she will have sweet, prattling words, I know,
To hear in the dusk till eventide.

But they have left me sitting by the fire
To think of how they both are dear,
Of how another love than first desire
Is flaming softly down the year.

(SUP: 12/28/19)

Elsewhere he wrote that "The fruits of marriage are disillusionment and children" (SN: 25)—a remark which, contrasted to poems like "She Has Gone Out,"
suggests the complexity of Sapir's private world.

Sapir did not confine himself to poems about his personal life, but wrote
on a variety of topics, from social satire to philosophical speculation. He self-
consciously attempted to portray his poetic personality in several lights. After
Monroe had accepted several of his poems for publication, he complained
jokingly that her choices "misrepresent me as an extremely sad fellow with a
horrible case of Weltschmerz!"—demanding "the opportunity later on to qual-
ify this dismal impression with a set of lighter, cynical-frivolous shots (I have
a bunch of them for you)" (PMP: 5/14/20). A year later he sent a new batch,
characterizing each poem for Monroe with terms such as "nostalgic," "facile-
pretty," "old-fashioned eroticism," and "impertinent" (6/30/21). In another letter he described poems ranging from "mordant or hopeless" to "thumbnail
symbolic things" to "the regular sentimental things," though with regard to
the last he wrote: "I hope I have avoided treacle" (10/28/18).

Yet with his penchant for the facile-pretty, the nostalgic, and the sentimental, Sapir had difficulty avoiding treacle. Monroe criticized his poems for their
lack of "hardness," as did Kroeber:

> I see no evidence of anything abnormal or tortured or warped in your work.
> It rather comes out clean and neat. All I don't see is the drive behind that makes
> the product compact and hard and arresting. . . . You evidently have great sen-
> sitiveness toward images. They run away with you over two and three pages.
> But the intensity of emotion that cuts them out and burns them in isn't there.
> (1/11/19, in Golla 1984:294)

Sapir was appreciative of Kroeber's reading, but he defended himself to Monroe, going so far as to advocate softness in a critique of her editorial biases:
"Why not look for hardness in the soft-textured stuff (better, soft-surfaced)
too? Such a lot of bluff around these days!" (PMP: 5/14/20).

Sapir's poetic voice tended to be soft and sentimental, on the one hand,
or aloof and distanced, on the other. In any case, it lacked that intensity and
"hardness" which was in demand, yet which he equated with "bluff." As we
shall see, "bluff" for Sapir was symptomatic of spurious personality, epitomized
in the distorted sexuality of women aspiring to hardness.

The Sex Problem in America

Both Sapir and Benedict used poetry to express the agony of marriages unraveling. Benedict, who said that her husband rejected her sexually (Modell 1983: 131–32), wrote poems that are cries of passion frustrated:

> Weep but for this: that we are blind
>
> With passion who have been clear-eyed
> As planets after rain: and know
> No longer any grief, who go
> Just to see love crucified.

(Mead 1959:71)

Or, reverting to the imagery of cutting flame, she wrote in an undated journal entry: "There is only one problem in life: that fire upon our flesh shall burn as a knife that cuts to the bone, and joy strip us like a naked blade" (Mead 1959:154). Sapir, too, wrote of dying love and frustrated passion, but he also explored the happier aspects of romance. In contrast to Benedict's poems, Sapir's tend to objectify his situation, allowing him to stand apart from it and analyze its various emotional and psychological components.

As Mead and Modell have noted, during these difficult years of their lives, Benedict and Sapir turned to each other, using poetry—which both aspired to publish—to communicate what could not be easily discussed in less stylized modes. When Benedict "initiated" their friendship by sending Sapir a copy of her doctoral dissertation (1923), she must already have been aware of his poetic interests, since he commented, as if in answer to her query: "No, I have not written any poems lately." Responding at length to her still somewhat conventionally Boasian thesis, Sapir urged that "the problem of the individual and group psychology [be] boldly handled, not ignored, by some one who fully understands culture as a historical entity"—confiding also that he felt "damnably alone" on the "long and technical . . . road I must travel in linguistic work" (6/25/22, in Mead 1959:49–53; see also Modell 1983:127). Although Benedict's diary entries over the next few years suggest an infatuation for Sapir, he kept his emotional distance, preferring to coach her professional development in both anthropology and poetry. He dedicated "Zuni" to "R. F. B.," urging her to "keep the flowing / Of your spirit, in many branching ways" (Mead 1959:88). On the day he wrote "Zuni" he composed "Acheron," in which he mourned his wife in images of water that would flow no more:

> Come, I have brought you here by the dim shores of water,
> By the faint lapping of scarce moving water.
> . . . .
> And you will sink into the ghostly midst without sound,
> In the middle of great widening ripples round.

(SUP: 8/26/24)

Two poems written on the same day, to two women, one living, one dead: Sapir must have seen, in Benedict, unstifled feminine aspiration, that of a woman with a hopeful future. And, as Perry (1982:243–49) has suggested, he must have felt a terrible sense of guilt at his wife's death. Florence Delson had left Radcliffe before graduation to go with Sapir to the isolation of Ottawa, where she had borne three children in little more than three years. Sapir was undoubtedly a loving husband and father, but he was also devoted to scholarship. Perry says that "he seems to have been so immersed in his work that he sometimes tended to resent the intrusion of the children on his studies" (245). This is perhaps exaggerated, but, on the other hand, it is not incompatible with the observational aloofness toward family life that one finds in some of his poems. According to Perry, when Sapir first met Harry Stack Sullivan, in the fall of 1926, they talked for some ten hours, as Sapir spoke of the responsibility he felt for his wife's death. She had, after all, abandoned her studies to become a wife in a setting where "isolation and loneliness had . . . shattered . . . her mind and body" (249). Ruth Benedict, with Sapir's encouragement, sought to avoid a similar trap as she moved from marriage to anthropology and poetry.

But Sapir and Benedict grew apart, and by the end of the decade were quarreling, as several letters reproduced by Mead show (1959:95, 192–95, 307, 325). They disagreed profoundly about the issues that Sapir raised in a 1928 essay, "Observations on the Sex Problem in America." There Sapir attacked an emergent sexual freedom which, as he saw it, unnaturally separated romantic and sexual love. He also denounced the therapeutic quest for personally enriching sexual experiences. And he singled out "the modern woman" as especially guilty in both regards (1928:528).

Sapir began his essay with the admission that "there is little herein set forth which is not a rationalization of personal bias" (519). He argued that in all societies the satisfaction of basic needs such as hunger and sex involved "the attempt of human beings to reconcile their needs with cultural forms that are both friendly and resistant to these needs" (520). Sapir thought that his contemporaries, in their revolt against Puritan repressions, had treated sex as "a 'good' in itself" to be pursued without regard for conventional regulations, and that this had led to an "artificial divorce . . . between the sex impulse and love" (521), and to a romantic glorification of sex as "primitive" and "natural":

> What has happened is that the odious epithet of sin has been removed from sex, but sex itself has not been left a morally indifferent concept. The usual process of over-correction has invested sex with a factitious value as a romantic and glorious thing in itself. The virus of sin has passed into love, and the imaginative radiance of love, squeezed into the cramped quarters formerly occupied by sin, has transfigured lust and made it into a new and phosphorescent holiness. (522)

Such an attitude was psychologically unnatural, for "the emotion of love . . . is one of the oldest and most persistent of human feelings" (525). Human culture has everywhere linked sex to love in such a way that sexual love "takes the ego out of itself," and becomes the prototype for "all non-egoistic identifications" (527). Anthropologists, Sapir felt, had helped to obscure this truth, with their "excited books about pleasure-loving Samoans and Trobriand Islanders" (523); the reading public was all too prone to mistake the absence of Western-style taboos for "primitive freedom" and, at the same time, to overlook the coercive presence of culturally unfamiliar sex regulations.

Equating the pursuit of sex in itself with "narcissism" (529), Sapir sketched a critique of the therapeutic quest for self-development: "the plausible terminologies of 'freedom,' of 'cumulative richness of experience,' of 'self-realization' . . . lead to an even more profound unhappiness than the normal subordination of impulse to social convention" (528). In other words, the pursuit of sexuality (and personality) as an end in itself, unlinked to cultural values that transcend the self, was doomed to failure—because "sex as self-realization unconsciously destroys its own object" which, in the "natural" case where love is valued, is to "take the ego out of itself" (529).

Sapir went on to suggest the harmful consequences of such attitudes, focusing his critique on women. Women who justly sought economic emancipation (see Sapir 1930:146–48) erred by linking it to sexual freedom, with unhappy results: "Every psychiatrist must have met essentially frigid women of today who have used sex freedom as a mere weapon to feed the ego" (1928: 528). At the same time, the devaluation of "passion between the sexes leads to compensation in the form of homosexuality," a form that Sapir found "unnatural" (529). He dismissed the "smart and trivial analysis of sex by intellectuals" who justify promiscuity and homosexuality, and rationalize their attacks on such phenomena as jealousy and prostitution by linking them to the economic underpinnings of romance and marriage (525). For Sapir, it was "an insult to the true lover to interpret his fidelity and expectation of fidelity as possessiveness and to translate the maddening grief of jealousy into the paltry terminology of resentment at the infringement of property rights" (531). Similarly, prostitutes "despise their own bodies," not simply on account of the social sanctions they suffer, but because their behavior violates "a natural scale of values," and their shame is shared by "many of the protagonists of sex freedom" (532):

> the "free" woman . . . , whether poetess or saleslady, has a hard job escaping from the uncomfortable feeling that she is really a safe, and therefore a dishonest, prostitute. . . . The battle shows in the hard, slightly unfocused, glitter of the eye and in the hollow laugh, and one can watch the gradual deterioration of personality that seems to set in in many of our young women with premature adoption of sophisticated standards. (533)

Such, then, was the fate of women aspiring to hardness.

Although Benedict read the paper as a personal attack on herself, Sapir vigorously denied this: "you were never once in my thoughts when I wrote the paper on sex, which I did . . . rather reluctantly at the request of Harry Stack Sullivan" (4/29/29, in Mead 1959:195). It seems likely that the "personal bias" Sapir was rationalizing focused on another "aspiring female"— Margaret Mead—who had a brief affair with Sapir but refused to "be mama" to his three motherless children, scheming instead to "have him reject her" before she went off to do fieldwork in Samoa (Howard 1984:52, 60). And while Sapir's paper endorses the distinction between love and lust that Sullivan drew so sharply (Perry 1982:90–92), his thinking along those lines had developed well before he knew Sullivan, Benedict, or Mead, as the following poem shows:

THE JACKAL

When the heart is broken and dream is out,
A glimmer crushed by night,
The jackal's footsteps patter the sand,
The jackal's eyes bring a light.
. . . .
When the heart is dead and dream is lost,
The jackal devours the flesh;
The passion of the heart and the passion of the dream—
They live in his lust afresh.

(SUP: 7/11/19)

"The Jackal" was published in 1923 in Queen's Quarterly, but Sapir had previously sent it to Monroe. "Of course, you know who the jackals are," he told her, his indirection suggesting that the poem is about prostitutes (PMP: 7/12/19). If so, it should be compared to Sapir's reaction to Robinson's poem, "Veteran Sirens" (1916), which one Robinson scholar, a contemporary of Sapir, describes as "an expression of pity for old prostitutes" (Winters 1946:33). By contrast, Sapir read the poem as "a most caustic sketch of the vanity of old-maidishness" (SN: 43)—as if this normally sympathetic interpreter of Robinson were unable to share the poet's pity for prostitutes, or old maids.

Benedict was in a better position to sympathize with old maids, having worked with several during her years (1911–14) as a teacher. "They are doing their best," she wrote in her journal, "to trump up a reason for living" (Mead 1959:121). She also speculated about prostitution, which she saw as rooted in the economic and sexual subordination of women in an acquisitive society (146–49). For her, Sapir's discussion of the "natural" shame felt by prostitutes, and his claim that the "free" woman "is really a safe . . . prostitute," must have seemed both insensitive and farfetched; and having herself turned sexually toward women—among them the bisexual Mead (see Bateson 1984:115–27)—

she must have felt equally discomfited by his attitude toward homosexuality. In *Patterns of Culture* she explicitly linked jealousy in American culture to capitalistic acquisitiveness: "Without the clue that in our civilization . . . man's paramount aim is to amass private possessions . . . , the modern position of the wife and the modern emotions of jealousy are alike unintelligible" (1934a: 245). Elsewhere in the book she chose homosexuality as an example of a trait stigmatized in our society but not necessarily everywhere (262–65). It is difficult not to read Benedict's arguments as direct responses to Sapir. As we shall see, their profoundly different approaches to "the sex problem" epitomized the differences in their theories of culture and personality.

The Spurious and the Intolerant

The central element of Sapir's approach to culture and personality is an epistemological critique of the reification inherent in the term "culture." In simple terms, Sapir's argument is that culture is not a "thing," monolithic and equally "shared" by all those included within its boundaries. Rather, every person has a unique culture, because, first, his personal history brings him into contact with a unique configuration of influences, and, second, he must interpret or respond to those cultural influences in a manner consistent with the unique organization of his personality. True, many people respond to cultural forces in ways so similar as to be nearly identical—much culture does appear to be shared—but there is always the possibility of an idiosyncratic response, a reinterpretation or rejection. Moreover, cultural rebels can persuade others of the validity of their responses; hence the importance of "Two Crows denies this": his personal vision can be "culturalized" (1938:569, 572). In other words, culture is not fixed and static, but open-ended; it is not thinglike, but exists only as it is continually reinterpreted by creative personalities. Here are the grounds for Sapir's remarks about Benedict's "As-if psychology," which, from his perspective, reified culture in personalistic terms. Or, as Sapir phrases the criticism more generally, "It is not the concept of culture that is subtly misleading but the metaphysical locus to which culture is generally assigned" (1932:516).

For Sapir, then, culture—located not "above" people, but "between" them—does not overwhelm individuals in oppressive or deterministic fashion. Rather, the relationship between individuals and culture is dialectical: culture provides individuals with the traditional givens—linguistic, aesthetic, social—out of which they will construct their lives, and individuals, as creative personalities, can bend those cultural givens to their own purposes, reshaping culture in the process. As Silverstein (1986) has shown, Sapir's earliest linguistic work is grounded in this dialectical understanding of cultural phenomena—

which suggests that Sapir's epistemology of social science precedes the period of his absorption in poetry and music. But, as I have argued (Handler 1983), Sapir worked out the consequences of his position in his aesthetic endeavors, where he experienced and analyzed the relationship between given form and personal creativity.

Moreover, familiarity with Sapir's aesthetic and poetic concerns can help us to understand some apparent contradictions in his writing on culture and personality. On the one hand, we find his paean to personality, his stress on individual uniqueness at the expense of culture: "Every individual is . . . a representative of at least one sub-culture" (1932:515). On the other hand, Sapir well understood the force of tradition, and sometimes spoke, as did most of his colleagues, of individuals caught in its grasp. For example, in an encyclopedia essay, "Custom," Sapir wrote:

> Custom is generally referred to as a constraining force. The conflict of individual will and social compulsion is familiar, but even the most forceful and self-assertive individual needs to yield to custom at most points in order that he may gain leverage . . . for the imposition of his personal will on society. . . . The freedom gained by the denial of custom is essentially a subjective freedom of escape rather than an effective freedom of conquest. (1931a:370)

In another encyclopedia essay, "Fashion," Sapir portrays individuals torn between the desire to be creative and the desire to conform: "Human beings do not wish to be modest; they want to be as expressive—that is, as immodest —as fear allows; fashion helps them solve their paradoxical problem" (1931b: 380).

Thus there are two poles in Sapir's theory: individual creativity and cultural constraint. On the one hand, Sapir's theory of culture and personality privileges the possibility of individual creativity while rejecting notions of reified culture. On the other hand, Sapir recognized the importance of cultural tradition—the "genuine" culture, rich enough to stimulate rather than hinder creative personalities. And he argued that in most situations, most people surrender to tradition rather than act innovatively. There is an implicit elitism in the argument: "genuine artists" (1921:222) are urged to create, but less is expected of ordinary people, who succumb too easily to spuriousness, either by abandoning any pretense of creative effort, or by adopting the guise of "high" culture without practicing the "self-discipline" necessary for true creativity. This imitative or spurious approach to culture "too often degenerates into a pleasurable servitude, into a facile abnegation of one's own individuality, the more insidious that it has the approval of current judgment" (1924a: 323–24).

In Sapir's theory of culture and personality, spuriousness is seen as the greatest danger. And he found spuriousness rampant in the therapeutic culture of self-realization, where, in his judgment, the pursuit of personality as an end in itself was inherently self-defeating. As we saw, sexual liberation came to epitomize for Sapir the cult of spurious personality. A freedom romantically admired as "primitive" was in Sapir's opinion nothing but "spiritual sloth" (1929:278). No wonder he retitled "Observations on the Sex Problem in America" as "The Discipline of Sex." For him, free love was spurious love, undisciplined, hence unrealizable: "The 'enrichment of personality' by way of multiple 'experiences' proves to be little more than a weary accumulation of poverties" (1928:523). And the aspiring woman was most vulnerable to such traps.

Benedict's understanding of the relationship between the individual and culture differed from Sapir's approach in several ways. First, she never accepted (indeed, like most anthropologists, never understood) Sapir's critique of reification. Like Kroeber (1952:148), she dismissed it as an idiosyncratic expression of personal hostility; consider the following remarks, from a letter to Mead describing a paper given by Sapir at a professional meeting:

> . . . Edward's got a new way to free himself from the necessity of admitting the role of culture. He analyzed his reactions to football, and he drew the moral that every phase of culture . . . is all things to all people, and that this concept dissolves Function, i.e. it outlaws Radcliffe-Brown's contentions. Well! All I got out of it was that Edward had satisfactorily phrased his quarrel with the universe again . . . (11/30/32, in Mead 1959:325)

It is tempting to speculate that Benedict, like Kroeber, tended to reify "culture" because both of them were more concerned than Sapir to bound the profession that guaranteed their public identity. In any case, Benedict's theory of culture and personality stressed not creativity but correspondence: the degree to which cultures might be seen as personality writ large, and, consequently, the ways in which cultures might glorify or suppress basic personality traits. Though she recognized (1934a:251–54) the kind of dialectical interaction between individuals and culture that Sapir stressed, she glided over it to focus, not on culture in relation to unique individuals, but on cultural patterns in relation to personality *types*:

> We have seen that any society selects some segment of the arc of possible human behaviour, and . . . its institutions tend to further the expression of its selected segment and to inhibit opposite expressions. But these opposite expressions are the congenial responses, nevertheless, of a certain proportion of the carriers of that culture. (254)

Benedict argued that most individuals are malleable or "plastic": "The vast majority of the individuals in any group are shaped to the fashion of that culture" (1934b:278). Here is the reifying rhetoric of culture and conformity, and it is extended even to the cases of those individuals whose "congenial responses" are so far from what is culturally valued that they cannot be "shaped" to the cultural norm. Ungovernable, they will nonetheless find their lives largely determined by culture: they become abnormals and deviants, "exposed to all the conflicts to which aberrants are always exposed" (1934a:265).

This brings us to the second difference between Sapir and Benedict. In Benedict's view of culture and personality, intolerance replaces spuriousness as the gravest of cultural ills. The deviant's tragedy stems not from inherent unfitness, but from the accident of his birth into a culture which happens not to value the behavior which is congenial to those of his personality type. Benedict believed that anthropology could teach people to be "culture-conscious," that is, to avoid believing that "local" culture traits are natural and inevitable. Without the justification of a presumed inevitability, institutions could be rationally examined "in terms of the less desirable behaviour traits they stimulate, and in terms of human suffering and frustration." Aspects of culture found to be too costly might be reformed, and, at the same time, the treatment of deviance made more humane:

> . . . the inculcation of tolerance and appreciation in any society toward its less usual types is fundamentally important in successful mental hygiene.
>
> The complement of this tolerance, on the patient's side, is an education in self-reliance and honesty with himself. (1934a:245–48)

Benedict hoped that tolerance on the part of the majority would enable deviants "to achieve a more independent and less tortured attitude" (1934b: 278–79).

Erudition and Engineering

Benedict's notion of self-conscious and rational cultural criticism led her to aspire to "what may some day come to be a true social engineering" (1934b: 280), and here we find the final difference between her and Sapir. As we saw, Sapir did not expect creativity of anyone but the genuine artist, and he made a similar argument with respect to cultural self-consciousness. For the most part, according to Sapir, "we act all the more securely for our unawareness of the patterns that control us" (1927:549). Moreover, as a passage quoted above suggests, even the creator, the "forceful and self-assertive individual" who manages to "conquer" a particular cultural pattern, must rely upon cultural patterns in all the other domains of life which have not been chosen as the focus of creative reinterpretation (1931a:370). The argument is central to Sapir's hermeneutic: one can never control thought with total, self-conscious rationality, for thought is by its very nature grounded in unconscious cultural categories; these, when brought to consciousness, are more often rationalized than rationally analyzed, precisely because any rational analysis of them must itself be based upon unconscious categories. As Sapir puts it in a critique of "orthodox psychology": "Introspection may be a dangerously elusive method, for the moment of consciousness that we set out to describe can not be strictly synchronous with the moment of observation" (1922:619). All of which leads to the stringent final paragraph of "The Unconscious Patterning of Behavior in Society," where we are told that "it can be laid down as a principle of far-reaching application that in the normal business of life it is useless and even mischievous for the individual to carry the conscious analysis of his cultural patterns around with him." There may be occasions, Sapir says, when the "student" of culture can use his analysis as "the medicine of society," but for the most part "We must learn to take joy in the larger freedom of loyalty to thousands of subtle patterns . . . that we can never hope to understand in explicit terms" (1927:558–59).

Sapir's conclusion must be contrasted to the scientific and practical optimism that Benedict admired in both Boas and Mead. Mead's indefatigable pursuit of fieldwork inspired Benedict with visions of scientific progress based on the constant accumulation of new evidence: "when I think of all the material you'll be able to control by the time you come back this next time, I think we needn't limit any of our problems" (10/16/32, in Mead 1959:324–25). For her part, Mead self-consciously used her published studies to sketch possible solutions to American social problems. Such pragmatic speculation reached an early high point in *Sex and Temperament in Three Primitive Societies*, where Mead attacked a problem central in Benedict's life as well as her own, that of sex roles and deviance. Mead argued that societies which arbitrarily defined sex roles in terms of narrow temperamental types condemned to deviant status those whose natural temperament did not match their biological gender. To remedy that problem, she proposed "a groundplan for building a society that would substitute real differences for arbitrary ones," a society which would "permit the development of many contrasting temperamental gifts in each sex" (1935:217).

Though more cautious than Mead, Benedict, too, was drawn to the role of the expert offering answers to current problems. In both *Patterns of Culture* and *The Chrysanthemum and the Sword*, Benedict was concerned to enlighten a broad public facing, during Depression and world war, the task of constructing a more rational and humane social order:

> Social thinking at the present time has no more important task before it than that of taking adequate account of cultural relativity. . . . the implications are fundamental, and modern thought about contacts of peoples and about our changing standards is greatly in need of sane and scientific direction. (1934a:278)

Thus despite her earlier aspiration to escape women's committees and the associated social services they offered, she never renounced "service" as an important responsibility. Now, however, woman's duty had been replaced by that of the scientist (see Modell 1983:247–49).

The search for a meaningful reality led poets and intellectuals in Sapir's and Benedict's generation to pursue genuine culture and hard personality. Sapir and Benedict sought both in poetry, but neither could achieve it there. In his letters to Kroeber and Lowie prior to 1920, Sapir expressed cautious enthusiasm for his poetry, but his correspondence of the mid-twenties with Benedict reveals that enthusiasm projected, ambivalently, onto her poems, and a corresponding sense of failure with respect to his own: "I'm beginning to feel the best thing I can do with poetry is to let it strictly alone. After all, one ought not to write verse when he hasn't the stuff" (5/11/26, in Mead 1959:183). At the same time, he criticized the poetry of his contemporaries for being either too soft or too hard. For example, he attributed Monroe's editorial rejection of some of Benedict's poems "to her inveterate softness or sentimentality. Difficult or in any way intellectual verse gets past her only with difficulty" (179). But he himself criticized the work of another poet, whom Benedict had praised, because it "sounded more like keen cerebration in verse form than poetry. And I'm utterly sick of intelligence and its vanity" (186).

Realizing that his own poetry was unsuccessful, Sapir retreated to erudition:

> Poetry I neither read nor write. . . . I really think I shall end life's prelude by descending into the fastnesses of a purely technical linguistic erudition. . . . I can understand better than ever before what content there may be in pure mathematics. (180)

This echoes the closing sentences of "The Grammarian and His Language," where Sapir claimed for linguistics "the same classical spirit" that he attributed to "mathematics and music at their purest," but found lacking in the spurious culture of his contemporaries (1924b:159). Thus for Sapir linguistics remained the supreme art to which he could always return.

Benedict, too, retreated from poetry; but her search led in a different direction, to a science that would "contribute . . . toward the saving of humanity," as Sapir put it, contrasting her scholarly engagement to his own erudite withdrawal (Mead 1959:180). Benedict's mature anthropology focused on culture and personality but looked beyond purely theoretical speculation to social engineering. She discovered her convincing sense of selfhood not simply in anthropology as scholarship, but in the role of the technical expert, the scientific creator who puts her individual talents at the service of the collectivity. One could play such a role cautiously (Benedict) or boldly (Mead), but in either case it guaranteed a genuine self and at least the promise of a genuine culture—one in which hardness and softness would no longer matter.

Acknowledgments

The research upon which this essay is based was made possible by a summer grant (1985) from the National Endowment for the Humanities. I would like to thank James Clifford, Michael Ebner, Dell Hymes, Daniel Segal, Laurie Shrage, George Stocking, and Jennifer Wallace for critical commentaries during the course of research and writing.

References Cited

Aldington, R. 1920. Standards of literature. *Poetry* 16:164–68.

ANMM. See under Manuscript Sources.

Arnold, M. 1868. *Culture and anarchy.* Ed. J. Dover Wilson. Cambridge (1960).

Bateson, M. C. 1984. *With a daughter's eye: A memoir of Margaret Mead and Gregory Bateson.* New York.

Benedict, R. 1923. *The concept of the guardian spirit in North America.* New York (1964).

———. 1934a. *Patterns of culture.* Boston (1959).

———. 1934b. Anthropology and the abnormal. In Mead 1959:262–83.

———. 1946. *The chrysanthemum and the sword: Patterns of Japanese culture.* Cleveland (1967).

Cowan, W., M. K. Foster, and E. F. K. Koerner, eds. 1986. *New perspectives on Edward Sapir in language, culture, and personality.* Amsterdam.

Croce, B. 1902. *Aesthetic as science of expression and general linguistic.* London (1909).

Golla, V., ed. 1984. *The Sapir-Kroeber correspondence.* Berkeley.

Handler, R. 1983. The dainty and the hungry man: Literature and anthropology in the work of Edward Sapir. *HOA* 1:208–31.

———. 1986. The aesthetics of Sapir's *Language.* In Cowan et al. 1986:433–51.

Howard, J. 1984. *Margaret Mead.* New York.

Hulme, T. E. 1924. *Speculations.* London.

Kenner, H. 1971. *The Pound era.* Berkeley.

Kroeber, A. L. 1952. *The nature of culture.* Chicago.

———. 1959. Reflections on Edward Sapir, scholar and man. In *Edward Sapir: Appraisals of his life and work*, ed. E. F. K. Koerner, 131–39. Philadelphia (1984).

Lears, T. J. J. 1981. *No place of grace.* New York.

———. 1983. From salvation to self-realization: Advertising and the therapeutic roots of the consumer culture, 1880–1930. In *The culture of consumption*, ed. R. W. Fox & T. J. J. Lears, 1–38. New York.

Lowie, R. H., ed. 1965. *Letters from Edward Sapir to Robert H. Lowie.* [Berkeley].

Mandelbaum, D. G., ed. 1949. *Selected writings of Edward Sapir in language, culture, and personality.* Berkeley.

Mead, M. 1935. *Sex and temperament in three primitive societies.* New York (1950).

———, ed. 1959. *An anthropologist at work: Writings of Ruth Benedict.* Boston.

Modell, J. S. 1983. *Ruth Benedict: Patterns of a life.* Philadelphia.

Monroe, H. 1920a. Those we refuse. *Poetry* 15:321–25.

———. 1920b. Men or women? *Poetry* 16:146–48.

————. 1938. *A poet's life.* New York.

Pater, W. 1873. *The Renaissance.* New York (1919).

Perry, H. S. 1982. *Psychiatrist of America: The life of Harry Stack Sullivan.* Cambridge, Mass.

PMP. See under Manuscript Sources.

Pound, E. 1914a. The renaissance. In Pound 1954:214–26.

————. 1914b. The prose tradition in verse. In Pound 1954:371–77.

————. 1918. A retrospect. In Pound 1954:3–14.

————. 1954. *Literary essays.* Norfolk, Conn.

————. 1971. *Selected letters, 1907–1941.* New York.

Riesman, D. 1950. *The lonely crowd.* New Haven.

Sapir, E. 1917a. Do we need a "superorganic"? *Am. Anth.* 19:441–47.

————. 1917b. The twilight of rhyme. *Dial* 63:98–100.

————. 1920. The heuristic value of rhyme. In Mandelbaum 1949:496–99.

————. 1921. The musical foundations of verse. *J. Eng. & Ger. Philol.* 20:213–28.

————. 1922. An orthodox psychology. *Freeman* 5:619.

————. 1924a. Culture, genuine and spurious. In Mandelbaum 1949:308–31.

————. 1924b. The grammarian and his language. In Mandelbaum 1949:150–59.

————. 1927. The unconscious patterning of behavior in society. In Mandelbaum 1949:544–59.

————. 1928. Observations on the sex problem in America. *Am. J. Psychiatry* 8:519–34.

————. 1929. Franz Boas. *New Republic* 57:278–79.

————. 1930. What is the family still good for? *Am. Mercury* 19:145–51.

————. 1931a. Custom. In Mandelbaum 1949:365–72.

————. 1931b. Fashion. In Mandelbaum 1949:373–81.

————. 1932. Cultural anthropology and psychiatry. In Mandelbaum 1949:509–21.

————. 1938. Why cultural anthropology needs the psychiatrist. In Mandelbaum 1949:569–77.

Silverstein, M. 1986. The diachrony of Sapir's linguistic description; or, Sapir's 'cosmographical' linguistics. In Cowan et al. 1986:67–106.

SN. See under Manuscript Sources.

SSLN. See under Manuscript Sources.

SUP. See under Manuscript Sources.

Susman, W. I. 1984. *Culture as history.* New York.

Symons, A. 1919. *The symbolist movement in literature.* Rev. ed. New York.

Weber, M. 1905. *The Protestant ethic and the spirit of capitalism.* New York (1958).

Winters, Y. 1946. *Edwin Arlington Robinson.* New York (1971).

Manuscript Sources

ANMM   Archives of the National Museum of Man, Ottawa, Can.

PMP   *Poetry* Magazine Papers (1912–35), Department of Special Collections, University of Chicago Library.

SN   Suggestive Notes. Ms. Diary, 1917–19, in the possession of Philip Sapir, and transcribed by Regna Darnell, Department of Anthropology, University of Alberta.

SSLN Sapir's students' lecture notes, 1933–38, compiled by D. G. Mandelbaum (quoted material is from the notes of A. M. Cooke, 31–32).

SUP   Sapir's unpublished poems, in the possession of Philip Sapir, and transcribed by William Cowan, Department of Linguistics, Carleton College.

PERSONALITY AND CULTURE

The Fate of the Sapirian Alternative

REGNA DARNELL

In 1930, Edward Sapir invited his junior colleague Robert Redfield to come with him to the annual Hanover Conference of the Social Science Research Council. The Conference had its origins in 1925, when the Committee on Problems and Policy of the newly founded Rockefeller-funded Council met in Hanover, New Hampshire, with a group of psychologists to discuss research alternatives; Sapir's own involvement followed from his acceptance that same year of a Rockefeller-funded position as the second anthropologist in the world's premier department of sociology at the University of Chicago. During the intervening years, Redfield had completed his own training in that department, entered its ranks as assistant professor of sociology, and then joined Sapir and Fay-Cooper Cole in forming an independent Rockefeller-funded department of anthropology in 1929. Invited now for the first time into the brave new world of interdisciplinary social science, Redfield sent his wife, Margaret (daughter of the eminent Chicago sociologist Robert Park), a vivid account of the creatures that inhabited it:

> The place is overrun with pedants and potentates. The potentates are the ex-
> ecutive secretaries of the big foundations—collectively they represent huge—
> staggering—amounts of money that has been set aside for research. The ped-
> ants have invited the potentates so that the potentates may see how pedants
> do their most effective thinking, and how they arrange to spend that money.
> . . . There are about seventy here in all. The Social Science Research Council
> pays their fares, and boards them, and feeds them and washes their clothes,
> and gives them cards to go to the golf club, and then expects them to produce

---

Regna Darnell is Professor of Anthropology at the University of Alberta. She is the editor of *Readings in the History of Anthropology* and the author of various articles on the history of Boasian anthropology and linguistics. She is currently working on a biography of Edward Sapir.

Significant Results. . . . There was much conversation last night, and after Kimball Young and I left, Sapir and Lasswell kept it up till midnight. How those two can talk . . . ! They are so wise in the ways of the academic world, and make so many brilliant suggestions. . . . This morning was held the first session of the "Committee on Research in Acculturation and Personality." . . . I understand that all the members of this committee were selected by [Robert] Lynd, except Young and myself, whom Sapir added. [Since] my scheduled remarks on the Yucatan project were postponed till tomorrow . . . Sapir asked me to take notes. . . . It is rather amusing to watch the Effective Minds in action, but also a little depressing, like watching Shaw's he-ancients. Besides the psychological-psychiatric-anthropo-sociological committee of mine, three visitors were there, distinguished educators. . . . The discussion centered around the W. I. Thomas project to study crime and insanity among the Scandinavians, and the Lawrence Frank proposal to bring foreign students to a great seminar to train them to make standardized studies of their own cultures. . . . The session of the Committee this morning was quite interesting, especially a rather sharp conflict between the psychometric-statistical viewpoint on the one hand, and the psychiatric-sociological view on the other. The principal psychiatrist present is Harry Stack Sullivan . . . another one, like Sapir and Lasswell, with the gift of tongues. When the three of them get together, the polysyllabic confluences are amazing . . . (As quoted in Stocking 1978)

In the process of thus gaining "glimpses into a field I [knew] nothing about," Redfield provided a number of leads into the influence of Edward Sapir on the early history of that field. For although Sapir's impact on the development of culture-and-personality research is widely attested, it is difficult to document. Forestalled by the failure of potentate funding, by institutional competition, by the dispersal of his own energies, and by premature death, Sapir's "brilliant suggestions" led to no published body of "Significant Results." But conveyed informally to students by his "gift of tongues"—and wrapped in the mantle of disciplinary myth—they remain to this day an inspiration for those who are doubtful of results once deemed Significant.

Sapir's Entrance on the Center Stage of Interdisciplinary Social Science

Sapir's move to Chicago in 1925 marked the end of a major phase in his life. Although recognized by Boas as his most brilliant student, he had received his Ph.D. (1909) at a point when museums were as likely as universities to provide satisfactory employment (Darnell 1969; Stocking 1985); dissatisfied with his prospects as instructor at the University of Pennsylvania, Sapir accepted a position as chief of the newly created Division of Anthropology in the Geological Survey of the Canadian National Museum (Darnell 1984). For a number of years, he continued in a traditional Boasian pattern, carrying on extensive linguistic fieldwork among Canadian Indians, systematizing the various possible approaches to the problem of *Time Perspective in Aboriginal American Culture* (1916), and working toward a more satisfactory classification of American Indian languages—although his approach to the latter problem was more radically genetic than Boas would allow (Darnell 1986; n.d.)

Toward the middle of the Ottawa period, however, Sapir began to move away from traditional Boasian models on a number of fronts. His initial euphoria over being able to develop his own program for mapping the languages and cultures of Canada gradually gave way to an increasing dissatisfaction with his profession. The cutbacks of World War I and the general sense of disillusionment that came in its wake caused Sapir to question the validity of his work, particularly in ethnology:

> I have an enormous amount of linguistic and ethnological data on my hands from various tribes, certainly enough to keep me busy for at least five years of concentrated work. But (and here's the rub and the disappointment) I don't somehow seem to feel as much positive impulse toward disgorging as I should. . . . I somehow feel in much of my work that I am not true to my inner self, that I have let myself be put off with useful but relatively unimportant trifles at the expense of a development of finer needs and impulses, whatever they are. (UCB: ES/R. Lowie 8/12/16)

Sapir went on to muse that music might have been a more satisfying career than anthropology, implicitly criticizing his discipline for lacking the "beauty of form" he found more easily in poetry, music, and mathematics: "How can the job-lot of necessarily un-coordinated or badly co-ordinated facts that we amass in our fieldwork satisfy such longings?" Sapir's dissatisfaction with his scientific work was intensified after about 1916 by his first wife's mental illness, which he blamed at least in part on her sense of isolation in Ottawa.

Sapir's writings at this time evinced a new concern with the problem of individual creativity in cultural context. His major writings on aesthetics and literature date from this period; he also turned to poetry (see Handler, in this volume), and was active in Ottawa belles lettres. Turning also to the cultural evaluation of his own society from the point of view of the pattern of individual lives, he contrasted the "spurious" nature of modern civilization, with its specialization and fragmentation, with the "genuine" integration of individual lives in many so-called primitive cultures (1924). Criticizing the cultural reification implicit in Alfred Kroeber's notion of the "superorganic," he insisted that the individual was the locus of culture, and must be the starting point of any adequate theory of society (1917). Similarly, his book *Language* (1921) included considerable discussion of aesthetic issues, and of the way individual speakers came to understand their language. At the same time, Sapir was beginning to read psychiatric literature, initially in relation to his wife's illness, but increasingly in search of more adequate models for social science. By 1925, this developing concern for formal patterning and psychological integration was manifest in his formulation of the linguistic concept of the phoneme (1925). By that time, he was ready to move from "sound patterns" toward patterns of individual behavior in cultural context; but during the Ottawa period there was no easily accessible audience to respond to these new ideas (Darnell 1986).

If the outlines of Sapir's mature thought were defined during the second half of his Ottawa sojourn, nonetheless his thinking about culture and personality per se was still incidental and unsystematic at the time he arrived in Chicago in 1925. When the sociologist William Ogburn asked him for advice on psychological literature in 1918, he apologized for being unable to offer "any fruitful criticism about what the psycho-analysts have done in folklore and ethnological respects," and evinced a characteristically Boasian dissatisfaction with their failure to recognize the historical nature of cultural phenomena (NMM: ES/WO 1/14/18). As he continued his explorations of "dynamic psychology," he did not tie himself to any particular model or mechanism of unconscious process—though he found Jung more congenial than Freud, since Jung's approach to "psychological types" allowed a focus on individual variation within a single culture. Classifying his professional colleagues in a letter to Lowie, Sapir described Lowie as a "thinking extravert"; Kroeber, as a sensation-introvert with an inconsistent extravert compensation; Radin, as a sensation-extravert; Benedict, a thinking-feeling introvert; and Boas, a feeling introvert with a strong and only partially successful thinking compensation. Like Jung, he saw himself as a rare "intuitive introvert" (UCB: ES/RL 5/20/25; see also Sapir 1923). But consistent with his own insistence that the individual rather than a reified notion of culture had to be the starting point, Sapir applied this approach only at the individual level, not ethnographically. Dissatisfied with the options available to him within Boasian anthropology, Sapir at the time of his arrival in Chicago was still trying out a variety of psychological and psychiatric approaches that would be amenable to his emphasis on the role of the individual.

In moving from Ottawa to Chicago, Sapir came from the ethnological periphery to the center of American social science. In Ottawa, anthropology had been subordinated to geology and administratively tied to the natural sciences; the emphasis was on the collection of empirical data, and Sapir was further frustrated by the lack of any teaching opportunities. In dramatic contrast, Chicago was the leading American center for academic social scientific research—and it was not closely tied to the institutional network of Boasian anthropology, which in general was not oriented toward the other social sciences. Furthermore, the vitality and momentum of the "Chicago School"

Fay-Cooper Cole and Edward Sapir wishing *bon voyage* to Paul Martin and the archeology truck of the University of Chicago Department of Anthropology, 1926. (Courtesy Department of Special Collections, University of Chicago Library.)

created a sense of urgency comparable to that Sapir had experienced in Boasian anthropology when he encountered it at Columbia two decades earlier. Although sociology was the most visible of the Chicago social sciences (Bulmer 1985), it was by no means the only component, and the fashion of the day encouraged interdisciplinary work. Furthermore, the scope of such activity extended beyond the Chicago urban scene to a national stage. Political scientist Charles Merriam, for example, played a key role in the founding (in 1923) of the Social Science Research Council, which was to provide an important base for research in culture and personality during the next decade (Sibley 1974; see also Karl 1974). Long tied to Rockefeller philanthropy, Chicago became a major concentration point for the interdisciplinary social science strategy of the Laura Spelman Rockefeller Memorial and the Rockefeller Foundation (Stocking 1985). Sapir, in short, was entering an institutional and intellectual situation much more congenial to the direction his thought was taking as he moved away from traditional Boasianism—i.e., away from an "ethnological" anthropology toward other social scientific disciplines.

He entered, furthermore, as a "star," deliberately chosen by the Department of Sociology's resident anthropologist, Fay-Cooper Cole, to add a stellar dynamism to its anthropological work. And Sapir rose to the challenge, entering what was the happiest period of his professional life. Margaret Mead, who knew him well in this period, later recalled that Cole "gave him his head and Sapir was to be the great brilliant decoration at Chicago, and students were very excited about his lectures and people went there to study with him and he had a lovely time" (Mead 1966). Being at Chicago, Sapir now had access to the interdisciplinary foundation-funded social science to which Chicago was connected—Redfield's world of "pedants and potentates." Brilliantly endowed, prepared by his late Ottawa development for a new intellectual role, he now moved onto a stage where it could be played with flair.

Although he was at first a member of the same department, it is not clear how much Sapir was directly influenced by the Chicago sociologists (see Murray 1986). There were certainly a number of parallelisms of approach. The sociologists were carrying on field studies of an "ethnographic" character in the urban "laboratory"; Sapir was associated with the groups (the Institute for Juvenile Research and the Local Community Research Committee) which supported these studies, and as a Boasian ethnographer, he would have found their approach congenial. Although he did not himself collect such materials, he appreciated the importance of the "life history" as a crucial methodological tool, especially in the study of personality. His comments at various interdisciplinary conferences make it clear that he accepted the consensus of personality students from a range of disciplines that Chicago sociologists were the only ones who had concrete data bearing on the relationship of culture and personality. His own stress on the role of the individual as shaper and creator of culture may have been reinforced by his contact with sociology insofar as "society," by offering a middle term between the "individual" and "culture," allowed him to resist the tendency among some other Boasians toward the reification of the latter term.

On the other hand, there were aspects of sociology that were essentially uncongenial to Sapir—particularly the sort of quantitative approaches associated with the work of Ogburn, who came to Chicago in 1927. When Sapir was invited to write the article on "Anthropology and Sociology" for a volume on the interrelationships of the social sciences edited by Ogburn and Alexander Goldenweiser, his message was ambiguous. While on the one hand he saw Boasian historicism as "little more than a clearing of the ground toward a social interpretation," he was also critical of the "modern tendency . . . to see most associations of human beings in terms of function." Sapir looked beyond anthropology and sociology toward a "social psychology of form which has hardly been more than adumbrated" (1927a:338–40). Arguing on lines analogous to Boas' insistence on the independent variation of race, language, and culture, Sapir insisted that "the concepts of social pattern, function, and associated mental attitude are independently variable": "in this thought lies the germ of a social philosophy of values and transfers that joins hands in a very suggestive way with such psychoanalytic concepts as the 'image' and the transfer of emotion." In pursuing this enterprise, sociology seemed less important than "modern psychology" and anthropology; the former offered an emphasis on "the formal or rhythmic configurations of the psyche and on the concrete symbolization of values and social relations" (343); the latter might throw light on "the social psychology of the symbol" (345; see also 1927b).

Besides the current members of the Department of Sociology, however, there were other Chicago figures whose ideas were more directly relevant to Sapir's thinking on culture and personality. Although he had left Chicago in 1918, W. I. Thomas continued to be crucial to its definition of ethnographic sociology in a cross-cultural frame; a major figure in the interdisciplinary conferences of the period, he too was moving in the direction of culture-and-personality research (Volkhart 1951). Another figure who attracted Sapir was the brilliant young political scientist Harold Lasswell, whose interests in the psychological aspects of political life paralleled Sapir's (Smith 1969). But the most important was the psychiatrist Harry Stack Sullivan, a pioneer in environmentally oriented treatment of schizophrenia as a problem of "interpersonal relearning." The two met when Sullivan attended a professional meeting in Chicago at which Sapir lectured on "Speech as a Personality Trait" (Perry 1982:242–50; see also Sapir 1926). Their first conversation—motivated, apparently, by Sapir's desire to talk about his feelings regarding the mental illness and death of his first wife—went on for ten hours; for the years until Sapir's own death, their intellectual relationship continued to be central to his developing thought. Sullivan's "interpersonal" approach stimulated Sapir's emerging emphasis on society as an intermediary between the individual and culture: the particulars of family and community network would enable anthropologist (or psychiatrist) to get at the forms of a particular culture as manifest in different individuals. Psychiatry could teach anthropologists how to do justice to the individual in concrete cases through life histories; anthropology could teach psychiatrists how to place the individual in a cultural world (see Sapir 1938).

In addition to the new range of intellectual contacts it provided, Chicago also offered Sapir a ready audience for the ideas that he was developing about the individual in culture. In addition to courses on ethnology and linguistics, he also began to teach a course on "the psychology of culture." In a flush of enthusiasm that the details of the interdisciplinary model would quickly fall into place, he signed a contract with Harcourt Brace to write a book on that topic, and the surviving outline seems to date from this period.[1] But in

1. Class notes from Sapir's course in culture and personality were collected by former students and made available by Fred Eggan. Judith Irvine is currently editing them into prose text as part of the *Collected Works of Edward Sapir* (General editor, Philip Sapir), in the volume on *Culture* edited by Darnell, Irvine, and R. Handler—which will also contain the outline for Sapir's never-written book.

practice, he found himself engrossed in increasingly more complicated efforts at interdisciplinary rapprochement, entering a network of conferences and interactions through his Chicago connections. Although his colleagues in this traveling "think tank" tended sometimes to treat him as an expert anthropological consultant able to provide cross-cultural data on the primitive and the exotic, Sapir's own goal was interdisciplinary in a broader and more theoretical sense—perhaps more so than that of any other participant in this brave new world of foundation-sponsored inquiry into the relationship of personality and culture.

Sapir and the Psychiatrists: "A Proposal for Three-Fold Inquiry into Personality"

Sapir's collaboration with Harry Stack Sullivan expanded the interdisciplinary range of the study of personality: psychiatry, as well as sociology, anthropology, and psychology, came to play a crucial role. After meeting Sapir, Sullivan began a struggle "to achieve a place for psychiatric research . . . in the scientific community" (Perry 1982:261). At its 1927 meeting, the American Psychiatric Association established a committee on the relations of psychiatry and the social sciences, chaired by Sullivan's mentor William Alanson White, with Sullivan in the active organizing role as secretary, "with a view to greater cooperation among those concerned in studying the nature and influence of cultural environments" (APA 1929:iii). Over the next two years the committee sponsored two colloquia on "personality investigation."

Interdisciplinary collaboration was high on the agenda of the potentates as well as the pedants. An especially crucial participant was Lawrence K. Frank of the Laura Spelman Rockefeller Memorial, who was to play an important role as intellectual broker and entrepreneur in the developing culture-and-personality movement. Aside from Frank, Sullivan, Lasswell, and Sapir, there were several other core participants who attended both colloquia. Ernest Burgess and W. I. Thomas represented the perspective of Chicago sociology, and were able to discuss much of the unpublished ethnographic work being done by the department there, making the case for concrete case studies and adding a deep commitment to interdisciplinary collaboration. William Healy of the Judge Baker Foundation offered a perspective on the social application of the results of cultural study of personality. Mark May of Yale (where the Rockefeller-funded Institute of Psychology was in the process of transformation into the Institute of Human Relations) represented the other major university interest in this field; himself an educational psychologist, May was concerned to develop at Yale an institutional context for an integrated research program which then existed nowhere in America. The pieces seemed all in place for something entirely new.

At the first conference, Sapir stayed somewhat in the background—introducing himself at the beginning as "only an amateur and dabbler in the question of personality" (APA 1929:11). But by the end of the colloquium he was the person who suggested how the sociologists and the psychiatrists might talk to each other. Stressing the "chasms which separate our respective disciplines," he chided the participants for their unwillingness to think in new ways, and suggested a bridging conceptualization: "Whether we talk about an individual as a physiological organism or about a society, at the other end of the behavior gamut, what we are really talking about is *systems of ideas*." Just as the human being lifting his arm to strike someone was behaving *intentionally*; so also the social institution of marriage was "a complex of meanings" (77–78). Granting that there was a problem in defining "personality," Sapir suggested that it was a matter of indifference "whether we call personality that part of the individual's functioning which has meaning" or "that in society's behavior patterns which can some day be translated into terms of meaning for the individual."

> We arrive, therefore, at this somewhat curious, yet really necessary conception that in the last analysis there is no conflict between the concept of "culture" and the concept of "personality," if only we make our abstractions correctly. I would say that what really happens is that every individual acquires and develops his own "culture" and that "culture," as ordinarily handled by the student of society, is really an environmental fact that has no psychological meaning until it is interpreted by being referred to personalities, or, at the least, a generalized personality conceived as typical of a given society. (79)

Sapir's remarks were greeted as having "crystallized" the "wide range of topics" covered by the conference (APA 1929:80); at the second colloquium, his role was even more central. The major lines of his contribution were threefold: a consistent emphasis on the "symbolic" aspect of human behavior; an insistence on certain methodological principles; and the formulation of a three-part research strategy for future study. His brief contribution to the summary of recent research results during the early part of the colloquium—a rather uncharacteristic experimental approach to the problem of "individual symbolism in the domain of speech" (37)—was an attempt to show that the realm of the symbolic could be treated in a rigorous manner. What was really important was not objective measurement, or statistics, which at one point Sapir suggested "gives us material that is of rather little essential interest" (127). It was rather to learn a certain way of thinking about human behavior—as Sapir insisted when discussion moved on to the major substantive topic (Sullivan's report, "Schizophrenic individuals as a source of data for comparative investigation of personality"):

I would suggest that we are oversimplifying when we think that we can define a certain bit of behavior in purely objective terms. If one first considers the important factor of symbolic meaning of the behavior, one must in each case ask whether or not a given bit of behavior can be the same thing for all individuals. Murdering one's father under certain circumstances and in certain contexts, whether in actual life or a fantasy, might be no more than kicking a cat out of a window. On the other hand, depriving one's canary bird of a morsel of cake might be considered extraordinarily tragic. We must learn to see each bit of behavior as not only what it is in measurable terms or as roughly estimated by society at large, but also as, in the individual case, something other than what it seems to be. There is the necessity of evaluating any type symbolically. I think we should get into the habit of thinking of this as a step in our procedure. (67)

Resisting the efforts of his colleagues to cast him in the role of the ethnographic expert who would provide comparative data on a given hypothesis (48, 84, 96), Sapir emphasized rather the great difficulty of collecting cross-cultural material on problems of personality:

I find that a great many anthropologists are interested in just these problems, but they don't as a rule get very far, because it takes so very long to get acquainted with the native in other than a superficial sense. There is a very definite wall between you and the average primitive, even if you have got to the state of normal friendliness with them. . . . [It] would be none too easy to get life histories that would be of interest to psychiatrists. . . . I don't think that it is possible to sail into an ethnological field with a few generalities in one's own mind, ask a few questions, and expect to get anywhere that is worthy of serious consideration. The work will require years of careful approach . . . (85–86)

When the colloquium turned finally to specific proposals for future work, it was Redfield's trio of "gifted tongues" who held forth: Sullivan, with a proposal for "research in personality investigation by the personality document (life history) method"; Lasswell, with one for "the adequate training of research personnel"; and Sapir, with "a proposal for three-fold inquiry into personality." Despite the fact that he "represented" anthropology at the conference, Sapir started not from culture but from personality—which he suggested in an appendix could be defined from five quite different points of view: philosophically (the subjective awareness of the self); physiologically (the human organism); descriptively (the totality of "physiological and psychological reaction systems"); sociologically (i.e., "symbolically") as "those aspects of behavior which give 'meaning' to an individual in society and differentiate him from other members of the community, each of whom embodies countless cultural patterns in a unique configuration"; and psychiatrically ("the individual abstracted from the actual psychophysical whole . . . as a comparatively stable

system of reactivity") (APA 1930:153). Arguing that personalities must be conceived of not as "isolated entities," but rather against "given backgrounds,"
Sapir framed his research proposal with reference to three types of cultural
background. First, there was "the background of daily experience here in New
York City, . . . which we have an intimate, intuitive knowledge of but which
we are often unable to delimit in properly scientific terms"; second, those
"backgrounds for which we have a kind of friendly feeling and of which we
have a good measure of understanding, but which we do not 'intuit' in any
detail"—such as the Scandinavian or Sicilian research projects proposed by
W. I. Thomas; finally, "the remote but extremely valuable type of background"
represented by "primitive man." Sapir's "three-fold" program was intended to
move out from the first background, starting with "the very careful study of
a rather small number of selected normal types, illustrative, one hopes of several distinct types and studied exhaustively by a group of people interested
in personality as such." This would be followed by "a similar study of a schizophrenic group," after which the schizophrenic study would be extended "to
alien cultures, including the primitive"—"one of the crying needs in the whole
field of human behavior [being] to discover what maladjustment means in
the remoter cultures." While Sapir did not deny the need for a "certain amount"
of statistical work, or of "preoccupation with cultural problems and defini-
tions," or with "social processes as such," he felt that "we should never lose
sight of the fact that the center of our interest is the actual individual studied"
(APA 1930:124–25).

Accepting Sapir's suggestions as "an actual basis for beginning something
of very great importance," Sullivan and Lasswell turned the discussion to the
problem of training researchers capable of carrying on this kind of interdisciplinary work, and the appointment of some kind of continuing committee
to supervise it (APA 1930:127ff.). As it happened, the second colloquium was
not to be followed up by the American Psychiatric Association, and further
planning regarding research agendas and training shifted to other venues. But
if Sapir's specific "three-fold" program was not in fact implemented, his contribution to the colloquium made clear the direction that his own interest
in personality and culture (the order is significant) would take over the next
decade—in contrast to the work of most of the other anthropological figures
in the "culture and personality" movement.

Sapir at Yale:
The Impact of Culture on Personality

Sullivan had hoped from the beginning to involve the S.S.R.C. in his plans
for developing psychiatric research, and the second colloquium had in fact

been held under the joint auspices of the A.P.A. and the S.S.R.C. Carrying on under S.S.R.C. sponsorship, many of the same characters pursued their previously defined interests, supported by the same group of potentates—one of whom was to play a creative as well as supportive role. In response to Sapir's observations at the second A.P.A. colloquium on the methodological difficulties of cross-cultural study among primitive groups, Lawrence Frank had suggested the possibility of personality research in "a variety of contemporary cultures . . . through the[ir] representatives here" (APA 1930:86)—an idea that was to develop into the "seminar on the impact of culture on personality." As elaborated by Frank at the Hanover Conference of 1930, the scheme involved bringing together "persons from a variety of cultures interested in problems of culture and personality" who could draw on the specialists who had been participating in the several conferences already held in order to "formulate an inventory or schedule for the study of contemporary culture in the countries represented." After initial seminar training, these foreign scholars would each carry out studies of American culture, meet together again, and then return to study their own cultures—"the essential desideratum" being "to develop a pattern of cultural research" (SSRC 1930). Sapir responded with enthusiasm to Frank's project. Having previously worked most comfortably with informants who were themselves prone to analyze their own languages, and concerned that comparable material would be difficult to come by in the field of culture and personality, he was elated by the possibility of working with a seminar of self-reflexive cross-cultural analysts.

It was obvious from the start that Sapir was the person to lead the seminar, but there was a problem regarding its location. Sapir was at Chicago, and others in the "Chicago group" wanted to be involved. But there was also Yale, where the Institute of Human Relations was heavily funded by the Rockefeller Foundation, and its resident anthropologist was another senior Boasian with strong interdisciplinary connections—Clark Wissler. Within weeks after the second A.P.A. colloquium, Frank had already suggested that Wissler should join with Sapir and Thomas on a supervisory committee that would operate under the auspices of the S.S.R.C. In agreeing to participate, Wissler proposed that the seminar be centered in the Institute, since Sapir would have a half sabbatical the following year, and "would be delighted to come and supervise the project" (RF: D. Slesinger/E. Day 2/10/30). In the course of the ensuing negotiations, Sapir was in fact offered a Sterling professorship and numerous other inducements unusual for the period to move him permanently from Chicago to Yale, where he arrived in the fall of 1931 to head a newly independent Department of Anthropology.

Although the situation sounded ideal to Sapir, he was apparently unaware of many things about the Institute and about Yale generally that would soon prove to be massively uncongenial theoretically, politically, and personally.

The social science of the Institute of Human Relations was characterized by a strongly scientistic, behavioralist approach that ran sharply counter to Sapir's more intuitive, mentalistic psychology and anthropology. Moreover, sociology at Yale was still dominated by the evolutionary, cross-cultural model of William Graham Sumner's disciple Alfred Keller, which was completely antithetical to the orientation Sapir had imbibed from Franz Boas. To make matters worse, the sociologists had not been consulted about Sapir's appointment, though his new department was carved out of their territory. And despite the fact that Mark May (who was to play an increasingly important role in the Institute) had attended the A.P.A. colloquia, he did not appreciate the full extent of their theoretical and methodological differences, or the strongly individualistic tendency of Sapir's scholarship—which would make it very difficult for him to cooperate with the members of the team being assembled at Yale for cooperative social research (see Murray 1986).

Although it was listed in the Yale catalogue for 1931–32, the Frank-inspired seminar on "The Impact of Culture on Personality" had to be postponed a year, owing to difficulties in arranging for students under the Rockefeller foreign-fellowship program. During that time, Sapir taught other courses, and John Dollard, a young Chicago sociologist who was to serve as seminar assistant, traveled to Europe, where he underwent psychoanalysis. The actual selection of fellows was organized largely by Sapir and Frank, through the Rockefeller Foundation Paris office. Although there was considerable difficulty obtaining people of high quality from countries in which the scholarly tradition of sociological and psychological study was weak (RF: T. Kittredge/LF 2/2/32), the final contingent of thirteen included representatives from Japan, China, India, Turkey, Hungary, Italy, France, Norway, and Finland, with two each from Germany and Poland—a candidate from Holland having been rejected because Sapir feared that the seminar might be criticized for having more than two Jewish fellows (RF: ES/LF 3/14/32).

As described in the catalogue, the seminar was to cover "the meaning of culture, its psychological relevance for personality, its value relativity and the problem of reconciling personality variations and cultural variations." The invited-lecturer format did not compel Sapir to synthesize his own perspective, and the readings in the alphabetical syllabus suggest a rather wide-ranging orientation. Boasian anthropology was represented by Boas, Goldenweiser, Kroeber, Lowie, and Radin, along with Malinowski and Tylor—as well as Sapir's own *Time Perspective* (1916) and *Language* (1921). Sociologists included Cooley, Dewey, Ogburn, Trotter, and Veblen—although, surprisingly, no Chicago case studies. The emphasis was on theoretical works, which in psychology and psychiatry reflected Sapir's own eclectic proclivity: Freud (three volumes), Adler, Jung, Koffka, Rivers, McDougall—even Kretschmer for the constitutional substratum. At the end of two typed pages Sapir added in handwriting—as stand-ins for his still unwritten book on the psychology of culture—five of

Edward Sapir with Hortense Powdermaker, in a canoe, ca. 1935. (Courtesy Philip Sapir.)

his own periodical writings (1912; 1917; 1924; 1926; 1932) and six articles he wrote for the *Encyclopedia of the Social Sciences*: "Communication," "Custom," "Dialect," "Fashion," "Group," and "Language." Prior to their arrival, the fellows were instructed to read Boas' *Mind of Primitive Man* (1911), Kroeber's *Anthropology* (1923), Wissler's *Man and Culture* (1923), Dewey's *Human Nature and Conduct* (1922), and the Lynds' *Middletown* (1929)—as preparation for the second stage of the project, in which they were to study American small-town life. They were also asked to survey the culture-and-personality literature of their own countries, and to prepare a careful psychological autobiography for Sapir's advance perusal (RF: Sapir memo, c. 3/1932).

Although some students recalled disappointment that Sapir did not present his own program for culture-and-personality research (Philip Sapir, personal communication), he saw his role as that of intellectual critic, and as master of ceremonies for the visiting lecturers—who included Sullivan, Thomas, and Louis Wirth, the Chicago sociologist. After his own visit, Wirth sent Sapir his comments on the "unique and promising venture," along with evaluations of each of the students. Although Wirth felt they were learning "a great deal from one another about their respective cultures and about their respective approaches to scientific problems in social science," his evaluative comments suggest that the students were a very heterogeneous lot, apparently without prior anthropological background, little prepared for the sort of approach that Sapir and Frank wished to develop (UC: LW/ES 2/9/33). In arguing to the Rockefeller Foundation the case for continuing support, Sapir said that the focus had been on establishing "sophistication in the definition and interpretation of culture in general . . . and the importance of cultural studies for the proper understanding of the genesis and development of personality types": "We believe that it is no mean achievement to have created this common mode of thought" (RF: ES/S. May 5/22/33). Although Rockefeller officials assured Sapir that the decision reflected a general cutback in Foundation activities, rather than a judgment that the seminar was "unfruitful," they rejected his effort to follow up the program according to the original plan proposed by Frank (RF: S. May/ES 6/3/33). Except for the Chinese psychologist Bingham Dai, who had come with an M.A. from Chicago—and who went on to pursue an American academic career—none of the fellows was to contribute further to the study of personality and culture.

Despite the failure of the grand project, Sapir continued to offer "The Impact of Culture on Personality" as a graduate seminar, without the assumption that a group of invited foreigners (half colleagues, half guinea pigs) would themselves provide the basis for cross-cultural analysis. Many who later reported participating in the "impact" seminar were actually members of its successor group—including Weston La Barre, Irvin Child, John Whiting, Otto Klineberg, and Scudder Mekeel. While Sapir continued to attempt to synthesize the approach that had been developed in the interdisciplinary conferences, he did so as an individual scholar. The opportunity for a foundation-funded program did not—for him—arise again.

Psychoanalysis and Behaviorism in the Institute of Human Relations

Seeking Rockefeller support for his general research program in ethnography and linguistics the following fall, Sapir cited the precedent of previous grants to the departments at Harvard and Chicago: "in view of the fact that we do not seem to be behind these institutions either in staff or number and quality of our graduate students, it seems only fair in principle that we receive analogous treatment" (YU: ES/J. Angell 10/17/33). Although President Angell dutifully forwarded Sapir's five-year plan to the Rockefeller Foundation (YU: JA/D. Stevens 11/29/33), the moment was no longer propitious. Reevaluating its priorities in the depths of the Great Depression, the Foundation had decided to retrench in certain areas—notably that of cultural anthropology (see Stocking 1985). In this context, the Institute of Human Relations might have been the logical place for Sapir to turn, since in principle it embraced the kinds of research he espoused. However, it was in fact pursuing a research program which left little room for Sapir's kind of anthropology.

Mark May's retrospective account of the Institute's history suggests that, prior to his assuming the directorship, the Institute was still relatively loosely structured and laissez-faire in style—the directors acting on the "plausible but erroneous belief" that large social problems could be solved simply by "frontal attacks by the combined intellectual resources and talents of a great university" (May 1971:142). President Angell's statement of the purposes of the Institute in 1929 suggests that a more coordinated approach had been in his mind from the beginning: "the stage was all set for undertaking a synthesis of as many as practicable of these convergent interests . . . [so that a] cooperative scientific attack could be turned on the more accessible of the urgent problems of personal and social adjustment" (Angell 1929). Although participation was voluntary, it was still "deemed desirable to consider as members of the Institute all individuals who were doing research in the social sciences" (May 1971:145). President Angell, however, assured worried faculty that "no coercive direction of research" was intended, and his early statements indicate that he saw the Institute as a "loose general organization which should render easy a fruitful contact among men working in these neighboring fields" (Angell 1929). However, May, who in this period served as the Institute's executive secretary, clearly felt that such a loose structure was inefficient:

> The laudable plan of making the Institute an informal, voluntary association of scientists, with a fluid membership, was not without its disadvantages. . . . Feelings of identification with the Institute were slow to develop, except in the cases of some who were brought to Yale for full-time research and who received courtesy appointments in departments. . . . Regular teaching members of departments . . . who received research funds from the Institute were inclined to feel more closely identified with their departments than with the Institute . . . (1971:145)

May was also concerned about the control of resources. At the time of the Institute's formation, the Rockefeller Foundation had committed a total of

$4.5 million over a ten-year period. Of this about half was for research (as opposed to building) expenses—$500,000 to Robert Yerkes' primate station and most of the rest to studies in psychology, child study, and social science (147). But because allocation to individual researchers was handled by the relevant department heads, at the end of the first five years there was no "liquid research fund" available for new interdisciplinary projects—some of which May felt were "more in line with the purposes of the Institute than many of those that were receiving support" (145). As early as February 1934, May was already seeking to retrench on support for Clark Wissler's anthropological interests:

> In accordance with our understanding of the terms of the grant that supports the social science sections of the Institute, we have been developing gradually a unified program of studies in which practically all of the social sciences and some of the biological sciences are integrated. . . . Its development requires that, from time to time, we liquidate our interests in research activities that were started early in the life of the Institute, but which now appear unrelated to and difficult to articulate with the central core of studies. (YU: MM/CW 2/2/34)

Elevated to the directorship in a general reorganization of the Institute in 1935, May was able to set aside a liquid research fund for "projects that appeared to be most promising for the achievement of the main purposes of the Institute—that of developing a unified science of behavior and human relations" (1971:150).

In the spring of 1935, May initiated a series of conferences of the senior scientific staff of the Institute to develop a more coordinated program (1971: 157). The proposal "that received the most serious consideration" was made by the learning theorist Clark Hull, whose linking of Pavlovian reflexology with the American behavioralism of John B. Watson and E. L. Thorndike had, according to May, produced a "mechanistic conception of human behavior . . . adequate to account for the fact that human behavior is characteristically purposive, willful, creative and guided by ideas" (160). But when he discovered that "a majority of the members of the group were not really interested" in this approach, May discontinued the meetings. Instead, he acted on the comment of one of them that they were "too old and well established in their fields to be expected to change their interests and habits of work," and that "the Institute should therefore look to its younger men for the development of an integrated program." As May later recalled, "the integration that was later achieved was developed mainly by younger men, most of whom were of junior rank"—including a number of research assistants who, after the reorganization, were paid directly by the Institute, rather than attached to departments (158).

Although personality development continued to be a focus of Institute research, it was carried on in Hullian rather than Sapirian terms:

The psychoanalytic theory of personality development and the dynamics of behavior had been well developed before the Institute was organized . . . and was introduced into the Institute by John Dollard, who came to Yale from Chicago in 1930. His first assignment was to Professor Edward Sapir, in connection with a seminar on personality and culture sponsored by the S.S.R.C. [But] in the year following, Dollard became a member of the Institute's staff [and] thereafter began a series of studies which led not only to the further development and modification of the theory but also to its interrelation with Hull's principles of behavior, on the one hand, and with social structure and culture, on the other. (1971:161)

In pursuing the latter relationships, however, Sapirian orientations were again excluded. Under Hull's influence, the Institute turned back to the evolutionary sociology of Sumner and Keller, whose *Science of Society* (1927) showed that "culture and social structure are functional—i.e. instrumental to the basic needs of man—and that social evolution is a kind of mass trial-and-error learning which results in adaptive changes in social institutions" (May 1971:164). Although Keller himself never joined the Institute, his student George Murdock came into it in 1934, to be followed by Clelland Ford and J. W. M. Whiting; by 1937, Murdock had initiated the collection of masses of ethnographic data that became the Human Relations Area Files, in order to make possible the cross-cultural testing of comparative hypotheses.

While a Murdockian comparativism did in fact become a significant option in the study of culture and personality, it is nevertheless the case that Murdock's anthropology—superorganic in culture, behaviorist in psychology, evolutionist in diachronic assumption, positivistically comparativist in method —was, like the social science of the Institute it represented, radically antithetical to everything that Sapir stood for. Sapir's emphasis on the individuality of behavior, the specificity of cultural pattern, and the study of symbolic form made it impossible for him to collaborate with the emerging research pattern of the Institute. This, as much as the anti-Semitism that he encountered at Yale (see Siskin 1984), made his stay there increasingly frustrating.

The Failure of Sapir's N.R.C. Training Program

May's influence on culture-and-personality study extended beyond New Haven into other areas in which Sapir had been active—notably, the Social Science Research Council. In addition to the seminar on the impact of culture on personality, a second outgrowth of the Hanover Conference of 1930 had been the establishment of an S.S.R.C. "Advisory Committee on Personality and Culture," on which Sapir served from the beginning, and to which W. I. Thomas was attached in 1932 as staff member (SSRC 1934:57). After Thomas presented a report "On the Organization of a Program in the Field of Culture and Personality" (Volkhart 1951:290–318), the original S.S.R.C. committee was discharged, and a new one, organized in terms of specific research projects, was established. Although one of these projects (on acculturation) had originally been proposed by Sapir at the Hanover Conference, the subcommittee constituted to carry on this project consisted of Redfield, Ralph Linton, and Melville Herskovits. Although May had not been associated with the earlier committee, as chairman of the new subcommittee on "competitive-cooperative habits" he became a member of a new three-man "central committee on personality and culture"—serving in fact as its chairman until the committee was discontinued in 1940 (SSRC 1935:23).

In this context, Sapir took advantage of his two-year term as chairman of the Division of Psychology and Anthropology of the National Research Council (1934–36) to pursue his agenda elsewhere. Early in 1935, he proposed a conference to "work out a research program in a field connecting psychology and anthropology": the variation "of behavior against different cultural backgrounds" (NRC: ES/M. H. Britton 2/8/35). For political reasons the conference personnel included several people who by this time were thoroughly uncongenial to Sapir (among them May and his mentor, the educational psychologist E. L. Thorndike). But when the conference took place in New York City early in March 1935, it was clearly dominated by Sapir and Sullivan.

The problem, as a conference report indicated (NRC 1934–35:35), was that cultural anthropology dealt with "'impersonal' patterns of behavior," with "little or no concern for individual variations and for the significance of these socially transmitted patterns for personality development in the individual"—whereas psychologists were "unconcerned about the profound differences in social background responsible for personality variations that are often naively considered to be due . . . to types of conditioning that are only remotely, if at all, connected with social determinants." However, the anthropologist had a particular contribution to make, if he could only transcend his training:

> From the anthropological standpoint, there is a great deal of material that goes to waste in the anthropological field. The ethnologist is trained to select those types of behavior that throw light on the totality of pattern of behavior in a group. Individual variations seem more like interferences with his discipline. . . . [But] we can see variations of individual behavior in primitive society better than we can in our own, perhaps, because these [latter] patterns are woven into our own lives. (NRC: Conf. on Pers. & Cult., 3/6/35, p. 2)

While anthropological data were perhaps "a little too vague for someone who is dealing with an individual as an individual" (i.e., the psychiatrist), Sapir was convinced that his approach to culture in terms of the individual would enable a rapprochement: if cultural anthropologists addressed themselves "to the very definite task of descriptive consideration of ideas and cultures in definite individuals," they would "eventually arrive at culture as a tendency toward a larger grouping of ideas" (p. 8). He was, however, very sensitive to the fact that most cultural anthropologists were critical of such an approach, and would have to be convinced that it was feasible to focus upon the individual.

Training people to develop this interdisciplinary area now became a major focus of concern—as it had been six years before at the A.P.A. colloquia, when Sullivan had suggested that "7 or 8 courses" would be sufficient to produce "a new profession of people capable of studying their fellow man with some regard to the principles of science and some aptitude for the securing of data" (APA 1929:59). In 1935, the "Committee on Personality in Relation to Culture" that emerged from the N.R.C. conference established two subcommittees toward this end: one, headed by Sullivan, to discuss training fellowships for young anthropologists; the other, headed by A. Irving Hallowell, for the preparation of a "handbook of psychological leads for ethnological fieldwork." Sapir, as chairman of the overall committee, was of course involved in both projects.

When the subcommittee on training fellowships met in December 1935, discussion focused on the proposal that four three-year training fellowships be established for young anthropologists, with the first two years devoted to psychoanalytic training analysis and clinical experience in psychiatry, and the third to supervised research of a cross-cultural nature (NRC: Britten/Barrows 11/20/35). Sapir was particularly concerned about the importance of training analysis:

> I think the temptation to project one's own complexes is just too great. People find what they want to find and ignore what they wish to ignore. I know in my own case I wouldn't dare express judgment with regard to the more intimate personal problems suggested by culture, without preliminary training. In a favorable instance, I might make interesting observations or suggest interesting leads but I would consider I had no right to go very far. I think that is true, after all, of most people. (NRC: Subcomm. Training Fels., 12/21/35, p. 65)

Although he himself had reservations about psychoanalytic theory, Sapir felt that it was the only systematic method to allow examination of individual behavior. Ruth Benedict waxed even more naively enthusiastic: "cultural anthropologists will have the perfectly beautiful opportunity of allowing psychoanalysts to give a completely impersonal attitude to their chosen students" (p. 81)—perhaps by implication acknowledging the problem of observer subjectivity that Sapir obviously felt in regard to both her own work and that of Margaret Mead (Stocking 1980).

In his role as chairman, Sullivan pushed each of the individuals present to make specific commitments of their time and expertise. He was willing to direct the training program, but saw it as a team project. Erich Fromm and Karen Horney were to be the training analysts, with Adolph Meyer commuting to New York from Baltimore as supervising analyst. Among the candidates discussed for the fellowships were Cora Du Bois, Ruth Bunzel, Pearl Beaglehole, Ruth Landes, and Walter Dyk, with Benedict speaking on behalf of Morris Opler, and Sullivan and Sapir strongly pushing Stanley Newman —who after receiving his doctorate under Sapir at Yale had had difficulty finding research money to encourage his interest in "problems of language psychology" (NRC: Subcomm. Training Fels., 12/21/35, p. 7). Although Newman was "a thoroughly normal person," which might make training analysis difficult, Sapir pronounced him "a great man for patterns," who felt "the relations of things, not merely the facts, in a sensory sense"—one of the "very few people in anthropology" who had a natural "integrating" bent (p. 8).

Although the program seemed almost ready to go, the issue of funding kept cropping up as an obstacle. In discussing the dearth of likely candidates for the training fellowships, Sapir insisted that "if this type of work were made possible financially, there would be no end of candidates": "It is a little green, but give it support, and you would be surprised to see how many people would be falling for it" (p. 27). Sullivan and Benedict were concerned how the fellows might get jobs after their training—Benedict protesting that it would be a waste of money for people with psychoanalytic training to teach undergraduates, when "as long as there is fieldwork money" they would be "infinitely valuable." In response Sullivan ventured the dream of a new type of psychiatric institution:

> It seems to me fieldwork by people actually sensitive to personal differentials, coupled with some collaborative teaching in each year, might add enormously to our reference data on human personality as the basis of phenomena; I should say that if new and well-endowed psychiatric institutes are one of the developments that we may anticipate as the depression passes, we may right there have a very good place for as many of these people as we can have trained in the meanwhile. (p. 34)

But despite all the grand schemes, the N.R.C. declined to pick up the initial tab of $70,000, of which $20,000 was for psychoanalysis for the trainees.

Sapir and Sullivan continued to search for ways to obtain support. At a meeting of the executive committee of the division, shortly before his term as its chairman expired, Sapir felt that the problem was that the division had never carved out a clear role for itself: "But if you could get psychologists and anthropologists to put a completely fresh program up to some of the donors or foundations, it might create a very different impression . . ." (NRC: 5/5/36). But Walter Hunter, the psychologist who was to succeed him in the regular alternation of office in the division, protested that N.R.C. divisions were never intended to develop their own general or integrated programs; the emphasis, rather, was on supporting established investigators: "What the Rockefeller Foundation itself is doing is to try to size up the men in the field, plus their projects, and give the money directly to men who have demonstrated ability, on the supposition that money so expended will bring in a return to science" (NRC: minutes, Anthro. & Psych. Ex. Comm., 3/16/36, p. 2). The obvious implication was that had Sapir himself wished to undertake training analysis, it might well have been funded. In response, Sapir argued that psychologists and psychiatrists, "in the grip of prestige [and] tradition"—like everyone else— tended to "shy away from the border line fields, unless they have definite encouragement":

> What I had in mind was whether the Division could pull itself together well enough to come back to the Foundations and get them to reconsider their policies. We cannot do anything without some money. We are just picking up crumbs these days. (p. 3)

But there was no money. Although a few younger anthropologists (including Weston La Barre, Irvin Child, and John Whiting) did succeed in getting psychoanalytic training in this period though the Institute of Human Relations, Sapir's proposed N.R.C. training program never got off the ground. Though he continued as a member of the N.R.C. divisional executive committee, Sapir himself seems to have been little involved in the Committee on Personality in Relation to Culture after his term as its chairman ended; his place was taken by W. Lloyd Warner, under whom there was a clear retrenchment in Committee activities. After a planned joint conference with the S.S.R.C. Committee on Personality and Culture fell through in 1938, the main activity was the completion of Hallowell's handbook of "Psychological Leads for Ethnological Fieldworkers" (1949)—parts of which were originally to have been prepared by Sapir in conjunction with Newman and Hortense Powdermaker, who had been his postdoctoral student at Yale.

Two years after Sapir's death in February 1939, when it was clear that the Committee on Personality in Relation to Culture had drifted into impotence, various concerned parties were asked whether it was worth maintaining. May, who had served as chairman of the subcommittee on agenda, "felt all along that it was constantly searching for something to do and never succeeding in finding it"; he was doubtful that the situation had changed "so that such a committee could now be useful" (NRC: 2/12/41). Clark Wissler was even more dubious: "The outcome was not particularly impressive" (NRC: 2/13/41). Even Sapir's former student Harry Hoijer was unenthusiastic: "the field of personality in relation to culture is such a broad one that all the interests cannot be represented satisfactorily in any committee and if they are there is little likelihood of satisfactory action taking place because the problems they attempt to solve cannot be worked in a collaborative fashion" (NRC 2/13/41). Others suggested that the committee might be reoriented toward questions raised by World War II in Europe. But while the war was in fact to give renewed impetus to culture-and-personality studies, it was under other auspices. By the end of June 1941, the N.R.C. committee was disbanded.

The Ineffable Imprint of the Gift of Tongues

The N.R.C. Committee on Personality in Relation to Culture was not the last attempt to find institutional sponsorship for the Sapirian program in personality and culture. When Sapir's first heart attack in the summer of 1937 forced him to spend his sabbatical year from Yale in New York City rather than in China, Sullivan was a frequent visitor. Sullivan apparently hoped that the new journal *Psychiatry*—to which he, Sapir, and Lasswell contributed articles on the interdisciplinary connections of psychiatric study—might put his William Alanson White Foundation "on the map and call forth financial support from many people." Convinced that Sapir's "actual survival depended on his not going back to Yale," Sullivan had hopes early in 1938 that he might raise an endowment to provide Sapir with an independent income for the rest of his life. But the attempt failed, and by the end of that year, Sullivan was resigned to the "final disaster" of Sapir's death (Perry 1982:367–68, 372).

Sapir died unhappy because he had been unable to complete so much of his work (J. Sapir 1967). The range of his activities after 1930 had been extremely broad. At Yale he was chairman of the Anthropology Department, taught courses in the linguistics program, was affiliated with the Peabody Museum, and—albeit ambivalently—with the Institute of Human Relations; and there were also multiple associational involvements on the national scene as well, including the American Council of Learned Societies, the Linguistic Society of America, and the American Anthropological Association. In addition to a major commitment of time and energy to the work of his students, he maintained his interests in American Indian languages (especially Navajo), Indo-European languages (especially Tibetan influences on Tocharian), and theoretical linguistics (English grammar, international language, morphophonemics, and the relation of language and thought). So it is perhaps not surprising that his work in personality and culture should not have achieved fulfillment. The book on "the psychology of culture" he conceived while still in Chicago seems never to have gone beyond the outline stage; neither did he carry out empirical work that might have produced an exemplary monographic study (his last important fieldwork was with the Navajo in the summer of 1929). The small number of articles that he published in the area are for the most part programmatic; they suggested conceptual orientations toward the enterprise, but little in the way of specific methodological leads. Speaking of his own movement into "culture and personality" under Hallowell at the University of Pennsylvania in the late 1940s, Anthony Wallace characterized Sapir's papers as "early harbingers"—"statesman-like blessings on the enterprise." In contrast to the writings of Linton, Kardiner, Róheim, Mead, Benedict, Hallowell, La Barre, Devereux, Whiting, Bateson, and others who were "actively doing fieldwork and publishing," they "did not contain data, or testable hypotheses, or examples of method" (quoted in Murray 1986).

In the case of Mead there is in fact evidence of a specific methodological influence: she later noted that "when we began our work on culture at a distance [in the 1940s], the first thing we did was to get all the records of that Seminar at Yale and use them . . . as the basis for the first manuals we built for the people that worked in that study" (Mead 1966). But if Wallace's general point remains valid, it is an interesting fact that a number of those he cited as offering more concrete exemplars themselves proclaimed their indebtedness to Sapir. Thus Hallowell: "In the 1930s I became directly involved in psychological anthropology through Edward Sapir. . . [who] had explored various methods of getting at such information in different cultures" (1972:8). And La Barre: Sapir ("my spiritual father") was "the founder of culture and personality studies" (1978:282, 264). And even Whiting: "It was Edward Sapir who represented for us the more subtle and humanistic point of view" (Whiting & Whiting 1978:44).

And yet, there is a certain ineffableness to these testimonials. The tone was set in the first collection of papers in culture and personality (Kluckhohn & Murray 1948), where Sapir was acknowledged in the preface as having "initiated formal instruction" in the field, and as having influenced Thomas' programmatic "landmark" of 1933—but was unrepresented in the volume itself. Commenting that "a volume on 'culture and personality' without Sapir seems like *Hamlet* without Hamlet," the editors explained his absence by the fact that his essays were in the process of republication elsewhere (Mandelbaum 1949). But it was also the case that Sapir was noted only twice in their index.

Nevertheless, when La Barre made a survey of culture-and-personality courses being taught around 1950, the list of teachers read "like a roster of Sapir's former students and persons directly influenced by him" (Perry 1982: 374). One suspects that the ineffability of Sapir's influence reflects the fact that it was conveyed largely through a process of verbal interaction, to students who directly felt the power of his "gift of tongues." But there is more to it than this. Commenting on his two colleagues in Redfield's trio of "gifted tongues," Sullivan said that Lasswell was "but a highly talented technician; Edward, a genius" (Perry 1982:372). The term is one that keeps recurring in reminiscences of Sapir: of all the figures in the history of American anthropology, none (save perhaps in a rather different style, Boas) has been so widely acknowledged for his sheer intellectual power. Students who experienced that power did not forget it, even when their orientations, like Whiting's, remained quite different.

But it was not simply the power, but a certain message it conveyed, and continues to convey, to those who never experienced Sapir's power directly. The message, however programmatic and unexemplared, was that there was another way of doing things. In the case of Whiting, it was one which contrasted with "the materialistic, practical, functional, and scientific hypothesis testing approach" he had inherited through Murdock (Whiting & Whiting 1978:44). More generally, however, it was an alternative to the dominant style of culture-and-personality research, which in the work of Benedict, Mead, Kardiner, and Du Bois emphasized the formative power of culture on the individual personality. Sapir, too, was aware of that power, and some of his statements echo the psychologized cultural stereotypes associated with that tradition (see Murray 1986). But from the beginning, he also raised questions about its fundamental assumptions, questions that, according to George Spindler, have still "not been responded to adequately by most of us who explicitly psychologize"—including, most notably, that of "the distributive locus of culture." In a subdiscipline that "started off with great expectations," only to "come under vigorous, at times strident, attack," which has consistently "suffered from identity problems," and which has "often had obituaries read over it" (Spindler 1978:17–18), Sapir has remained available as an alternate source of interpretive power. Perhaps he may himself have sensed that possibility when, as he was beginning to develop his interest in this area, he wrote to William Ogburn:

> I have certain ideas about the meaning and value of individuality in history that I am afraid are rather heterodox. Much of the talk on social psychology that I run across from time to time strikes me, to be very frank, as simply bosh. The attempt to understand history in terms of book formulas that take no account of the individual is, to my mind, but a passing phase of our hunger for conventional scientific capsules into which to store our concepts. When all the experiments in massed action will have brought with them their due share of inevitable disappointments, there will be a very real reaction against this whole way of thinking, but in any event this reaction is not due for some time yet so you may as well have the laugh on me for the present. (NMM: ES/WO 1/1/18)

Acknowledgments

A preliminary version of this paper was presented to the Yale University Department of Anthropology Colloquium in October 1985; its argument is part of a general biography of Edward Sapir currently in progress. I am grateful to a number of persons for access to documents and for discussion of Sapir's work in culture and personality: Robert Allen, Harold Conklin, Leonard Doob, Judith Irvine, Stephen Murray, Stanley Newman, James M. Nyce, Richard Preston, George W. Stocking, Jr., Philip Sapir and other members of the Sapir family, as well as the librarians of the various archives consulted.

References Cited

Angell, J. N. 1929. Yale Institute of Human Relations. *Yale Alumni Weekly* 38 (31): 889–91.

APA. 1929. *Proceedings. First colloquium on personality investigation held under the auspices of the American Psychiatric Association Committee on Relations with the Social Sciences; December 1–2, 1928, New York City.* Baltimore.

————. 1930. *Proceedings. Second colloquium on personality investigation held under the joint auspices of the American Psychiatric Association Committee on Relations of Psychiatry and the Social Sciences and of the Social Science Research Council; November 29–30, New York City.* Baltimore.

Boas, F. 1911. *The mind of primitive man.* Boston.

Bulmer, M. 1985. *The Chicago school of sociology: Institutionalization, diversity and the rise of sociological research.* Chicago.

Cowan, W., M. K. Foster, and E. F. K. Koerner, eds. 1986. *New perspectives on Edward Sapir in language, culture, and personality.* Amsterdam.

Darnell, R. 1969. The development of American anthropology, 1879–1920: From the Bureau of American Ethnology to Franz Boas. Doct. diss., Univ. Penn.

————. 1984. The Sapir years at the Canadian National Museum in Ottawa. In *Edward Sapir: Appraisals of his life and work.* ed. K. Koerner, 159–78. Philadelphia.

————. 1986. The emergence of Edward Sapir's mature thought. In Cowan et al. 1986:553–88.

————. n.d. Edward Sapir and the Boasian model of cultural process. In *Proceedings of the Brown University Sapir Lecture Series, 1984,* ed. J. M. Nyce et al.

Dewey, J. 1922. *Human nature and conduct.* New York.

Hallowell, A. I. 1949. Psychological leads for ethnological fieldworkers. In *Personal character and cultural milieu,* ed. D. Haring, 341–88. Syracuse, N.Y.

————. 1972. On being an anthropologist. In *Contributions to anthropology: Selected papers of A. Irving Hallowell,* ed. R. Fogelson, 3–14. Chicago.

Karl, B. 1974. *Charles E. Merriam and the study of politics.* Chicago.

Kluckhohn, C., & H. Murray. 1949. *Personality in nature, culture, and society.* New York.

Kroeber, A. L. 1923. *Anthropology.* New York.

La Barre, W. 1978. The clinic and the field. In Spindler 1978:259–99.

Lasswell, H. 1938. What psychiatrists and political scientists can learn from one another. *Psychiatry* 1:33–39.

Lynd, R., & H. Lynd. 1929. *Middletown: A study in American culture.* New York.

Mandelbaum, D. G., ed. 1949. *Selected writings of Edward Sapir in language, culture and personality.* Berkeley.

May, M. 1971. A retrospective view of the Institute for Human Relations at Yale. *Behav. Sci. Notes* 3:141–72.

Mead, M. 1966. Neglected aspects in the history of American anthropology. Yale Univ., December 8 [tape courtesy H. Conklin].

Murray, S. 1986. Edward Sapir in "the Chicago school" of sociology. In Cowan et al. 1986:241–92.

NMM. See under Manuscript Sources.

NRC. See under Manuscript Sources.

NRC [National Research Council]. 1934–35. *Annual report.* Washington, D.C.

Perry, H. S. 1982. *Psychiatrist of America: The life of Harry Stack Sullivan.* Cambridge, Mass.

RF. See under Manuscript Sources.

Sapir, E. 1912. Language and environment. In Mandelbaum 1949:89–103.

———. 1916. *Time perspective in aboriginal American culture: A study in method.* Canada Dept. Mines, Geol. Surv. Mem. 90. Ottawa.

———. 1917. Do we need a "superorganic"? *Am. Anth.* 19:441–47.

———. 1921. *Language: An introduction to the study of speech.* New York.

———. 1923. The two kinds of human beings. In Mandelbaum 1949:529–32.

———. 1924. Culture, genuine and spurious. In Mandelbaum 1949:308–31.

———. 1925. Sound patterns in language. In Mandelbaum 1949:33–45.

———. 1926. Speech as a personality trait. In Mandelbaum 1949:533–42.

———. 1927a. Anthropology and sociology. In Mandelbaum 1949:332–45.

———. 1927b. The unconscious patterning of behavior in society. In Mandelbaum 1949:544–59.

———. 1932. Cultural anthropology and psychiatry. In Mandelbaum 1949: 509–21.

———. 1934. The emergence of the concept of personality in the study of culture. In Mandelbaum 1949:590–600.

———. 1938. Why cultural anthropology needs the psychiatrist. In Mandelbaum 1949:569–77.

Sapir, J. 1967. Letter to Richard Preston. 12/4.

Sibley, E. 1974. *Social Science Research Council: The first fifty years.* New York.

Siskin, E. 1984. Edward Sapir: The Jewish dimension. Paper presented to Sapir Centenary session, Am. Anth. Assn. Denver.

Smith, B. L. 1969. The mystifying intellectual history of Harold D. Lasswell. In *Politics, personality, and social science in the twentieth century: Essays in honor of Harold D. Lasswell,* ed. A. A. Rogow, 41–106. Chicago.

Spindler, G., ed. 1978. *The making of psychological anthropology.* Berkeley.

SSRC. See under Manuscript Sources.

SSRC [Social Science Research Council]. 1930. Proceedings of the Hanover Conference. Mimeo.

———. 1934. *Decennial report: 1923–33.* New York.

———. 1935. *Annual report.* New York.

Stocking, G. W., Jr. 1976. Ideas and institutions in American anthropology: Thoughts toward a history of the interwar years. In *Selected papers from the American Anthropologist, 1921–1945,* ed. Stocking, 1–44. Washington, D.C.

———. 1978. Pedants and potentates: Robert Redfield at the 1930 Hanover conference. *Hist. Anth. Newsl.* 5:10–13.

———. 1980. Sapir's last testament on culture and personality. *Hist. Anth. Newsl.* 7:8–11.

————. 1985. Philanthropoids and vanishing cultures: Rockefeller funding and the end of the museum era in Anglo-American anthropology. *HOA* 3:112–45.

Sullivan, H. S. 1938. Editorial notes: The Wm. Alanson White Psychiatric Foundation. *Psychiatry* 1:135–40.

UC. See under Manuscript Sources.

UCB. See under Manuscript Sources.

Volkhart, E. H., ed. 1951. *Social behavior and personality: Contributions of W. I. Thomas to theory and social research.* New York.

Whiting, J., & B. Whiting. 1978. A strategy for psychocultural research. In Spindler 1978:41–61.

Wissler, C. 1923. *Man and culture.* New York.

YU. See under Manuscript Sources.

Manuscript Sources

NMM Sapir and Jenness administrative papers, Archives of the Division of Anthropology, National Museum of Man, Ottawa, Can.

NRC Papers of the National Research Council, Archives of the National Academy of Science, Washington, D.C.

RF Rockefeller Foundation Archives, Tarryton, N.Y.

SSRC Archives of the Social Science Research Council, New York.

UC University of Chicago Department of Anthropology Manuscripts, Department of Special Collections, University of Chicago Library.

UCB Papers of Robert Lowie and A. L. Kroeber, Department of Anthropology Manuscripts, Bancroft Library, University of California, Berkeley.

YU President's Papers, Institute of Human Relations, Department of Anthropology Manuscripts, Yale University Archives, Sterling Memorial Library, New Haven.

SCIENCE, DEMOCRACY, AND ETHICS

Mobilizing Culture and Personality for World War II

VIRGINIA YANS-McLAUGHLIN

"When it comes to the ethics and politics of their discipline," Margaret Mead wrote in 1978, "anthropologists have shown themselves to be extraordinarily incapable of applying the principles of their own discipline to themselves" (1978:438). Actually, for more than a decade, criticism of anthropology's ties to colonialism had troubled many of Mead's colleagues, provoking debate and reflection upon the politics and ethics of their discipline (Hymes 1972; Huizer & Mannheim 1979). Mead's comment reflected both her own current personal dissatisfaction with some of the partisans in the controversy, and a long professional experience stretching back over half a century and including the cultural and political crisis of World War II. As Mead saw it, prior to the war anthropologists had limited their political and ethical concerns to such questions as "the fate of primitive peoples, minorities, just or unjust wars, racial or biological determinism *versus* economic determinism" (1978:435). They offered their expert opinions to the educated public on these issues without involving themselves in the formation or implementation of governmental policy. But the war forced many anthropologists to become active "interventionists and practitioners in the lives of human communities," both modern and primitive, at home and in colonized areas, among the allies and in enemy territory (429). Some anthropologists began to consider the ethical and political implications of their work, and to think about their relationship to what

Virginia Yans-McLaughlin is an Associate Professor in the Department of History at Rutgers, the State University at New Brunswick, New Jersey. Her major previous publications include *Family and Community: Italian Immigrants in Buffalo, New York*. She is currently working on a cultural biography of Margaret Mead.

184

they studied, not only as an abstract epistemological problem, but as a moral one. Far from permanently resolving these issues, their participation in policy research intensified the contradictions, leaving most anthropologists anxious to return as quickly as possible to the academy. After the war, Mead reported, "Everybody was glad to get away from the restrictions of government," and those who remained in Washington "found themselves continually hampered by the witch hunt of the McCarthy era" and by the policies of the Cold War (BBWD:8–9). For the next two decades the deceptively unproblematic expansion of university programs and research projects required full attention from the discipline, but the political uses and involvements of anthropology—indeed, the politics of anthropology itself—could no longer be denied (Huizer & Mannheim 1979:10; Wolf 1969). Reconsideration of the ethical and political dilemmas faced by anthropologists during World War II, then, has more than historical interest.

A Prior Pattern:
Boas and American Anthropology in World War I

This pattern of involvement and withdrawal by anthropologists of the World War II period had been foreshadowed a generation earlier. And here, as in many other instances, Franz Boas was the archetypical representative of a disciplinary tradition. A man of passionate political and moral beliefs, Boas also stood firm in his conviction that anthropologists should maintain the scientific stance of detached critical observers. Rejection of dogmatic tradition, commitment to intellectual and political freedom, to equal opportunity and human fellowship, to the pursuit of scientific knowledge, and to science in the service of humanity underlay both his politics and his anthropology. But he never thought of himself, nor was he thought of, as an applied anthropologist or policy scientist. Boas believed that anthropological knowledge, widely shared, could liberate men and their minds from prejudice and intolerance, and his research agenda for himself and for his students generated knowledge that would serve this purpose; but from Boas' perspective, the appropriate active political role for the anthropologist was the scientist-citizen, advocate and promulgator of scientific anthropological knowledge—not the government employee or advisor formulating and implementing policy (see Stocking 1976). During World War I, the politics of nation-states and of his profession conspired to convince him of the propriety of this position.

In the prewar decades, as Boas established himself as the leader of American anthropology, he battled with an evolutionary tradition then strongly entrenched in, and identified with, quasi-governmental agencies: the Smithsonian Institution and its affiliates, the United States National Museum, and the Bureau of American Ethnology. The justification offered for founding the Bureau, that is, its potential contribution to a more rational management of Indian reservations, hints at the philosophy of Washington anthropology (Hinsley 1981). Boas had a very different set of objectives for the discipline. A product of the German university system, he sought to establish anthropology as an academic discipline. Although he did occasionally work for several government agencies, his relationship to "Washington anthropologists" was always somewhat oppositional, and frequently acrimonious. The events of World War I greatly exacerbated his antagonism toward governmental anthropology (see Stocking 1968:273–307).

Although he had become an American citizen in 1891, Boas spoke out vociferously against American intervention in the war, defending the military actions of his native land, and the German national culture to which he was profoundly attached. During the war years, and immediately afterward, he suffered severe disappointment with fellow scholars and intellectuals whose patriotism fueled anti-German feelings and whose uncritical support of American intervention rested upon what he saw as a confusion between historically conditioned American standards and universal democratic values. Disappointed by the very group upon whom he had counted to enlighten the citizenry, he sought support outside the academic community, and for a period joined the Socialist Party—the major political organization boldly opposed to the war (Boas 1916; Stocking 1979).

In the meantime, the Washington anthropologists, inspired with nationalistic fervor, joined the war effort. The National Research Council, formed in 1916 to mobilize the resources of science for the government, formed a special committee of anthropologists. Its leading figures included several of Boas' long-time Washington antagonists, and several prominent racialists—among them the outspoken geneticist Charles B. Davenport, and the notorious polemicist Madison Grant. Boas and his students, many of whom shared his Jewish immigrant background, interpreted these committee appointments as part of an attempt by biologists and other "hard" scientists, most of them nativist descendants of old-line American families, to turn anthropology away from environmentalist cultural approaches toward racial research that might serve the causes of xenophobia and immigration restriction (Stocking 1968: 273–307).

For Boas, the final, most bitter, and most personal blow came during the political hysteria of the immediate postwar period, after he published a scathing letter in the *Nation* denouncing the use of "Scientists as Spies" (1919). He publicly exposed anthropologists who had used scientific activities in Mexico to cover wartime espionage. These men whom he refused "to designate any longer as scientists," who had "prostituted science by using it as a cover for their activities as spies," had close ties to Washington anthropology, and early in 1920 their sympathizers in the American Anthropological Association, flushed with postwar patriotism, rallied to censure Boas and remove him from the Council of the Association, and to force his resignation from the National Research Council. It is easy to see why, from Boas' viewpoint, government and government policy seemed inimical to the development of theoretical anthropology in general, and cultural anthropology in particular.

Within several years the Boasians recaptured control of the Association, and soon took advantage of National Research Council funding to forward Boas' antihereditarian research program. But the bitter heritage of these continuing struggles with Washington anthropology was not easily forgotten. A searing chapter had been written in the history of science and public policy, a sober warning to the next generation of anthropologists as they came to professional maturity in the interwar period. During the Depression, the already established cadre of government anthropologists at the Bureau of American Ethnology was temporarily augmented when New Deal administrators employed a number of cultural anthropologists, notably in the Bureau of Indian Affairs and the Soil Conservation Service. But the New Deal experiments in applied anthropology were short-lived. Bureaucrats in the Indian and Soil Conservation programs resisted interference; the anthropologists were more often interested in the American Indians' past than in their immediate difficulties relating to the dominant culture (Eddy & Partridge 1978:20–28; Kelly 1985:128–29; see also Goldschmidt 1979:51–144).

Watching this new round of experiments in government anthropology from the outside, many Boasians, like Melville Herskovits, worried that applied anthropologists acting in government service might endanger the integrity of the discipline (1936). It was not that anthropologists ignored important social and political issues. On the contrary, during the 1930s, Boas himself contemplated abandoning anthropological research in favor of his role as critic of Nazi racialism and defender of intellectual freedom. But he made his political case, cautiously, from outside the government, not within it; most of his disciples followed a similar pattern—until the outbreak of World War II forced them to reconsider.

From Boas and Brown to Bali

By that time, many changes had taken place within American anthropology itself. Even before World War I, Boas began to turn away from historical reconstruction and diffusion toward the study of the "inner development" of culture and the "relation of the individual to society" (quoted in Stocking 1976:15). According to Mead, Boas had nothing to say "about hypotheses or paradigms" (1972:209); but by the 1920s he had defined a new research agenda:

on the one hand, the critical examination of biological and cultural determinants of individual behavior was to continue; on the other, the exploration of the determining cultural patterns themselves, of their formation and
integration, would commence. The work of a number of Boas' students reflected the shift, moving from the study of the distribution of cultural "elements," to cultural "configurations" and "patterns," and finally, to individual
personality formation in different "cultures." Ruth Benedict's work offers an
example of this progression. Her 1923 doctoral dissertation examined the distribution of a culture "trait"—belief in guardian spirits; several years later she
offered her first formulation of the configurationist approach in "Psychological Types in the Cultures of the Southwest"; finally, the Dionysian and Apol-
lonian types in *Patterns of Culture* (1934) dramatically presented her case that
cultures select, from the "great arc" of potential human behaviors, clusters
of values which become the standard for individual behavior (see Modell 1983).

During the same period, British anthropology, too, moved away from evolutionism and diffusionism toward a synchronic and behavioral or "functionalist" study of human variety. Initially, in the work of W. H. R. Rivers
and Bronislaw Malinowski, the British tradition also moved toward a psychological orientation (Stocking, in this volume). But the dominant trend in British anthropology, best illustrated in the work of A. R. Radcliffe-Brown, moved
away from psychology. Rather than discussing cultural integration in terms
of "pattern"—with its psychological, aesthetic, and humanistic resonances—
Brown preferred to speak in terms of "system" or "structure"—concepts suggesting analogies to the natural sciences of physiology and mechanics. Eventually concluding that the idea of "culture" itself lay outside the realm of scientific inquiry, he focused instead on the concrete study of kinship. Other
customs, beliefs, and rules of behavior interested him only insofar as they
enhanced understanding of "social system" maintenance, for his goal was to
develop a comparative anatomy of social systems (see Stocking 1976:22; 1984:
106–11; Wolf 1964:4–5).

But if British and American anthropology were in these respects diverging
in the interwar period, the visits of both Malinowski and Radcliffe-Brown
to the United States heightened interest in British approaches. Disagreements
existed, to be sure, but "functionalism" definitely earned a place on the
American agenda, especially when Radcliffe-Brown taught for six years at the
University of Chicago. As American anthropologists began to break through
the parochial boundaries of "railroad" and "motor-car ethnography" among
the American Indians to undertake research in colonial areas overseas, the
experience of British anthropologists naturally seemed salient. Anthropology
in both countries entered its "classical" period in the 1930s, when intensive
fieldwork in a large number of different cultures (or societies) became the
hallmark of the discipline. Carried on under the umbrella of colonial author-

ity, not yet troubled by the issues of power and knowledge that disturbed ethnographers of a subsequent generation, ethnographic fieldwork seemed to offer the comparative basis for testing or establishing generalizations about human behavior in the full range of human societies or cultures (see Stocking 1983; 1982).

The marriage of Margaret Mead and Gregory Bateson, of course, offers a fascinating illustration of the relationship of the two major national traditions of the "classical" period. Mead and Bateson were each unusually receptive to ideas and influences coming from outside their native traditions, and their careers may be interpreted as an effort to synthesize the two approaches. From the beginning of their professional cooperation, nevertheless, the distinguishing marks of their training persisted, and the ultimate divergence of their anthropological interests paralleled the parting of their private lives.

Before moving on to graduate work in anthropology at Columbia under Boas, Mead had taken her B.A. and her M.A. in psychology at Barnard College. She later claimed that a psychology professor's question set the direction for her lifetime of research: "When does an Indian become an Indian?"—and her early reading of Freud, Jung, Adler, Piaget, and the Gestalt psychologists prepared her for the study of child development, psychological types, and cultural "patterns" (Mead 1974). In her senior year, she took a course with Boas in anthropology, in which Ruth Benedict served as teaching assistant. The pattern of her graduate experience recalls Boas' agenda in this period: a master's thesis on intelligence testing among Italian and American children, research for a library doctoral dissertation on the stability of the association of cultural elements in Polynesia, and a subsequent Samoan field trip to study the relative weight of biology and culture in adolescent development (Mead 1972). Her first two popular ethnographies, *Coming of Age in Samoa* (1928) and *Growing Up in New Guinea* (1930a)—both intended for general audiences—heavily emphasized problems of individual development. It was in fact only in *Social Organization of Manu'a* (1930b)—intended for scholars—that she used the configurationalist approach, a legacy from lengthy conversations with Ruth Benedict (Mead 1972:195–96). A subsequent scholarly monograph on her first New Guinea fieldwork reflected the British influence. After her second marriage—to New Zealander Reo Fortune, a disciple of W. H. R. Rivers—and after a brief study of kinship with Radcliffe-Brown had brought her into closer relationship to British anthropology, she undertook a technical study of *Kinship in the Admiralty Islands* (1934). By the time she met her third husband, Gregory Bateson, during a return field expedition to New Guinea, Mead had already begun to bridge the two national traditions.

Gregory Bateson's development followed a different route. As the son of the distinguished English geneticist William Bateson, he learned from an early age to be a patient, observing naturalist, and a seeker for the order underlying natural phenomena (Mead 1972:227; Bateson 1984:18–19). Bateson did not forsake biology for anthropology until late in his undergraduate career at Cambridge, and his early anthropological work was guided by A. C. Haddon, a formally trained zoologist. Bateson never fully relinquished his interest in natural phenomena, or in the interconnections of all things natural; when Mead met him in 1932 she was much taken with the easy leaps he made by analogy from natural science to human cultures. Bateson's natural scientific heritage, however, did not immediately help him in his ethnographic fieldwork. In 1930, when he returned from his first three-year stint in New Guinea, the best that he could produce was a descriptive ethnography of the Iatmul. And despite considerable contact with Radcliffe-Brown during his time in the Southwest Pacific, he still "did not see clearly any reason why I should enquire into one matter rather than another" when he returned in 1932 for a second round of fieldwork among the Iatmul (Lipset 1980:133, 135).

When Bateson met Mead and Fortune on the Sepik River after their own frustrating fieldwork among the Arapesh, he was "floundering methodologically"; they were "starved for theoretical relevance." As the three anthropologists conversed intensely into the night, they "moved back and forth between analyzing ourselves and each other, as individuals, and the cultures that we knew and were studying." A recently forwarded draft of Ruth Benedict's *Patterns of Culture*, and Mead's recollections of Jungian psychological types, informed their tentative assumption that cultures selectively emphasized and assigned different temperamental characteristics among men and women. There, on the Sepik River, in a tiny eight-by-eight-foot mosquito room, Mead and Bateson fell in love—having concluded that they represented "a male and female version of a temperamental type . . . in strong contrast with the one represented by [Fortune]" (Mead 1972:216–17; Bateson 1984:128–38). So began a new intellectual collaboration which assisted the cross-fertilization of two anthropological traditions.

Before their marriage in 1936, the couple's discussions of culture, gender, and personality found formal expression in Mead's *Sex and Temperament in Three Primitive Societies* (1935). In 1935 Bateson visited the United States, and the two conferred with Radcliffe-Brown, attempting to clarify further "what is meant by society, culture, and cultural character" (Mead 1972:222). Upon his return to England, before they initiated their joint fieldwork in Bali in 1936, Bateson completed the manuscript of his first major work. Entitled *Naven: A Survey of the Problems Suggested by a Composite Picture of the Culture of a New Guinea Tribe Drawn from Three Points of View* (1936), it attempted to bring to bear on the analysis of a single ceremony both Radcliffe-Brown's social structural theory and the configurationalist approach to culture that Bateson borrowed from Benedict and Mead. An ethnography of ceremonial transvestism and ritual homosexuality, *Naven* rotates about three levels of abstraction: the ethnographic data; their rearrangement "to give various pictures"—aesthetic, emotional, and cognitive—of the culture; and a "self-conscious discussion of the procedures by which the anthropologist put "the pieces of the jig-saw puzzle . . . together." Finally, in his epilogue, Bateson bemusedly acknowledged his last-minute realization, just before the book went to press, that its various organizing concepts (*ethos, eidos,* cultural structure, social structure, etc.) were not actual entities, but vantage points from which to explore and explain culture (Bateson 1936:261, 263, 281). Bateson's overwhelming and continuing epistemological concerns distinguished him most sharply both from his often unquestioningly scientist British colleagues and from the more intuitively oriented American ethnographers. But another departure loomed even larger. For static theories of adaptation or harmonic integration, Bateson substituted a more dynamic, circular, interactional scheme: "schismogenesis." Later, he defined it as "positive feedback," but in *Naven* it signified a "process of differentiation in the norms of individual behavior resulting from cumulative interaction between individuals." Bateson expected that this concept would apply not only to the development of cultures, but more generally to human behavior, including "the progressive maladjustment of neurotic and prepsychotic individuals" (175, 179; Mead 1972:235–36).

The rivalries and tensions evident in Iatmul culture—rivalries expressed ceremonially in *naven*—raised, but did not yet resolve, the tantalizing problem of why this society, or any other society, did not just explode. Why was it that "vicious circles" did not develop in which the tensions between two persons—or two groups, or even two nations—did not accelerate to the breaking point? At the time, Bateson presumed that two balancing forms of "schismogenesis" (symmetrical and complementary) would "account for the presumed dynamic equilibrium of the system"; after World War II, however, his deepening involvement with the development of cybernetic theory led him instead toward explanations implied in the ideas of "negative feedback" and "circular causal systems"—mechanical models of "causal circuits which would . . . seek equilibria or steady states" (1936:287). Although a scion of the British tradition, Bateson sought not simply to study social equilibria, but to explain how they were achieved.

Mead and Bateson each brought to their anthropological collaboration very different talents, training, and ideas; but both thirsted for more than their original background or training offered. Bateson wanted to incorporate the emotional, aesthetic, and cognitive aspects of Mead's neo-Boasian anthropology into his work, and at the same time to inject his discipline with methodological rigor. But, as was his wont, he also thought about thought. Mead learned both from his love of abstraction and from his epistemological concerns. During their two years in Bali, she was interested in character formation; he, in the theory and dynamics of social interaction. The intent was to connect child

Gregory Bateson and Margaret Mead, Iatmul, 1938. (Courtesy The Institute of Intercultural Studies, Inc.)

development and character formation, and to demonstrate the congruence between infant experience and broad culture patterns (Bateson 1984:19–20; Mead 1972:224). While trying to understand the cultural organization of human behavior, the two also struggled to develop greater observational rigor, and an understanding of the process of observation itself. In answer to criticism of Mead's "impressionistic" fieldwork and Bateson's "philosophical" ethnography, they attempted ambitious new photographic and notational methods. With thousands of spontaneously annotated stills and cine films, physical recordings of sequential moments, the couple hoped to document for others the relationships—the "emotional threads"—which connected the unfolding actions (Bateson & Mead 1942:xii). When they returned from Bali in the spring of 1939—after a six-month interval of comparative research among the Iatmul— they had an unprecedented body of ethnographic materials. The Balinese field notes and photos "multiplied by a factor of ten" their original work estimates (Mead 1972:234), providing much more than they could use in their lavishly illustrated collaborative volume *Balinese Character* (1942). But the effort bore other bounties: for Mead, Bali had provided the missing temperament needed to complete the four-fold table of "culturally defined temperamental expectations for men and women" that had originally been conceived in 1932 on the Sepik (Mead 1972:218); Bateson found in Bali a "counterinstance of non-schismogenic society" in which "escalating processes" were modified or inhibited by "culturally integrated childhood conditioning" (Lipset 1980:158).

Mobilizing Culture and Personality to Defeat the Axis

None of this research involved policymaking at home or abroad—the Batesons had traveled to the field in order to understand society, not to change it. In this, they conformed to the dominant pattern of American anthropology in the interwar period (Stocking 1982).

Mead's background qualified her for a more activist role: she came from a highly educated family of Eastern progressives, true believers in the possibility of scientifically directed social change. Emily Fogg Mead, herself an ardent social reformer, took Margaret along, as a young child, when she did fieldwork among Italian immigrants for her own doctorate in sociology; supported by Margaret's paternal grandmother, who lived with the Meads, the mother taught her child to respect equality, cultural differences, scientific knowledge, and the practical and social uses of the intellect. Mead's father, a University of Pennsylvania economist, reinforced his daughter's confidence in the practical application of scientific inquiry to social conditions. Mead's anthropological training under Boas supported these familial values (see Mead 1972); both *Coming of Age in Samoa: A Psychological Study of Primitive Youth for Western Civilization* (1928) and *Growing Up in New Guinea: A Comparative Study of Primitive Education* (1930) related her fieldwork to contemporary educational issues. She soon withdrew, however, to strictly academic concerns. In a recollection omitted from the final published version of her autobiography, Mead described her political stance in the interwar years:

> I had been uninvolved in any sort of political activity since I left college, putting all my time and effort into getting into the field, writing up and publishing results . . . and getting back to the field again. Organizing funds to get to the field meant doing a lot of work on various aspects of scientific work on American culture, conferences, [preparation] of research plans, so that I knew a good deal about the culture—from an educational angle. But I belonged to nothing except the American Anthropological Association and related professional organizations. I had never held an office in any of them. I hadn't voted since 1924, for never since then had I had the residency requirements to vote. When I decided, in 1923, for science rather than politics or the arts, the decisions had been complete. Henceforth I was to be single minded, trying to do as much field work as possible before the next war, which my father put at 1939. Even the political upheaval of the Depression and later of the Spanish War went in a sense unnoticed, for I was living in a time perspective of a hundred years, and preparing the materials with which we would, hopefully, be better prepared for that long future. Fascism, Communism, Nazism, Capitalism, from such a long stand point, were perturbations, with which other people had to deal.
>
> Gregory had a brief spasm of political interest in 1935, at the beginning of the Abyssinian War, and tried to get Britain interest[ed] in putting down a year's supply of food, but no . . . one was interested, and we plunged into our Balinese field work, years away from the scene of action. (BBWD:2)

In contrast to Mead, Gregory Bateson was not a reformer by temperament, background, or intellectual leaning. His abiding concern with the potential destructiveness of human institutions, his skepticism about existing structures or solutions, and his abstract, detached approach to social reality led him to view political or social reform cynically (Bateson 1984:96–97). During the 1930s, he remained indifferent to the leftist and utopian ideas that captured the minds and hearts of many of his British scientist friends (Lipset 1980: 139). For most of his life Bateson was ambivalent or even negative about applied social science, which he thought at best peripheral, and at worst dangerous, to pure research.

When the Batesons returned from the South Seas in the spring of 1939, leaving behind them months of incredibly intense fieldwork, the demands of the real world seemed suddenly and powerfully importunate. As Mead later recalled, "from the time we returned, we had realized that Hitler presented a terrible threat to everything we valued in the world" (BBWD:3). Her daughter remembered her parents' fears that "an Axis victory would have set science back a hundred years." Now, even the skeptical Gregory—convinced that he had "something essential to contribute to the effort to defeat Hitler"—was ready to join in mobilizing the idea of culture for the battle against totalitarianism (Bateson 1984:23).

Initially, however, they favored seeking ways to avert war, not aggressive intervention. In the last week of August 1939, still a period of American detachment, Mead sent a remarkable letter to Eleanor Roosevelt, signed by her but jointly composed with her husband, who was still a British subject. She tried to persuade the First Lady—and through her, the President—of the utility of anthropological analysis for handling Hitler. She and Gregory had already begun "to analyse things like the white papers which gave Chamberlain's account of 'Every time I said x, Hitler flew into a tantrum'—whereupon it appeared that he said x again." She had also seen "a short news clip of Hitler gazing at a map on which great autobahns were being built and divined that he was a frustrated builder, convinced that he had to tear down before he built" (BBWD:3). Writing "as a professional anthropologist," and buttressing her analysis of Hitler's personality with the knowledge "psychiatrists and political scientists" had of the "role of Hitler's peculiar psychological make-up in European affairs," Mead hoped her suggestions would enable Mrs. Roosevelt's husband to "cut the Gordian knot of the present world crisis." If the American president would play upon the German dictator's psychology, it would be possible to "enlist Hitler actively on the side of peace" and "halt the present march towards destruction." Because Hitler thought of himself as a "man of action . . . making continuous, constructive and fearless efforts," no threats or appeals "NOT to precipitate war can work"—because "in his conception of himself as a Man of Destiny, . . . to criticize [his role] becomes a blasphemy." Drawing on Bateson's ideas about circular systems, Mead suggested that "the only way to divert [Hitler] from an undesirable course is to divert him TOWARDS a desirable one which can be represented to be MORE magnificent. . . ." The President must put Hitler's past acts, including rearmament, "into a moral setting"—by affirming the injustice of the Versailles Treaty, admitting that rearmament had been "its logical outcome," returning to the Fourteen Points as a basis of negotiation, and arguing that "Hitler, himself, was the European leader who, by virtue of his great constructive efforts to build up his own country, had the chance now to build the peace of all Europe." Offered in the light of her "field experience of simpler social systems," Mead's advice was presented "as a strictly private contribution to the cause of peace" (GC 8/25/39).

After Hitler's invasion of Poland rendered the idea of substituting psychological for territorial appeasement irrelevant, Bateson left the United States for England to see what uses his mother country could find for his talents. Mead awaited the birth of their child in New York City. Bateson's visit proved frustrating—as Mead later suggested to a friend in Bali: "They don't want the social scientists in England" (GC: MM/K. Mershon n.d.). But it did allow him to return to the United States "with the full sense that he [had] taken all the necessary risks" (GC: MM/J. Dollard 1/18/41), and could explore the "possibility of using science constructively here" (BBWD:1). Previous doubts now quelled by a demonic dictator, an ambitiously activist wife, and his concerns for the future of their newborn daughter, Bateson was now disturbed by the "outcropping of negative attitudes" among some of his social science colleagues. Their "I don't think we ought to do anything like that—we don't want to appear to—perhaps under the circumstances it would be better if we took no steps" equivocations now seemed to him mocking echoes of his own prior attitude toward activism (PCFC: GB/B. Bateson 10/28/1940). Since neither Bateson nor Mead had been "caught up in the fashionable radicalism of the 1930s with its roseate views of the Soviet Union," they did not suffer "the paralysis that crippled so many liberals who were stunned and confused by the [1939] Soviet-German pact" (Mead 1942b:xxvi). Although some of her sociologist friends found her stance "unintelligible," Mead's position was "that as an American I hoped we would not become involved in the war, but that as a human being concerned with the well-being of the human race I hoped we would" (1979:148).

Within a few months, Bateson was able to report to his mother back in England that "democracy and psychology and anthropology [were] popping together at a great rate" (PCFC: GB/B. Bateson 10/28/40). By that time, he and Mead had become involved in the Committee for National Morale, a privately supported citizen's group organized by the Persian specialist and "intellectual entrepreneur," Arthur Upham Pope. Built on a "core of those who had been concerned with applications of psychology during World War I," the group was "an attempt to mobilize what would now be called the 'behavioral sciences' for the war effort" (Howard 1984:21–22). Among its members were the anthropologists Eliot Chapple and Theodore Lockhard, public opinion specialists Elmo Roper and George Gallup, psychologists Gordon Allport, Gardner Murphy, and Robert Yerkes, the psychiatrist Ernest Kris, and Lawrence Frank, who had been a "principle entrepreneur in the field of culture and personality." The Committee sponsored such projects as the Hungarian journalist Ladislas Farago's *German Psychological Warfare* (1942), and assumed responsibility for developing a "model for domestic communication between various grass-roots groups and sectors of the economy and a proposed new government agency." It also "began work on the application of the culture and personality approach as a way of predicting national behavior"—most notably, perhaps, in the English anthropologist Geoffrey Gorer's influential study of "Japanese Character Structure," which included the recommendation against any attack on the person or institution of the Japanese emperor (Mead 1979:148; Mead & Métraux 1953:402). Between the summer of 1940 and December 1941, Mead, Bateson, and their colleagues began to develop methods for "the study of culture at a distance," based not simply on existing documents, but on interview procedures "by which sophisticated human scientists . . . interview their counterparts, both nationals and in other countries, who had long experience with the peoples in whom we were interested, initially Germans and Japanese . . . [but later] those national groups that occupation had made inaccessible to direct observation—Greece, Burma, Thailand, the Netherlands, Romania, mainland China, and later still, Poland and the Soviet Union" (Mead 1979:148–49; 1953).

Early in 1941, Bateson optimistically reported to his mother that he and his social science colleagues were "gradually creeping up the administrative ladder." Even if their plans were not directly "implemented" by government, they were able to work privately and "see to it that many of our ideas get 'stolen' by the government" (PCFC: GB/B. Bateson 3/30/41). But federal bureaucracy proved stiffly resistant. Mead later reported that one of their cooperating colleagues once returned from Washington saying that Secretary of the Interior Ickes, Secretary of War Knox, and Vice President Wallace all supported the anthropologists' plans, but two "obscure men"—who turned out to be the director of the budget and his assistant—were opposed. "Clearly," she continued, these government bureaucrats belonged to "another era" than the "*entrepreneurs* of the use of science to defeat Hitler" (BBWD:5). In the summer of 1941, a colleague reported that the Army General Staff "thought we were butting in on military matters without consulting them" (SWG, CM: A. U. Pope/MM 7/19/41). Harold Lasswell, who was already in government service, "said none of our memos were worth anything and they were the joke of Washington" (SWG, CM: A. U. Pope/MM & GB 8/5/41).

American entry into the war was to bring the would-be policy advisors into closer relationship with the government bureaucracy. When it became "increasingly clear" to the anthropologists and younger members of her group, Mead recalled, that understanding of "how Washington functioned in 1914–1918 was inadequate for charting a course in 1941," they decided "that one of us would have to go to Washington and find out how the system worked." World events resolved the matter: on the very day of the Pearl Harbor attack, Mead received an invitation to come to the capital to serve as executive secretary of the Committee on Food Habits, an offshoot of the National Research Council's Division of Anthropology and Psychology. To fill the gap in communication between anthropologists and government, Mead used her position as "a base from which I would coordinate various kinds of anthropological input into federal programs" (Mead 1979:150).

During the same period, other developments involved anthropologists more closely in the war effort. The provost marshall general organized a meeting, with Bateson in attendance, which led to the establishment of a "whole network of university-based area institutes" as "centers for the training of regional specialists for problems of occupation, military government, and postwar international activities" (Mead 1979:151). After Pearl Harbor, the members of the Committee for National Morale were "co-opted, one by one," as new wartime agencies were established. Gorer went to the Office of War Information first, and later to the British Embassy; Ruth Benedict moved from the O.W.I. Foreign Information Service into its Bureau of Overseas Intelligence, where she prepared a series of national-character studies (Modell 1983:268–69). After a brief stint working for the Office of Strategic Services and the Navy teaching International Pidgen English to Pacific-bound Navy men at Columbia University, Bateson joined the O.S.S. as a "psychological planner" (Howard 1984:231, 238). As Mead later recalled, "by 1944 anthropologists and members of associated disciplines with a culture and personality approach were firmly established within the specifically wartime agencies; styles of access had been well established, and it was possible to continue to provide relevant policy input" (Mead 1979:152–53).

Anthropology and the Defense of Democracy: Two Variations on a Theme

The Mead-Bateson wartime collaboration revealed an unrelenting emotional commitment to and an intellectual defense of democracy. Each played a different role: Mead, as the nurturer and public interpreter of the culture of democracy; Bateson, as the logician of democracy and totalitarianism. The anthropological traditions they represented, then synthesized in Bali, reappeared—again as a synthesis—in their wartime anthropology. Mead's work on culture and personality, now invested with new dynamism by Bateson's notions of interaction, circularity, and learning theory—and clarified by his logical skills—informed both their continuing collaborations and their individual projects. They shared a common ground; still, philosophical, personal, and academic differences between the two affected not only how they responded to the war, but the projects they entertained.

In Mead's case, value, emotion, and intellect found an easy partnership; to her, it seemed quite appropriate for the objective scientist to act as a morally responsible political agent. Mead's interest in character formation, and earlier successful efforts to communicate with general audiences, drew her immediately to problems of individual behavior and morale on the home front. While still in New Guinea, she indicated awareness of where her theoretical research might lead: "Bali had a lot to contribute to positive ideas about planning a new world—from the bottom instead of from the top. . . . Bali also demonstrated the advantages of running a society at right angles to the individual life, instead of forever counting upon enlisting each citizen's major motivations to get the streets cleaned and the walls mended" (GC: MM/E. Rosenberg [1938]). "Pattern" continued to be Mead's major concern, and it was the American pattern with all its detail and diversity which she hoped to preserve. She feared terribly the totalitarian disordering or authoritarian control of culturally patterned behavior, so she organized her home-front activities, morale building, writing, lecturing, and food research to reinforce what she understood as the American pattern—a democratic way of life, pluralistic, individualistic, and decentralized in its decision making. Mead adopted the position of a committee on which she served whose charge it was to develop a special exhibit on democracy for the Museum of Modern Art. She decidedly opposed the use of propagandistic appeals to the "primary emotions" of hate, fear, and so on. We cannot, her committee stated in 1941, use "fascist methods on a people whose character structure is primarily democratic, who have drunk in a preference for freedom and independent action with their mother's milk" (SWG, RM: memo Morale Comm. Jan./1941). She thought of the anthropologist's role as that of an intervener; and so she channeled her activities through grassroots groups, committees, or networks—microcosms to fit the American whole.

All of Mead's applied anthropology during the war—whether it had to do with morale, food research, or the study of culture at a distance—related to her idea of character structure. From the beginning, she grounded research on nutrition and home-front nutrition projects in her understanding of the

American character. Mead claimed that all Americans had a third-generation character structure; the metaphor was intended more to describe a cultural function than an historical reality. All Americans are third generation because the American character, like the assimilating third generation's character, must depend upon the standards of the age group, not parental control, for direction. Americans, she observed, trust themselves more than their parents. This "contra-suggestibility to parents is the price we have paid," she noted, for a society "which is composed of representatives of every European nation." Without it, "we could not have assimilated the millions of first and second generation Americans"; upon it, "we have founded the greatness of democracy" (1940a:43).

Mead's character analysis had consequences for the policy she helped to develop. In war or in peace, Americans do not have respect for authority, and they chafe "under impositions or appeals from the top" (Mead 1940a:43). Since "fathers don't count," Americans could not take orders from Washington; federal plans for organizing war efforts must be based upon and adjusted to particular community needs, upon local block plans and elected block leaders (Mead 1942a). The way to get Americans to do things, to fight wars, to respect the democratic way of life, to nourish themselves properly, was to let each stand on his own two feet and work with other community members.

This understanding penetrated all aspects of Mead's work, from administrative organization and research projects, to actual implementation of plans. The Executive Committee of the Food Habits group consisted not of federal officials, but of scholars and scientists, persons who had never been directly involved in government service before. Mead's decision to decentralize research to various centers in the nation was economical, but it also expressed her belief in the importance of citizen participation. Her studies of different regions and ethnic groups throughout the nation acknowledged another American pattern—diversity within uniformity.

Her original policy directive was "to make scientifically sound recommendations to the appropriate governmental agencies upon the methods of controlling the cultural forces which cause them to change" (Guthe 1943:15). The war also required coping with food rationing and shortages, and Mead's concept of how to approach these unaccustomed constraints was predictable. Since food habits were "systematically inter-related with other standardized behaviors in the same culture," the strength of any given item of behavior (e.g., preference for meat or aversion to fish) must be related to a "total complex of behavior" (Mead 1943b:21). Her choice of research projects reflected this concept. She asked Kurt Lewin at the University of Iowa, for example, to trace the relationship of food habits to a variety of preferences, including as instances the Puritan tendencies to connect healthful food with unappetizing food, and to use food for reward and punishment.

An investigation conducted by the Committee showed that in an emergency situation, and in a nation with varied culture groups living in close proximity, a practical solution to varied group tastes would be to cook single foods separately and serve them with a minimum of condiments; all foods would then be identifiable by people with different food preferences. Mead traced the American demand for cafeterias, and other food practices highlighting individual decision, to American cultural diversity. The mix of "mutually incompatible food habits" required individual choice—a direction also compatible with the predominant character structure. Her understanding of culture pattern, enriched by Bateson's notion of circularity, led her to see clear connections between food, politics, and social behavior (1943a:23). "Whereas in the past," she noted, "Johnny had to eat up his potatoes and his vegetables just because he did not like them, now he has to eat them because they are good for him"—because the kind of character "which learns to eat its spinach, which it hates, to get its dessert, which it knows is bad for it, but which authority reluctantly concedes as a reward for virtuous behavior, is not the stuff of which vigorous democracy is made." Mead used Lewin's experiments to demonstrate her point: when individuals were not lectured at, but allowed to choose, Lewin found that changes in food habits came about more easily (Mead 1943a:39).

Mead's strategies for changing food habits recognized the necessity to avoid a strong government presence in food control programs: that presence, after all, could be perceived as the "denying father" by men and women reared as democrats. Civilian block leaders, who passed ideas on to housewives and answered their questions about everything from rationing to the use of subsidies, would draw housewives into the decision-making process; housewives, then, would not feel like victims of government or of greedy farmers (SWG, RM: Food Habits Reports, unpub., n.d.). Lewin's studies also reinforced Mead's inclination to recognize diversity and self-initiative in attempting to create change. He demonstrated that ethnic background was as important as class in determining food habits, and that group pressure was more effective than printed or spoken words as a way of changing them (Lewin 1943).

Bateson did not share Mead's taste for the blend of politics and science, but the Fascist threat enabled him to overcome both personal and scientific reserve. As the secretary of the Morale Committee, Bateson could create his own agenda. Thus he wrote a pamphlet on American passivity and defeatism, offered an analysis of the "memo" as an instrument of bureaucratic communication, and attempted to market a game that would "educate the players to realize the outstanding differences between dictatorship and democracy— that the two systems play by different rules and are subject to different sorts of disasters" (PCFC: GB/B. Bateson 10/28/41). Most of this work bore Bateson's unmistakable imprint. The strategic psychology underlying his game is a case in point. The German ideology embodied notions of "linear causation in society (hierarchy, allocation of authority at the top of the hierarchical structure and of responsibility at the bottom)," which he contrasted with "circular systems of causation, 'feed-back' systems of wireless valves, organisms, democratic social systems, etc." The Germans did not believe that "ultimate victory" was possible; war and peace were conceptualized as a continuing unity, not as separate states of events. But if the German High Command were convinced of the necessity for defeat—only a temporary one, of course—its game plan would be to secure an Anglo-American occupation, not a Russian one. The Russians would "smash" German notions of superiority; Americans would simply "laugh" at them. Americans "would never fully accept" that the Germans really believed in their ideology, much less act on it; they would, therefore, be the preferred occupiers. The next move would be the Americans'. What strategy should they adopt? One option would be to frustrate German efforts for an Anglo-American occupation. Another would be to exterminate the German ideology. To accomplish this, Americans would have to be trained to understand "what all this ideology stuff is about," said Bateson: "essentially they will have to know what human culture means" (SWG, CM: memo 2/5/1942).

Another of Bateson's memos, "Cultural Anthropology and Morale," applied interaction theory to international hostility. Whether "the parties concerned be two nations engaged in an armaments race; or two political parties . . . or two classes . . . or native born Americans criticizing some foreign group," we meet constantly processes which appear to be "vicious circles." The problem of national unity is "essentially a problem of handling vicious circles of this type," and Marxian and Nazi propagandists had "developed to a fine art the technique of aggravating such tensions." In contrast, the social scientist looked at social tensions "with somewhat less of dogma and somewhat more of science," arguing that "tensions of this sort are more usually not progressive." Hostility "does not increase to a point of total disruption but persists instead at a certain fluctuating level." Indeed, "the tension of this hostility is part of the dynamics of society, an essential part of the motivation system which makes the social machinery work"; tensions were "neutralized" by the existence of symmetrical and complementary patterns working in "actually opposed" directions. Whereas the Marxist propagandist model posits a period of increasing class tensions "followed by a climax and beyond that elysium"—an old European political and religious pattern—the anthropologist is aware that this climax pattern is by no means the same for all groups. The German tendency for complementary tensions offers a "different dream of climax from Americans," and therefore "the time of great warlike efforts as well as the motivation of those efforts will be different from the Americans," and the "two nations subject to different sorts of psychological weakness" (SWG, RM: Comm. Natl. Morale 2/17/41).

Bateson also offered a description of "uniformity" and diversity character-istically his own. The Americans' dislike of totalitarianism was bound up with their dislike of a dictator's ability to insist that everyone do the *same* thing. But, Bateson reminded, a democratic system is also a culture system and "all cultures presume some degree of uniformity among the individuals who take part in them." Not enough attention had been given to the kind of uniform-ity that democracies desire, probably because the matter provided some con-ceptual difficulties. These, of course, fascinated Bateson, who observed: "the uniformity needed in a democracy is more abstract than that with which the totalitarians are content. We strive for a system, for a frame within the bounds of which very different opinions may occur side by side." The uniformity underlying democracy, he postulated, may be in a sense the same order as that underlying language. A uniform language allows individuals to commu-nicate, but within that communication process, they can say exactly opposite things (SWG, RM: memo [1940–42]).

Although Bateson later spoke of Mead's studies from a distance as "culture cracking," he did a bit of it himself. Working at the Museum of Modern Art, he analyzed old German movies

> for the light which they throw on what makes Nazis tick and what sort of prog-nosis one can make about how they will behave in certain circumstances—for example, defeat, etc.—It's really all the same sort of work that we used to do in New Guinea and Bali—rather more hectic—and rather less thorough—using the best hunches that we can think of instead of waiting for complete docu-mentation—but still we hope a good deal better than lay intuition. (PCFC: GB/E. Bateson Jan./1943)

His pioneering analysis of the 1933 German film *Hitlerjunge Quex*, about a member of the Hitler Youth and his family, showed how both the content and the symbolic organization of the film's structure reflected the Nazi way of life (Bateson 1953).

It was only after he moved to Washington in 1943 that Bateson's anthro-pology became more directly connected to policy implementation. After join-ing the O.S.S., he was dispatched to the Pacific, where he spent two years in Ceylon, Burma, India, and China. Among the perhaps "tall tales" he told of his Pacific tour was a story of dying Burma's Irrawaddy River red, a porten-tous fulfillment of "some apocalyptic local prophecy" (Bateson 1984:41). The project he found most interesting during his Asian assignment allowed him to apply his idea of symmetrical "schismogenesis": simulating a Japanese radio station, he created exaggerated Japanese war propaganda in Burma and Thailand, an effort designed to cause a breakdown in enemy intelligence. Re-turning after the war much distressed by the O.S.S. treatment of natives, Bateson returned as well to his original negative assessment of applied an-

Gregory Bateson, while serving in Southeast Asia for the O.S.S., 1944. (Courtesy The Institute of Intercultural Studies, Inc.)

thropology (Lipset 1980:174; M. C. Bateson, personal communication 4/10/85). It was, he wrote to A. R. Radcliffe-Brown, "interesting in patches— . . . but a total waste of time so far as any visible effect on planning and politics. At most I may have poured a little oil on the Anglo-Amer[ican] misunderstandings around the Mountbatten HQ. And I brought home with me a profound cynicism about all policymaking folk" (PC: GB/ARB 8/21/46).

Looking at Bateson's wartime work as a whole, we may say that his fascination with system drew him, like Mead, toward communication. But the contrast in styles was striking. Bateson's efforts were as obstructionist as Mead's were nurturing: while she was involved "in enriching the communicative networks available in our society," he was "involved in the introduction of misinformation and the violation of patterns of communication in the hope of thereby damaging the enemy" (Bateson 1984:230). His role for the O.S.S.—to propagandize the enemy—implied both the identification and the disruption of system. Applying his theory of "schismogenesis" to psychological warfare, he found opportunities to test his notion that the anthropologist himself is part of the interactive cultural system: as propaganda maker, Bateson not only observed; he also took part in the communications systems which he helped to create or hoped to disrupt. Aside from his professed cynicism about "policymaking folk," he found the experience of covert interactive intervention disturbing (M. C. Bateson, personal communication 4/10/85). After the war, such "black" activities seemed, to Mead as well, "always destructive of later national purposes, even if they seemed to serve immediate wartime goals" (Mead 1979:153–54).

Trust in Democracy—And Keep Your Powder Dry

Mead disdained covert "black practices," but, in an apparent paradox, she accepted the occasional necessity to control public exposure of scientific ideas and information. In her public discourse, acting in her adopted role as the voice of anthropology, she sometimes subdued ideas which threatened to contravene, complicate, confuse, or weaken the broad outlines of messages she wished to convey. Here, she was perhaps overly confident, but not dictatorial, illogical, or inconsistent. As anthropologist, Mead understood and respected the need to evaluate the context in which information was presented: How, she asked, would specific information relate to "pattern"? As a liberal democrat, the "pattern" she hoped to preserve was democracy. She referred particular decisions to reveal or suppress information—and *when* to reveal or suppress it—to this prior goal. The most familiar instance is a decision she made in the early 1930s to withhold "publishing . . . to the world" her idea that different cultures systematically emphasized innate temperamental qualities, because emphasis on "inborn difference between human beings" was so "politically loaded" (Mead 1972:220). Mead's sensitivity to timing and context is dramatically apparent in the contrast between two of her major popular works: *Sex and Temperament*, published in 1935, implies almost complete cultural determination of sex roles, while her postwar book, *Male and Female* (1949b) acknowledges a dialectic of biology and culture. In 1941, Mead articulated her understanding of her role as public informant in a letter to a fellow scientist, the social psychologist J. L. Moreno. Discussing the culture-and-temperament hypothesis, she emphasized the "moral obligations of the scientist in a moment like the present":

> I feel that to emphasize hereditary factors more than is absolutely necessary for scientific accuracy may be doing incalculable harm. The first response of the average person to any accepted scheme of temperamental classification is to construct "we-groups" and "you-groups" (we saw that in the use of Jung's categories for instance), it is most important to avoid at present, especially within the social sciences, any sort of schism. I believe that if this theory were advanced now . . . it might do great harm. (PF 4/8/41)

Instead, she and Bateson would concentrate on character formation, leaving biological questions for a later date (PF: MM/J. Moreno 4/8/41).

And Keep Your Powder Dry, Mead's major piece of public anthropological advocacy during the war, contained the same kinds of compromises with scientific objectivity. Although future generations have shunted it aside as a worn-out relic of early culture-and-personality studies, it is worth understanding the book as a political text rooted in a passionate effort to maintain democracy as the only way of life that made scientific inquiry possible. The title's reference to a Puritan heritage—Cromwell's revolutionary rallying cry: "Put Your Trust in God—and Keep Your Powder Dry"—already suggested the direction that Mead's compromises would take. The conventional Boasian critiques of racialism were culturally pluralist: they argued for the relativity of cultural behavior and the legitimacy of alternative forms. But Mead was now concerned with emphasizing the dominant unifying features of American culture. Aiming to rally American democrats to become enthusiastic defenders of American democracy, she muted the racial conflicts and the ethnic diversity of a people who, she felt, lacked a positive sense of their own national identity and needed a social scientist to help them find it. On the grounds that its racial caste system and heritage of slavery conflicted with the dominant egalitarian character structure which she identified in order to preserve, Mead excluded the South from her deliberations—refusing to retreat in the face of a business-minded publisher's warning that the omission would limit sales below the Mason-Dixon line (WMC: T. Hobson/MM 8/14/42).

Mead was aware of the implications of this choice for her science and for her politics. Indeed, her wartime analysis of the American character, like her other war efforts, cannot be understood apart from the cultural and political crisis her country faced. In a later article on ethnicity and anthropology in America, Mead herself treated anthropology as part of the larger American consciousness, noting the parallels between the dominant cultural attitudes and the American anthropologist's views toward ethnicity. For both scholars and laymen, the American dilemma resided in contrary and shifting commitments to cultural pluralism and ethnic assimilation, to separatist and integrationist or melting-pot ideas (Mead 1975:173–97). Mead herself was no exception to this rule. When patriotic unity was required, when democracy found itself at odds with Nazi racism and totalitarianism, when the sons and grandsons of immigrants were being asked to sacrifice their lives in Europe, she drew a circle around the question of ethnic pluralism and defined the problem of American identity as the prior question; and this was a question as much of politics as of culture. Writing for teachers in the journal *Progressive Education* in 1941, Mead warned that the cultural differences that had always made the American child uneasy "today become doubly troubling, threatening to drive wedges not only between himself and his home, but also between himself and his fellows" (92). Indians, blacks, Southerners

—even Italians, Jews, and Germans—were not present in her major treatise on the American character, and with good reason. A nation at war could not be a nation divided. In a nation of immigrants, the immigrants were now given short shrift.

Winning the war was, and had to be, America's primary objective. Mead's reconstruction of the American character designed for public consumption suited that purpose better than some scientific effort to recreate America as it was, with all its regional and ethnic particularisms and racial conflicts. She was more interested in reconstructing America as it needed to be. She aimed to move from concept to action, and this meant she was interested not in ethnicity per se, but in the relationship between character structure and political form: American character, therefore, was a character based upon choice, upon denial of authority. Totalitarian rule threatened freedom of choice and hence American identity itself.

Mead's scientific opinion on race and ethnicity remained consistent throughout her long career—a direct outgrowth of Boasian training and work done earlier on intelligence testing as a Columbia University graduate psychology student. Americans, Eskimos, Indians, Balinese, or Chinese are what they are, she argued, not because of blood, but because of upbringing. Responding to an inquiry of Eleanor Roosevelt's in 1943, she reaffirmed that "there is no difference which has ever been demonstrated between the potential capacities of the different races of the world . . . [or] proof that any psychological abilities accompany . . . marks of racial difference." But in a wartime context, the conclusions she drew from egalitarianism were now assimilationist, rather than pluralist:

> There will be no democracy and no free world society until no human being is judged—or allowed to be proud—of any single thing which he (or she) did not *do*, himself. This has, of course, even wider ramifications than that of race. Not only must race, sex, nationality, religious affiliation (when it is a matter of birth), residence in any given spot in the earth's surface (when one lives there merely because one's parents did) be given up, but also even the very fact that one's ancestors fought for freedom and tolerance and the breakdown of just such barriers as these—that too, must be given up. The grandchild of the abolitionist and the grandchild of a slaver must be able to stand side by side and expect to be taken on their own terms, just as the white and yellow and black man must be able to stand side by side and taken for what they are, themselves. This is not a statement of religious belief; it is merely a statement of the logic of democracy. As long as any single person's pride and position depend upon his possession—by inheritance and through no effort of his own —of something that another, because of inheritance, is debarred from obtaining—we will all live in a prison, but it is a prison made by man, a social prison, not a prison which reflects any biological reality. (GC: MM/E. Roosevelt Jan./ 1943)

Here and in the body of her wartime public utterances, Mead's idea of American character rests not only on cultural analysis but on ideological and political commitment. In this she was not unique; as Edward Purcell has demonstrated, during the 1930s and 1940s, and even before, many American intellectuals—Mead, the philosophers John Dewey, Sidney Hook, and Morris R. Cohen, and the historian Jacques Barzun among them—came to equate American culture with democracy, not democracy as a social fact, but democracy as an abstract idea. Counterpointed to the distasteful and ruthless alternatives of the German, and later the Russian, dictatorships, American culture, a practically functioning democracy, came to be understood by Mead and other American intellectuals as normative (Purcell 1973:206, 213; Hollinger 1975). By this logic, Mead and others equated democracy—an experimental, open culture, a diverse and pluralistic culture—with science and scientific method. Absolutism in any form, but particularly in the form of the totalitarian state, represented the stultification of science. So, for Mead, and many of the American intellectuals, the war against Hitler was not only a war for democracy but also a war for free inquiry (Purcell 1973:202-3).

The war years forced Margaret Mead, Gregory Bateson, Ruth Benedict, and many of their contemporaries toward a formulation of the appropriate relationship of science and social ethics. As cultural relativists and empiricists who, as a matter of method, value, and politics, had rejected a priori absolutes, they were now faced with the dilemma of defending democracy absolutely. They thought of themselves as objective scientists committed to free expression of ideas; but now they found themselves faced with the dilemma of whether they would play a part in manipulation of ideas. Should they reveal, share, or suppress scientific information? Should they, as creators or discoverers of scientific data, intrude at all in the free market of ideas? Should they, as anthropologists, intrude in fully evolved cultural patterns? Finally, as scientists and as anthropologists, they felt obliged to clarify the proper role of authority and the surrogates for authority—teachers, parents, and scientists themselves—in a democratic state dedicated to the principles of unfettered choice and individual expression.

In the end, it seems that Mead, Bateson, Benedict, and many other social scientists, despite their protests, made a pragmatic choice: they chose patriotism over passivity, and saw democracy as the prior, and necessary condition for scientific detachment. If Bateson and Benedict were slow in revealing their position, by 1940 Mead had made hers public: "It reduces to a problem of values, a problem of choice. When I ask for an honorable world, I am a citizen of my country, a member of my culture, a sentient, judging individual, not a scientist." Having made this distinction and this choice, she could "step back into my special discipline . . . dismiss the whole question of value entirely and settle down to the problem" (1940c).

The Ethical Presuppositions of Wartime
Applied Anthropology

At a 1941 symposium, just months before Pearl Harbor and before any of them had gained actual wartime experience with intelligence or propaganda, Mead, Bateson, and others of their peers (including Ruth Benedict, Geoffrey Gorer, Clyde Kluckhohn, and Dorothy Lee) began to think in public about the ethics of applied science. Their session at the Interdisciplinary Conference on Science, Philosophy, and Religion in Their Relation to the Democratic Way of Life provides the most systematic available documentation of the ethics of applied anthropology in the war era. An assembly composed mostly of scientists, theologians, and philosophers—including Enrico Fermi, Albert Einstein, and John Dewey—the conferees came together hoping to reinforce mutual commitments to democratic living, "to promote respect and understanding between the disciplines involved and to create among them a consensus concerning the universal character of truth," an essential task for scholars alarmed by the totalitarian threat to democracy (Brooks 1942:2; Howard 1984:220).

The proceedings make clear that Mead, Benedict, and to a lesser extent Bateson developed a wartime theory of democratic culture which was the anthropological analogue of John Dewey's philosophical pragmatism. Boas' students had a special affinity for Dewey. They read his work in their graduate seminars at Columbia University, which Dewey had made his academic home since 1904 (Mead 1972:205; Leaf 1979:186–88). The affinity was mutual, for Dewey had acknowledged his debts to cultural anthropology in his recently published work *Freedom and Culture* (1939). That book's message underlay much of the discussion at the conference session on anthropology. Dewey argued that democracy provided the only fertile environment for science, and that democracy, and democratic culture, would succeed only if they employed the methods of science. "Freedom of inquiry, toleration of diverse views, freedom of communication, the distribution of what is found out to every individual as the ultimate intellectual consumer are involved in the democratic as in the scientific method" (1939:102). Dewey argued that the future of democracy depended upon the incorporation within culture of the scientific attitude of reflection, testing, and observation; the scientific attitude must become part of the "ordinary equipment" of the "ordinary individual" (151). This was the only guarantee against propaganda, the only safeguard for intelligent public opinion. Rejecting the separation of science and morals, of ideas from action, Dewey's pragmatic philosophy offered compatible guidelines to the socially and politically concerned scientists at the conference. In fact, in *Freedom and Culture* he expanded his argument to a theory of social action and ethics. It was the role of the socially responsible scientist to make a moral choice, to act on the belief that science itself had "intrinsic moral potentiality," to promote the "contagious diffusion of the scientific method" (153). For knowledge—competent inquiry—could determine what is of value and what is not, and the means to achieve these goals. Democratic ends demanded democratic methods for their realization (153). The depressing alternative, Dewey observed, would be rule by nonrational or antirational forces, not reasoned knowledge—a direction more compatible with absolutism and totalitarianism than with democracy (140).

Mead's presentation, "The Comparative Study of Culture and the Purposive Cultivation of Democratic Values"—an anthropologist's elaboration of Dewey's position—formed the centerpiece for anthropological discussion at the 1941 conference (1942c:56–69). Seeking practical solutions to abstract questions—as was her custom—Mead asked: Was planning consistent with the democratic idea of individual autonomy? And, assuming that planning was possible, how can we know it to be morally correct? How can we assure the moral responsibility of the scientist in planning or changing society? Gregory Bateson, as usual, defined the philosophical problem for anthropology. Looking for logical connections, this time between totalitarianism, war, and science, he defined the war itself as a struggle over the mind, over the control of knowledge (see Purcell 1973:202–3). This war, he wrote,

> is now a life-or-death struggle over the role which the social sciences shall play in the ordering of human relationships. It is hardly an exaggeration to say . . . this war is ideologically about just this—the role of the social sciences. Are we to reserve the techniques and the right to manipulate peoples as the privilege of a few planning, goal-oriented and power hungry individuals to whom the instrumentality of science makes a natural appeal? Now that we have techniques, are we, in cold blood, going to treat people as things? Or what are we going to do with these techniques? (1942:84)

Not surprisingly, Mead and her anthropologist commentators evidenced a relativist ethics—as in her example of approved infanticide among the child-loving Arapesh when survival needs prevented parents from sustaining a new infant life. But neither her cultural relativism nor her field experience resolved the perceived problem of the scientist's role in public policy. Less willing to accept total moral relativism, Gorer (1942) and Kluckhohn (1942) urged at least an empirical search for "ultimate" moral values, a strategy in keeping with Dewey's prescriptions. The Society for Applied Anthropology would struggle with this problem later, but in 1941 the issue, though perceived, remained unresolved (Mead 1942c). In their attempt to resolve this question, both Mead and Benedict clearly moved toward an absolute commitment to what Dewey called "humanistic democracy," a democracy based not upon habit and tradition but upon the moral value of faith in the potentialities of human nature.

"Democracy," said Dewey, "means the belief that humanistic culture *should* prevail," and this is a moral proposition (1939:124). Mead and Benedict added to cultural relativism their total commitment to the central assumption of the conference: the value of the "supreme worth and moral responsibility of the individual person" before the state (Mead 1942c:57–59).

Apart from this absolute moral choice, Mead and Benedict rejected all absolutes and absolute goals, for they emphasized that in a democracy means are as important as, and inseparable from, ends. In Deweyan terms, the ends are *in* the methods themselves. All "blueprints," all working toward "ends"— even well-intentioned ends such as "collective security" or "isolationism"— would result in ruthless manipulation and control over others by diplomats, politicians, scientists, and others in authority. This would result in a negation of democracy, of the spontaneity of democratic process. "Only," Mead argued, "by working in terms of values which are limited to defining a *direction*, is it possible to use scientific methods in the control of the process [of change] without the negation of the moral autonomy of the human spirit" (1942c:69). "Directional" activities—as opposed to controlled or Nazi propagandistic activities—Benedict insisted, "modify social institutions or educate the individual" so that his power to cope—whether as voter, leader, worker, or scientist—is increased. So, choice resides directly with the individual, and even if change occurs, it is a change to which humans can adapt. The principle of direction grounds decisions in cultural habits, and "taking its cue from the current situation," this principle can adapt itself to change without disaster (Benedict 1942:69–70). Mead's advice to teachers and to other "cultural surrogates" was, of course, consistent with these premises. The authoritarian classroom was culturally incongruent with the democratic personality (1940b; 1941). The process of both democratization and Americanization, therefore, involved redirecting a child's loyalty from the home to the group, through the school to the community. In this way, self-directed behavior would prevail over learned authoritarian behavior. Museums, food habits, school, and politics were all connected in the circular system of democratic culture.

Bateson sometimes looked east, not west, for his inspiration; but although he was often as abstract as his wife was practical, frequently there was a meeting of minds. When Mead recommended a new habit of thought which "looks for direction" and "value" in the chosen act rather than in defined goals, Bateson saw this as a "kind of philosophical paradox, a Taoism or Christian aphorism: that we discard purpose in order to achieve purpose" (1942:81, 83). He reached back to Bali for a cognitive model to demonstrate the possibility of Mead's idea. We could adopt the Balinese pattern, learn to alter our sense of time sequence and to focus upon acts, not goals. But unlike the Balinese, whom he described as motivated by avoidance of a "nameless fear," we would be motivated by an immanent sense of ultimate reward, of "unlocated hope of enormous achievement." Bateson continued:

For such hope to be effective, the achievement need scarcely be defined. All we need to be sure of is that, at any moment, achievement may be just around the corner, and, true or false, this can never be tested. We have got to be like those few artists and scientists who work with this urgent sort of inspiration, the urgency that comes from feeling that great discovery, the answer to all our problems, or great creation, the perfect sonnet, is always only just beyond our reach, or like the mother of a child who feels that, provided she pay constant enough attention, there is real hope that her child may be that infinitely rare phenomenon, a great and happy person. (1942:97)

Applying hypotheses he had developed in Bali about "deutero-leaning" (learning about learning) Bateson postulated, in an echo of their other wartime projects, that the significance of Mead's proposal for maintaining democracy was that it fostered a sense of individual autonomy. An individual's character structure, his attitude toward himself and toward his experience, is shaped "not only by what he learns but *how* he learns it" (1942:87–88). If he is brought up in an authoritarian society, or contexts in which decisions are made for him, his habits of mind will be profoundly different than if he learns under conditions of spontaneity and insight.

Elsewhere, Bateson and Mead, distinguishing between morale building in a democracy and Nazi propaganda, clarified even further the significance of means. Democracies may alter culture processes so that individuals are affected, but they do not operate directly upon identified individuals—such as Jews or Gypsies—and democracies use situations and processes to which the people as a whole can respond constructively. Totalitarian governments, on the other hand, operate in terms of identifiable persons who are sent to labor or concentration camps, or forced into certain professions (1941:206–20). In the postwar international theater, operation of this democratic principle would mean, for example, that instead of interfering directly in a reconstructed Germany, the Allies could alter the defeated nation's economic position by altering the general economic balance; then, the German people as a whole could respond (Mead 1949a:9–10). Mead, Bateson, and their colleagues were concerned not only with the abuse of power, but with the power of method to abuse.

In 1941, while Mead and Benedict strove to find an anchoring for democracy in a kind of flexible redirection of the American pattern, always encouraging a shift from instrumental or absolute goals to process, Bateson was content to act as critical observer of the cognitive strategies implied in their theories and cultural patterns. Mead and Benedict felt they could tamper with the social system, making adjustments here and there. Bateson operated under a different order of logic. His was an anthropology and philosophy of thought, not action. But all three agreed on some things. All of them thought of free inquiry as logically consistent with and necessary for democracy (Mead 1942b:177–78). In fact, their notion of holistic pattern led Mead and Benedict

to conflate democracy, science, and even the American character itself, view-
ing each as consistent with or even as logical parts of the whole. If this sounds
Deweyan, it is not clear who borrowed from whom. For Dewey's flirtation
with ethical relativism and his pragmatism were themselves grounded in ideas
of culture, cultural diversity, and empirical observation, all of them to be found
in Boasian anthropology. Like the Boasians, Dewey was committed to democratic principles. And, like them, he discovered those principles in culture
and action, not in some abstract a priori notions—which he, along with Mead,
Bateson, and Benedict, believed to be logically and culturally consistent with
absolutist philosophy and the totalitarian state.

"Something Happened": Culture and Commitment after Hiroshima

What is to be made of the wartime acts and thoughts of these anthropologists, newly defining the ethical basis of their actions, tempted but ambivalent about the exercise of power? In retrospect, they exhibit a kind of naive
grandiosity only the uninitiated practitioners of an applied science could afford. The Great Depression, Mead explained, convinced her and her colleagues
in the newer disciplines of anthropology, sociology, psychology, and psychiatry of the failure of the "older sciences of history, political science and
economics" (1965:xii). In 1942 Mead conjectured that "social science, which
is not a mere lifeless aping of the mannerism of the natural sciences . . . can
give us premises by which we can set men free" (1942b:181–82). With this optimism, Mead and her generation of anthropologists entered World War II.
Earlier brief excursions into policymaking and public controversy during World
War I and the New Deal had scarcely prepared them for the limits of their
science or for the compromises, conflicts, and contradictions they would
confront.

The naiveté of this generation of anthropologists—perhaps shaded with
hubris—may have resulted from the anthropological method itself. As Mead
herself pointed out in an essay on history and anthropology, while history
dealt with documents and defunct cultures, anthropology interacted with informants and examined existing cultures, living cultures over which power
could be exercised (1951:3–13). Despite studied detachment and appreciation
for simpler societies, the anthropologist's stance as observer allowed a sense
of control, even superiority. And perhaps this is what gave so many of this
generation the courage of their convictions, allowing them to believe that
knowledge gained in simple primitive cultures then transferred to the home
front, to complex societies, even to the world forum, could solve human
problems—and that those on the side of democracy, including themselves,
would use it only in positive ways. But if such assumptions were reasonable

in 1941, there was also something innocently arrogant about them. The anthropologists' sensitivity to the power of both democratic and totalitarian methods as means in themselves—a transference to the political realm of their conviction of the power of scientific method—only confirms their overly enthusiastic confidence in scientific capability. That Mead felt this billowing confidence in her method is made obvious by her dramatically appropriate reaction to its apparent failure.

After the bomb was dropped on Hiroshima and Nagasaki in 1945 Mead claimed that she tore up her sequel to *And Keep Your Powder Dry*, her discourse on the new world order, knowing "no sentence written with that knowledge of man's capacity could be meshed onto any sentence written the week before" (Mead 1965:xii). It was no longer possible, no longer meaningful, simply to explain that war was a manmade instrument, done and un-doable by man, or simply to urge Americans to have faith in science, to "Trust in God and Keep Your Powder Dry." At that terrible moment, Mead's notion of coherent pattern must have seemed inadequate to the task of living in a nuclear age. Ultimately indefatigable, she readjusted her understanding to the new pattern that science had wrought, refocusing her lens of inquiry upon the problem of culture, rapid change, and commitment in the postwar world.

In 1970, when Mead published *Culture and Commitment: A Study of the Generation Gap*, she affirmed the difference between then and now, between her own generation and those born after the war: the two groups, she believed, were like two different cultures. What was it like, she asked of youth in 1970, to live in a world where war was obsolete? What was it like to have grown up with the ever-present possibility of nuclear annihilation, with the knowledge that humans have created this possibility for themselves? Looking back today upon her peers and her time, we can sense how different it must have been for a generation of scientists living in a world where war remained a practical diplomatic instrument, where "good nations" battled "evil," where freedom confronted tyranny, where it was possible to believe in the superiority of democracy—in a world where social science could be dedicated to winning and fighting for the "good," where it was still possible to believe in both the power and the responsible use of science.

As Mead and Bateson—our forebears—moved into the nuclear age, an age in which new generations *and* new nations have developed their own ethical and political consciousness, they continued to offer two measures of anthropological consciousness. In the end, perhaps an accounting for cybernetic systems gone awry is proving more powerful as a system of understanding—if not as a system of ethics—for a nuclear age than one grounded in Boasian pattern and Deweyan pragmatism. Bateson's anthropology, an epistemology based upon new or—as his daughter justly reminds us—very ancient principles, crossed more gracefully into an atomic age in which the order of order itself was in question (Bateson 1984:96).

Looking back upon their wartime behavior, Mead described herself and her colleagues as "nationalistic and provincial" (1949a:8). Chastened by the necessity for a new international order, Mead revised her approach to anthropology; she returned to a strong emphasis upon cultural diversity. "The science of culture itself," she wrote, "must carry and integrate the basic imperatives of many great civilizations." Although physics and chemistry could be developed in one nation and exported to another,

> it is of the very nature of the human sciences that they cannot be exported in the same way. . . . To the possible entrepreneurship of the western world, we have had to add, in a humility which is a useful corrective to our peculiarly American tendency to believe ourselves able to think for the whole of mankind, the integral need for the contribution of as many cultures large and small as possible. For the study *of* other cultures, we add the need to study *with* other cultures. (1949a:4–5)

Yet Mead and Bateson both withdrew, along with most of their colleagues, from government service. Upon the necessity for this withdrawal, at least, they were in fundamental accord. Bateson's retrenchment was the more extreme. It represented a norm for him—the war period was his aberration. It is no surprise that he was attracted later in life to a San Francisco Zen community "whose epistemology united . . . thoughts and actions providing a kind of coherence he had missed" (Bateson 1984:97). In contrast, Mead fashioned a career for herself as the public voice of anthropology. But she used the college lecture circuit, popular magazines, television and radio—not government—as her forums. If she took an occasional government assignment such as relief-work planning for Greece, she and her collaborators "set these projects up outside the rules of secrecy and security, which had been established during the war and have lingered in various stages of exacerbation, ever since." Henceforth, she "refused to do any research which would either have to be classified and so unavailable to others, or which could in any way injure the members of other cultures with whom we worked." The wartime experience had taught us "that psychological warfare rebounded on those who perpetrated it, destroyed trust and simply prepared for later trouble—discoveries which the young radicals were to make over again in the 1960s but about which we had no doubt in the late 1940s." With this, she entered her coda on World War II: "The social scientists . . . took their marbles and went home" (BBWD:7).

Acknowledgments

Grants from Rutgers University and the American Philosophical Society supported the research for this essay. The staff of the Library of Congress, especially archivist

Mary Wolfskill, deserves special appreciation. Merle Curti, always gracious and spirited, offered his comments as a historian and as a participant in this historical period.

References Cited

Bateson, G. 1936. *Naven: A survey of the problems suggested by a composite picture of the culture of a New Guinea tribe drawn from three points of view.* Stanford (1958).
———. 1942. Comment. In Bryson & Finkelstein 1942:81–97.
———. 1953. An analysis of the film *Hitlerjunge Quex*. In Mead & Métraux 1953: 302–14.
Bateson, G. & M. Mead. 1941. Principles of morale building. *J. Ed. Psych.* 15:207–20.
———. 1942. *Balinese character: A photographic analysis.* New York.
Bateson, M. C. 1984. *With a daughter's eye: A memoir of Margaret Mead and Gregory Bateson.* New York.
BBWD. See under Manuscript Sources.
Benedict, R. 1923. The Concept of the guardian spirit in North America. Doct. diss., Columbia Univ. *Mems. Am. Anth. Assn.* 29:1–97.
———. 1930. Psychological types in the cultures of the Southwest. *Procs. 23rd Int. Cong. Americanists*, 572–81.
———. 1934. *Patterns of culture.* New York.
———. 1942. Comment. In Bryson & Finkelstein 1942:69–71.
Boas, F. 1916. Why German-Americans blame America. In Stocking 1974:331–35.
———. 1919. Scientists as spies. In Stocking 1974:336–37.
Brooks, V. W. 1942. Introduction. In Bryson & Finkelstein 1942:1–2.
Bryson, L., & L. Finkelstein, eds. 1942. *Science, philosophy, and religion: Second symposium.* New York.
Dewey, J. 1939. *Freedom and culture.* New York.
Eddy, E. M., & W. L. Partridge, eds. 1978. *Applied anthropology in America.* New York.
Farago, L. 1942. *German psychological warfare.* New York.
FC. See under Manuscript Sources.
GC. See under Manuscript Sources.
Goldschmidt, W., ed. 1979. *The uses of anthropology.* Washington, D.C.
Gorer, G. 1942. Comment. In Bryson & Finkelstein 1942:78–81.
Guthe, C. E. 1943. *History of the committee on food habits.* In *The problem of changing food habits. Bul. Natl. Res. Council* No. 108, 9–19.
Helm, J., ed. 1985. *Social contexts of American ethnology: 1840–1984.* Washington, D.C.
Herskovits, M. J. 1936. Applied anthropology and the American anthropologists. *Science* 83 (March 6):215–22.
Hinsley, C. M. 1981. *Savages and scientists: The Smithsonian Institution and the development of American anthropology, 1846–1910.* Washington, D.C.
Hollinger, D. 1975. *Morris R. Cohen and the scientific ideal.* Cambridge, Mass.
Howard, J. 1984. *Margaret Mead: A life.* New York.
Huizer, G., & B. Mannheim, eds. 1979. *The politics of anthropology: From colonialism and sexism toward a view from below.* The Hague.
Hymes, D., ed. 1972. *Reinventing anthropology.* New York.

Kelly, L. C. 1985. Why applied anthropology developed when it did: A commentary on people, money and changing times, 1930–1945. In Helm 1985:122–77.

Kluckhohn, C. 1942. Comment. In Bryson & Finkelstein 1942:72–76.

Leaf, M. J. 1979. *Men, mind, and science: A history of anthropology.* New York.

Lewin, K. 1943. Forces behind food habits and methods of change. In *The problem of changing food habits, Bul. Natl. Res. Council* No. 108:35–65.

Lipset, D. 1980. *Gregory Bateson: The legacy of a scientist.* Englewood Cliffs, N.J.

Mead, M. 1928. *Coming of age in Samoa: A psychological study of primitive youth for Western civilization.* New York.

———. 1930a. *Growing up in New Guinea: A comparative study of primitive education.* New York.

———. 1930b. *Social organization of Manu'a.* Honolulu.

———. 1934. *Kinship in the Admiralty Islands. Anth. Papers Am. Museum Nat. Hist.* 34 (2):183–358.

———. 1935. *Sex and temperament in three primitive societies.* New York.

———. 1940a. The conflict of cultures in America. *Report of Fifty-fourth Annual Convention of Middle States Association of College and Secondary Schools,* 30–44.

———. 1940b. Social change and cultural surrogates. *J. Ed. Soc.* 14:92–109.

———. 1940c. Toward an honorable world: A symposium. *Wilson Col. Bul.* 4:18–29.

———. 1941. For children of different backgrounds. *Prog. Ed.* 17:13–17.

———. 1942a. Abstract of the general lectures given at Vassar Summer Institute for Family and Child Care Services in Wartime. Mimeo.

———. 1942b. *And keep your powder dry.* New York (1965).

———. 1942c. The comparative study of culture and the purposive cultivation of democratic values. In Bryson & Finkelstein 1942:56–69.

———. 1943a. Changing food habits. In *The nutrition front.* Report of New York State . . . on Nutrition, 37–43. Albany.

———. 1943b. Problem of changing habits. In *The problem of changing food habits. Bul. Natl. Res. Council* No. 108:20–31.

———. 1949a. The comparative study of cultures and the purposive study of democratic values, 1941–49. Tenth Conference on Science, Philosophy and Religion. Mimeo.

———. 1949b. *Male and female: A study of the sexes in a changing world.* New York.

———. 1951. Anthropologist and historian: Their common problems. *Am. Quart.* 3:3–13.

———. 1953. The study of culture at a distance. In Mead & Métraux 1953:3–53.

———. 1965. Preface to reprint ed. of Mead 1942b.

———. 1970. *Culture and commitment: A study of the generation gap.* Garden City, N.Y.

———. 1972. *Blackberry winter: My earlier years.* New York. 1972.

———. 1974. Margaret Mead. In *History of psychology in autobiography,* ed. G. Lindzey, IV, 295–325. New York.

———. 1975. Ethnicity and anthropology in America. In *Ethnic identity,* ed. G. De Vos & L. Romanucci-Ross, 173–97. Palo Alto.

———. 1978. The evolving ethics of applied anthropology. In Eddy & Partridge 1978:425–37.

———. 1979. The use of anthropology in World War II and after. In Goldschmidt 1979:145–57.

Mead, M., & R. Métraux, eds. 1953. *The study of culture at a distance.* Chicago.

Modell, J. S. 1983. *Ruth Benedict: Patterns of a life.* Philadelphia.

Partridge, W. L., & E. M. Eddy. 1978. The development of applied anthropology in America. In Eddy & Partridge 1978:425–37.

PC. See under Manuscript Sources.

PCFC. See under Manuscript Sources.

PF. See under Manuscript Sources.

Purcell, E. A., Jr. 1973. *The crisis of democratic theory: Scientific naturalism and the problem of value.* Lexington, Ky.

Stocking, G. W., Jr. 1968. The scientific reaction against cultural anthropology, 1917–1920. In Stocking, *Race, culture and evolution: Essays in the history of anthropology,* 270–307. New York.

———, ed. 1974. *The shaping of American anthropology, 1883–1911: A Franz Boas reader.* New York.

———. 1976. Ideas and institutions in American anthropology: Thoughts toward a history of the interwar years. In *Selected papers from the* American Anthropologist *1921–1945,* ed. Stocking, 1–44. Washington, D.C.

———. 1979. Anthropology as *Kulturkampf:* Science and politics in the career of Franz Boas. In Goldschmidt 1979:33–50.

———. 1982. Anthropology in crisis: A view from between the generations. In *Crisis in Anthropology: View from Spring Hill, 1980,* ed. E. A. Hoebel et al., 407–19. New York.

———. 1983. The ethnographer's magic: Fieldwork in British anthropology from Tylor to Malinowski. *HOA* 1:70–120.

———. 1984. Radcliffe-Brown and British social anthropology. *HOA* 2:131–91.

SWG. See under Manuscript Sources.

WWF. See under Manuscript Sources.

Wolf, E. R. 1964. *Anthropology.* New York (1974).

———. 1969. American anthropologists and American society. In Hymes 1972:251–63.

Manuscript Sources

Margaret Mead's papers, located in the manuscript archives of the Library of Congress, Washington, D.C., constitute a large and extensive collection. With the exception of the William Morrow Company files, the abbreviations below refer to specific subdivisions or files within the Mead papers.

BBWD	Blackberry Winter Draft (1972). "War Post War." In Publications File.
FC	Family Correspondence.
GC	General Correspondence.
PC	Papers of Colleagues.
PCFC	Papers of Colleagues; Family Correspondence.
PF	Publications File.
SWG, CM	Special Working Groups, Correspondence and Memos.
SWG, RM	Special Working Groups, Reports and Memos.
WMC	William Morrow Company files, New York.

BETWEEN-THE-WARS BALI

Rereading the Relics

JAMES A. BOON

Before beginning, consider scrupulously these scrupulous words of Gregory Bateson:

> An event occurs, for example, a battle is fought, or a man is born or dies, or writes a book. Then memory of this event centers later around some relic or, lacking a relic, we set up a tablet or memorial to the past event, and either the relic or the memorial becomes an influence which pushes those who come after to perpetuate the sociological effects of the original event. Thus we invest the past with real authority and set it, like a policeman, to the business of governing the present. Sometimes the precepts of the past do not quite suit us or the past event is not dramatic enough for our taste, then we are compelled to emend or to embellish the story woven around the relic. (1937:133)

Bateson's words, worth intoning, grace "An Old Temple and a New Myth," an article about rearranging contemporary concerns to render plausible, and alluring, the past. That article was occasioned by Balinese culture, ritual practice, and speech, meticulously recorded and translated. Identical words could refer also to the book compiled by Jane Belo, in which Bateson's essay was republished over thirty years later. Belo's *Traditional Balinese Culture* (1970) purported to represent an event: "Balinese studies in the 1930s." And Belo's book evokes that past by embellishing the story woven round the relic, occasionally investing it with authority, like a policeman. For readers today Bateson's words become a gift from interwar Bali that illuminates how that very subject (including Bateson's words themselves) would subsequently be com-

---

James A. Boon is Professor of Anthropology, Asian Studies, and Comparative Literature at Cornell University. His books include *The Anthropological Romance of Bali* and *Other Tribes, Other Scribes.* He is currently completing collections of essays on comparative Indonesian studies and on the inescapable ironies of ethnology.

A typical Balinese split temple gate (*candi*), this one framing a memorial to wartime, silhouetted. (Photograph by the author.)

memorated. In the following pages we accept Bateson's gift and recirculate his words as epigraphs, or perhaps rubrics.

I score these fragments with phrases from the cited passage of Bateson. My compositional technique is inspired perhaps by surrealism, perhaps by musical examples that figure in our story. Readers are requested to entertain such possibilities behind this composite text of disparate data, strange interludes, unexpected connections, and undecidable questions woven through fieldwork and remembering it.

Like Proust's, our subject is memory, or the writing-construction (the commemoration) of memories, in this case partly shared ones: semi-social-facts comprising a charmed circle's sense of *entre-deux-guerres*. Our "leading motives" include fragments from the prose of several protagonists: Jane Belo, Walter Spies, Margaret Mead. We allude to certain psychoanalytic views of repression and displacement, and consider in passing one case (Culture and Personality) of the many disciplinary movements whose inevitability has been created through retrospection. Yet, we explore *texts* of commemoration, not *lives* presumably "behind" those texts—lives that may elsewhere be the subject of psychologistic investigation. The present essay, then, strives *not* to become certain familiar things: *not* an exposé of prominent figures; *not* a cynical revelation that Balinese studies are about Balinists as well as Bali (this kind of point should no longer be "news"); and *not* an ode to the good old *d'antan* days of those oh-so-yester years.

To resist the above-mentioned plots, without suppressing evidence of their appeal to other readers, is to offer in their stead ambiguous tonalities—fluid, resonant, charged with specificity. This essay, a prose commemoration of prose commemorations, seeks to sustain ambiguities with heightened precision and reflexivity. The proper signature of our story is the "key" of Debussy. May these misty fragments be neither obscurist nor subjective, dear reader, but musical.[1]

Fragment 1: "We invest the past with real authority . . ."

War is—besides hell, sorrow, and suffering—a "space" (Michel Foucault might have said) around which gather a *vor dem*, a *nach dem*, and, alas, an "inter." Like revolution, "war" betokens the essence of "eventness": the headline, the declared, the won/lost. "War" represents FACT *en majuscules*; then come the wrenching details. Upon the hinge of "wartime," near-forgottens turn into ordered recollection; the ensuing mode is always commemorative, sometimes elegiac.[2]

Theories of knowing and knowledge occasionally contest whether war-events or revolution-events exactly happen as constructed. A postwar classic in doubting the priority of anything originary is Lévi-Strauss's famous disso-lution of "1789":

> Both history and ethnography are concerned with societies other than the one
> in which we live. Whether this otherness is due to remoteness in time (however
> slight), or to remoteness in space, or even to cultural heterogeneity, is of sec-
> ondary importance. . . . What constitutes the goal of the two disciplines? Is it

1. This essay, which may appear experimental, can be read as a companion piece to my recent article on the cross-cultural intersection represented by R. Fortune, M. Mead, and G. Bateson, whose intertextuality wove together New Guinea cultures, themselves, and anticipations of Bali (Boon 1985a). The present study, however, is perhaps better not read that way, because part of the effort here (as there) is to resist fixating on such larger-than-life figures as Mead (and Bate-son). Mead enters often, but tangentially, into our story of interwar Balinese studies; and Bate-son, although he was a protagonist, has been converted to our guiding epigraph. Such devices are helpful (and in this case, I think, accurate) if we are to surmount artificially "centered" his-tories of anthropology, if we are to give voices—as anthropologists ought—to elements marginal-ized by standard, "heroic," history of disciplines.

2. My allusions to Foucault are less to his later work on sexuality and more to his mid-career classic, *The Order of Things* (1973), which invites readers to explore comparative (actually con-trastive) history, or the history of possibilities (really histories of difference), rather than a "symp-tomatological history" (1973:x).

the exact reconstruction of what has happened, or is happening, in the society under study? To assert this would be to forget that in both cases we are dealing with systems of representations which differ for each member of the group and which, on the whole, differ from the representations of the investigator. The best ethnographic study will never make the reader a native. The French Revolution of 1789 lived through by an aristocrat is not the same phenomenon as the Revolution of 1789 lived through by a *sans-culotte*, and neither would correspond to the Revolution of 1789 as conceived by Michelet or Taine. (1963:17)

In order to reconcile history and ethnography-ethnology (and "hot" and "cold" societies), Lévi-Strauss questioned the underpinnings of chrono-logics. He decentralized what some ideologies misconstrue as time's own story of itself. Such challenges to the authority and priority of events have burgeoned in both modernist literature and postwar *sciences humaines*.

In such systems of representation as "history" and "ethnography," "war" epitomizes those events presumed to have a before and an after. "War," moreover, coaxes other experiences and reminiscences into a centralized format of discontinuity. Some might call war, so imagined, intellectually hegemonic. Even a critical movement—surrealism, for example—that doubts historical causality and determinant contexts can be made to bow to "war," even by scholars sympathetic to that movement. Hence, Walter Benjamin on "Surrealism": "What sprang up in 1919 . . . fed on the damp boredom of postwar Europe" (1978:177). Hence too, Lévi-Strauss's suggestion that surrealism—this ostensibly least legacy-laden of isms—was less ahistorical than sometimes portrayed: "Le surréalisme aussi savait à l'occasion s'inspirer du passé" (1983:342).[3]

Through the process of such constructions, "après la guerre" becomes the pretext for revisiting a period only eventually construable as interwar. Our sense of that time becomes recontextualized in light of a subsequent fact: a war-fact. "Interwar," moreover, becomes construed as a time of difference, of otherwise, in any "history." Histories by anthropologists augment such constructions by locating the interwar and otherwise in another place, an ordi-

---

3. Mention of surrealism will, I hope, return readers to the seminal essay "On Ethnographic Surrealism" by Clifford (1981), which compiles a rich field of associations linking desirable incongruity and anthropology's often-papered-over task of acknowledging "the exotic, the paradoxical, the *insolite*" (1981:548). Certain less-subversive-looking scholars than those Clifford accentuates—Kenneth Burke and C. Lévi-Strauss, for example—have sometimes championed incongruity and at least occasional surrealism (see Boon 1982:150–53, 236–37; 1984). Clifford poses more dramatically "the surrealist moment" in ethnography as "that moment in which the possibility of comparison exists in unmediated tension with sheer incongruity" (1981:563). My sense of surrealism is less absolute: more a matter of mediated tension with incongruity than unmediated tension; more a fragmentariness still somewhat discomforted by not being "whole," or proper —but not nostalgic for that condition, and dubious of its plausibility. Regardless, as Clifford argues, the result of writing toward incongruity—whether, I think, mediated or unmediated—is "collage," or something like it.

narily uneventful place: a fieldwork place. In this event betweenness inten-
sifies; the condition of *entre-deux-guerres* grows exponential.

Fragment 2: "An event occurs, a battle is fought, or a [wo]man . . . writes a book . . ."

To help set in motion issues in the arts of commemoration, we linger over
an arresting example of recontextualization. Our material is ethnographic;
our era is, again, interwar (the "age of," among other things, surrealism); our
scene is Bali; our subject is Belo. With reference to all this, after World War
II, and during the continued routinization of psychotherapeutic styles of analysis, "something happened."

It is time to speak of Jane.[4] In 1968 Jane Belo composed the introduction
to *Traditional Balinese Culture* (1970), saluting the company of scholars, performers, and enthusiasts (foreigner and Balinese alike) resident during the 1930s
in Bali, outside the Dutch colonial administrative establishment. Upon Belo's
death, Margaret Mead added a capstone epitaph in her customary manner:
"She has been a lovely part of all of our lives for the thirty years we have
studied Balinese culture together. She brought delight to all she touched"
(Mead 1970). The book's gnomic binding displays spidery blotch figures against
a luminous field "derived from a Batik tapestry in the Margaret Mead collection"; the design encourages Rorschach responses, or so it strikes me. Regardless, the tome became, doubly, a *tombeau*: of and to Bali-then and Belo.

Students of Hollywood's history will recognize this story: post-1929 movies
benefited from an onrush of talented technicians and performers, refugees
from the breadlines (Taylor 1983). There resulted labor-intensive, low-waged,
highly wrought productions: MGM musicals, Disney animation. Bali too, de-
prived of tourist guilders, pounds, and dollars during the long aftermath of
Black Tuesday, harbored many gifted stayers-on. Some were adrift; others
waited, belts tightened, for the economic and political tides to turn. Connois-
seurs of otherness, of indisputably "star quality," parked in Bali; and many
Balinese, not uncagily, responded by intensifying their ceremonial displays:

> And, in fact, in the 1930s, when they were told that the reason fewer tourists
> were coming to Bali than in previous years was that there was a world depres-
> sion, the Balinese responded by celebrating an elaborate purification and pro-
> pitiation ceremony at Besakih, the head temple on the slopes of the Great Moun-
> tain, in order to bring the world depression to an end. (Belo 1970:xi)

---

4. Several transitions in this essay are pastiches of devices or phrases from celebrated writings
in a commemorative mode—this one Waugh's *Brideshead Revisited* (1945:178).

Belo's own early work included a vanguard account of Balinese kinship and endogamy, and a now-classic study of ideas and practices surrounding twin births. These pieces alone place Belo in the first rank of Balinese ethnographers; with her entries on "temperament" and on conventionalized children's drawings, they form the core of *Traditional Balinese Culture*. Except for Colin McPhee's account of Balinese music and two typically unclassifiable articles by Gregory Bateson, the remaining items are incidental, popular pieces: brief reconnaissance reports, and summaries of efforts to situate Balinese character in cross-cultural surveys of socialization.

The collection's most striking feature is its array of contributors. They include (preserving sobriquets from Belo's introduction): Walter Spies—artist-writer, musician, polyglot (Russian, German, French, English, Javanese, Balinese, Indonesian), and bon vivant; Colin McPhee—(ethno) musicologist, and Belo's middle husband; Claire Holt—scholar of dance, sculpture, archeology, and art history, and all-round Indonesianist; Arthur Waley, Orientalist—together with his companion, renowned choreographer Beryl de Zoete; Katharane Mershon—from California, professional dancer, past director of the Pasadena Playhouse, amateur nurse, autodidact in Balinese Brahmana high rituals, and wife of her dancing partner, the brilliant photographer Mack Mershon; Margaret Mead and Gregory Bateson—anthropologists. Those *were* the days.

An important sequence of contacts merits review. Although Belo and Mead were acquainted at Barnard when both studied under Boas, Belo's earliest materials from Bali (on twins) were collected independently of Mead and before Belo met Bateson in 1934. She had, however, read Mead's work on Samoa and Manus before completing her studies of Balinese families and temperament. In New York in 1934 Belo helped kindle Mead's interest in Bali; and then in 1936, upon Belo's return to Bali, strong ties developed. Belo was converted to topics in Culture and Personality promoted by Mead, and to the intensive fieldwork strategy of multiply inscribed ritual events favored by Mead and Bateson.[5] Although her important study of Bali's temple festivals (1953) remained closer in spirit to standard ethnographic documentation, her influential study of exorcist rites centering on the witch figure Rangda (1949) accentuated themes and frameworks from Culture and Personality. The full flowering of Belo's conversion to Mead and Bateson's programs of research appeared in Belo's *Trance in Bali* (1960).

5. These extraordinary field methods (involving photography, filming, and several varieties of simultaneous writing) deserve a study in their own right. In another article I hope to continue tracing peculiar "captionings" over the course of Balinese studies, including techniques enlisting an array of Balinese and non-Balinese inscribers and viewfinders promoted by Bateson and Mead. Their kind of "writing lesson" and "seeing lesson" develops out of a particular history of discourse and stereotyping (see Boon 1977:186–218; Neiman 1980; Geertz 1983).

These points bring us to an entry in *Traditional Balinese Culture* that I have delayed mentioning. The study "Free Designs as a Personality Index: A Comparison of Schizophrenics with Normal, Subnormal, and Primitive Culture Groups" is inserted before the book's final item, Bateson's "The Value System of a Steady State." The author, Theodora Abel, not a Balinist, went uncommemorated in Belo's volume introduction. I quote characteristic snippets:

> The other primitive group, the Balinese (Group VI), has had much less cultural contact with white people [than has the Navaho]. . . . [The Balinese] hate tests and are suspicious of their purpose.
>   . . . Dr. Mead [in her letter of February 12, 1938] described the personality structure of the Balinese as follows: "The whole emphasis of the education is to scatter, disintegrate, separate one response from another, and to make only very superficial verbalistic associations. It's not so much that the Balinese can't take in a new idea, as that they can't take in anything *whole*; their own receptivity is a honeycomb. Every new idea has to be chopped into little bits." (Abel 1938:380)

Mead's casual remarks may have some merit if carefully qualified. In her influential studies of Balinese behaviors (e.g., Bateson & Mead 1942), Mead situates this kind of comment, which animated her copious correspondence to nonprofessional readers, in fuller observations of communication and styles of interaction. Abel, however, at once imposed a prepackaged symptomatics:

> This factor probably accounts for the making of the discrete ununified lines in the designs. This same factor may be the one dominant in the behavior of schizophrenics. Certainly one of their marked characteristics is disorganization of the total personality, and inability to integrate different aspects of their world of new experiences. They failed to build up a constructive plan for a design, but were successful in drawing the correct number of lines. (1938:381)

By this point in Abel's diagnosis, the antecedent of "they" is unclear: Balinese or schizophrenics? (Should this disorganization in Abel's own account lead us to declare her schizophrenic too?)

Abel's instant short circuits across cultures and psychoses should not be confused with subtler works in Culture and Personality, including many of Mead's books and, of course, Benedict's *Patterns of Culture* (1934), which compared *styles* of cultural integration with *styles* of integration of neuroses or psychoses. In contrast Abel's essay compared not styles (of problem personalities) with styles (of cultures) but decontextualized symptom with symptom. She appears to label Balinese as schizophrenic: "Their performance was like that of the paranoid schizophrenics [in her samples], and we have suggested that their attitude and modes of thinking were the same" (Abel 1938:383).

We have revisited Abel not to correct once again faulty models of psychological parallels long ago discarded by more careful theorists of Culture and

Personality, but to illustrate arguments from an article that was deemed appropriate for the tome *Traditional Balinese Culture*. Abel's piece was juxtaposed with the other studies, including Belo's, as if they could be assimilated to its terms. In the process, the 1970 volume attached simplified and partial psychologistic symptoms to descriptions of culture which when first published were innocent of such perspectives. This variety of revisionism characterizes many styles of retrospection, including much of Mead's important popular and journalistic work (see Boon 1985a). We are not here concerned with whether Belo might have inclined toward these analyses in 1968 because of personal stress or for other private reasons. Rather, I wish to indicate the ironic consequences such juxtapositional revisionism may have as we proceed to re-read the history of anthropology—in this case Balinese studies. "Like a policeman," Belo's memorial of 1968 managed retrospectively to make certain interwar accounts of Bali appear to say something different from what they would have appeared to be saying originally. Bearing this paramount point in mind, we turn, hesitantly, to a mysterious footnote.

Fragment 3: "Sometimes . . . the past event is not dramatic enough for our taste . . ."

It is a venerable custom among anthropologists to present the *humble* facts of ethnography in a *sublime* style. Practitioners of this rhetorical strategy range from James Frazer (unsurprisingly) and early Malinowski to Robert Lowie (see Boon 1982:3–26, 54–111). Jane Belo followed suit. The opening of her initial study of Bali is redolent of epics past, a near-pastiche of grandiloquent narrative style:

> On the night of September 18, 1933, twins were born to a woman of Suka-wana. When the family saw that the twins were a boy and a girl, they knew that this was a great wrong, that disaster had come upon their village. A brother of the father ran to the open place before the *bale agung*, the village temple. There he beat upon the *kul-kul*, the hollow wooden alarm, so that all the men of the village would come together to hear the direful news. And the sleeping villagers awoke in their tiny houses, still warm with the dying coals of the evening fire, and came forth wrapped in their blankets, for at night it is bitter cold on the slopes of the Gunung Penulisan. (1935:5)

In the year 1968, further sentences occurred to a woman of New York. When she saw that her original study was inadequately prefaced, she wrote a new analysis obscurely related to the original's evidence that opposite-sex twins signify incest in Bali, an event deemed auspicious for high-born houses and catastrophic for commoners. Belo's new note of 1968 refers to Balinese indifference to monozygotic/dizygotic distinctions, to Balinese obliviousness to ideas of exceptional ties between twins, and to Balinese casualness about homosexual play (*main-main*). These features she abruptly contrasts to "Western culture," interjected via footnotes to two postwar psychoanalytical articles: Jules Glenn's "Opposite Sex Twins" (1966) and F. J. A. Kallmann's comparative study of homosexual male twin "index cases" (1952). She then concludes:

> There is also to be found in the psychoanalytic literature evidence of strong sexually based attraction between boy and girl twins which comes to light in analysis, as of the adolescent boy-twin who would only find satisfaction by masturbating before a three-way mirror, looking at his own anus and thinking of his sister. Likewise [?] to studies of homosexuality to be found in both of a pair of monozygotic twins. I have nothing to add. (Belo 1970:4–5)

I, on the contrary, have much to add. What might this masturbating boy twin, fixated on his reflected sister-anus, be doing here in 1968?[6] Whence Belo's allusions; whither do they point (besides Trickster)? What is the nature of the psychoanalytic texts that Belo here insinuates alongside her data from 1935? How should the present study of Belo's peculiar book proceed? What opportunities does her "scandalous" recontextualization afford to a history of anthropology or to a history of the histories of anthropology? How manifold may the resonances of stories about culture crossing become and yet remain tolerable? To sustain these questions, we now scrutinize Belo's new references— standard fare in some psychoanalysis, but certainly bizarre from the vantage of Bali.

Fragment 4: "Then we are compelled to emend . . ."

Belo's first reference relates not just the dreams but the fancies of one Mr. C.:

> He and his sister were brought up close together. Mr. C. recalled their being bathed together and sleeping in the same room. Even at nineteen he shared a room with his sister. The twins shared the responsibility of cleaning the house since both parents were at work. When they were alone they fought, duplicating their parents' relationship to each other. . . . The parents and relatives . . . glowed at seeing them together as if they were a unit.
> During latency he knew one twin stuck the other with a fork, but he did not know who did it. . . .
> Although he shared a room with his sister, who looked like a movie star, he first thought himself not attracted to her. Later he recalled sexual excitement

---

6. At this juncture our essay steers nearer "surrealism" in Clifford's more extreme sense (in the vein of Bataille, Leiris, etc.): a surrealism conjoining the sublime and the vulgar, and "licensed to shock" (1981:548–49).

in her presence. He recalled that masturbation started at thirteen. At times he would look in the mirror while masturbating so as to be able to see his own anus. Analysis revealed this looking at his mirror image to be a reflection of his wish to see his sister. (Glenn 1966:740)

Because Belo had nothing to add in 1968, we are left to wonder what she read into this risqué representation from a psychoanalytic scene of multiple transgression. Were one to compile a list of conceivable sexual repressions "imaged" by Mr. C., one would hardly know where to begin: (1) Homosexuality with a *différance*? (2) Autoeroticism through doubling and repetition? (3) Incestuous bisexuality *à un*? (4) A degraded platonic androgyny: the pursuit of the (w)hole called love? (5) Hermaphroditism in the age of mechanical reproduction (mass-produced mirrors)? (6) Imaginary heterosexuality via reversals, condensation, and self/other substitutions? (7) A carnivalized image (through parodic inversion) of Ovidian homosexuals: male bodies with female "soul" entrapped? The longer our perhaps outrageous list of bottom-line irregularities grows, the more convincing its alternatives become: *all* of them. These symbols of transgression begin mysteriously to reinforce each other; such is the power of many kinds of imagery and myth. But by the same token, the longer our list grows, the less relevant *any* of its items, or Mr. C., appears to Balinese culture.

Jane Belo's article of 1935 documented the place of incest in Balinese values of aristocracy and divinity. However important the topics of homosexuality and masturbation may be, they were *not* the subject of evidence she collected in the early 1930s. Moreover, unhappy Mr. C. before his mirror simply does not seem—how should one put it?—"Balinese." To repeat, Belo elects to add nothing to her unexplained invocation of Mr. C.; our above list of sexual possibilities simply parodies the sorts of hidden themes assumed in many styles of psychosexual readings, including psychoanalysis. Belo juxtaposed something radically psycho-something-or-other with an earlier "innocent" ethnography. Her study of twins reported specific social circumstances of symbolic ambiguities of gender, status, and birth order (Boon 1977:119–44; see also Boon n.d.b.). Her important insights into cosmology, ethnographic practice, and folklore helped stimulate studies of Balinese performing arts and daily life (e.g., Covarrubias 1937; De Zoete & Spies 1939), where dramatic depolarizations of gender punctuate dance, drama, refined comportment, and ritual.

As late as 1949 Belo was content to interpret Bali's "arts and crafts" ethos (including graceful males and occasional transvestism) in images of cycles of differentiation/undifferentiation in a "self-perpetuating personality system" (1949:59). Developing Bateson's notions of "steady state" values and perhaps Mead's (1935) important schemes of gender and temperament, Belo crowned her study of Rangda (1949) with Bali-Hindu iconography of boy-and-girl twins, figures of the "original couple." She mapped circuit switching among male/

female, males in female roles, and females in male roles, showing how male/ female distinctions shift, permute, intensify, and lapse across phases of ritualized life cycles. In these studies nothing was reduced to psychologistic symptoms; nothing even allusively suggested intermingled indices of homosexuality, androgyny, bisexuality, hermaphroditism, and so forth. The sensationally blurred image of Mr. C. became attached to publications of Balinese evidence only after a longer lapse of time.[7]

Fragment 5: "or to embellish . . ."

The second reference in Belo's new footnote contains a psychoanalytic tale sadder still than Mr. C.'s. The following extract is offered to demonstrate what Belo left vague and to illustrate the particular variety of narrative involved. So that readers may "hear" Kallmann's presumably clinical diagnoses of index cases as a stylized mythic rendering redolent of tragic form, I underscore paired contrasts and constructions about similarity/difference and first/second; I even place the selection's thematic heart in "warlike" *majuscules*. I do not consider this intrusion into Kallmann's text cheating. Devices to help us recognize the slants and angles of any conventionalized analysis are fair play, provided we own up to them. While italics may distort our readings, the greatest distortion of all would be to make the following words sound neutral:

> Because of the general significance of this monozygotic pair of schizophrenic twin brothers concordant as to homosexuality and death by self-destruction, it may be mentioned that the U. twins were of English-German descent, from a thrifty middleclass family, and the only sons of their parents (they had an older sister). Their early lives were uneventful, except for the fact that one of them (the *second* with respect to delivery and suicide) required plastic surgery on account of a disfiguring facial birth injury (*left lower* jaw) which seemed to have been responsible for a certain retardation in physical and mental development. In 1942, the twins entered *different* branches of the Armed Services from *different* universities, in spite of their histories of overt homosexual behavior and although the disfigured twin had been a conscientious objector. Within less than a year, they developed *similar* schizophrenic symptoms in *different* theaters of war, but at practically the *same* time. Following shock treatment in *differ-*

7. Perhaps I should restate that our subject is neither Culture and Personality, properly speaking, nor, of course, the merits and/or drawbacks of psychoanalysis. Rather, we are rereading commemorations of an episode in anthropology's past, which have become seasoned by suggestive allusions and references to bits and pieces of psychosexual themes and psychoanalytic diagnosis. (For a reading of allusive digressions in earlier Indonesian ethnology, see Boon 1985c.) An important inspiration for my proceeding with this manner of essay—which obviously risks rekindling the very kinds of plot it wishes to distance—was J. Malcomb's (1984) tale of Freudian archivists, especially in its breathtakingly serial form as "originally" published in the *New Yorker*.

ent hospitals, they were unable to readjust themselves to civilian life, apparently because they were equally defective to personalities and equally unmanageable in their tendencies to PERIODIC VAGABONDISM. The suicides were committed *before* and *after* the death of the mother (one *at home*, the other *away from home*) and were ascribed to fear of readmission to a mental hospital. (Kallmann 1952: 291–92)

This passage in my copy of the 1952 *Journal of Nervous and Mental Disease* is tearstained. May none of us, dear readers, identify with this devastating tale, yet may all of us sympathize. Ensuing irritation dries my eyes as Kallmann discloses his clinical conclusions, as if to explain "how the leopard got its spots":

In this tragic manner, the U. twins served to confirm our recently expressed opinion that "the suicides of two twin partners are apt to occur but will only be observed by chance (not directly related to one another even under similar conditions of unfavorable family background, social frustration, or emotional maladjustment), and therefore will be extremely rare." The photographs of the pair are withheld upon the request of the twins' father. (1952:292–93)

On that last note, the tears resume.

Kallmann does manage to include portraits of "three concordant one-egg pairs," eyes masked: the J. twins, the O. twins, and the K. twins (lanky entertainers posed at age twenty-two, like a visually stuttered Fred Astaire). Kallmann regrets that "further clinical or photographic data cannot be revealed since most of the twin index cases of this survey are still subject to the laws of the State of New York" (1952:294).

We pass over Kallmann's dated diagnosis of "fixation or regression to immature levels of sexuality" and the ungainly analytic coinages of his craft's views (even the liberal ones) of homosexuality: "an alternative minus variant in the integrative process of psychosexual maturation rather than . . . a pathognomonically determinative expression of a codifiable entity of behavioral immaturity" (1952:294). Our concerns lie elsewhere. What could have prompted Belo to append a reference on homosexual twins to her classic study of opposite-sex Balinese twins—a study utterly unconnected to Kallmann's index cases? What, moreover, are we to make of this tragedy of periodic vagabondage, homosexuality, Armed Forces, hospitals, and theaters of war? The story, or one of its possibilities, continues.

Fragment 6: "The story woven around the relic"

Were this essay employing subheadings rather than extracts of Bateson atop its fragments, we would now begin "Censored Postcards." If we projected the full rays of Walter Spies's renown back on interwar Bali, Jane Belo's lunar glow would be outshone. There is insufficient room even to telegraph vital facts of Spies's life and art between his birth in Moscow in 1895, where (like Vladimir Nabokov born four years later in St. Petersburg) he absorbed the twilight of Czarist culture in privileged diplomatic circles, and his death in 1942, drowned off Sumatra by a Japanese bomber. Suffice it to say that this painter-polyglot-musician-musicologist-dancer-photographer-archeologist-ethnographer-botanist-entomologist—raised in the worlds of Rachmaninoff, Scriabin, and Richard Strauss, schooled in Cubism and Expressionist Dresden, displaced via Holland to the traditionalist courts of Java where he became Master of the Sultan's Music—found fulfillment in Bali after 1927. There can be few rivals to Spies in the history of crossing cultures. His was a kindly charisma, his open-door residences a blend of the *salon*, the *café*, and the academic *équipe*. If ever an individual reoriented an era's sense of an entire people, it was interwar Spies-in-Bali. Spies opened Balinese studies beyond the narrower spectrum of official Dutch ethnography (interesting enough in its own right) devoted to encyclopedic documentation of temple types, customary law, land rights, and "archeologizable" art. Spies helped direct an entire generation, some of it "lost," to issues of performance and the interrelation of the arts. He never challenged Dutch ethnographic and administrative authority; rather he provided a richly peripheral alternative vantage point.

To sustain this (sincere) vein of accolade would advance the cult of Spies that has intensified since 1964, when Hans Rhodius prepared *Schönheit und Reichtum des Lebens: Walter Spies (Maler und Musiker auf Bali, 1895–1942)*. This splendid tome stands to Spies's work in Bali much as De Zoete and Spies's own *Dance and Drama in Bali* (1939) stood to Balinese performing arts. Rhodius' *Walter Spies*, moreover, helped hitch the name of Spies to new agencies for the revitalization of Balinese arts and Balinese studies—one in Bali and one in the Netherlands. Conventional tributes to Spies (including some from the 1930s) identify his sensibility with the essence of "Balineseness"—always a dubious kind of claim. Spies himself, then, has been commemorated along with Balinese culture. Indeed, the construct "interwar Bali" has come to coincide with the impact and influence of Walter Spies.[8]

It is time, again, to speak of Jane. Rhodius' *Walter Spies* (1965) possibly helped determine Belo to edit *Traditional Balinese Culture*; her 1968 introduction men-

8. A major exhibition of works by Spies and Balinese artists he influenced was held in 1980 at Amsterdam's Tropenmuseum; its lavish catalogue and introduction (Rhodius & Darling 1980) condense discussions from Rhodius' still more elaborate volume (1965). In Bali in 1981, I happened upon a review of this English-language account in a tourist newsletter distributed at the Bali Beach Hotel, the aging flagship of government-backed tourism flowering during President Suharto's era. The Spies phenomenon thus enters the convoluted history of patronage and commercialization of Balinese arts, performance, and—one might say—life.

A typical inner temple gate (*padu raksa*) in North Bali; ritual and narrative concerning this temple's founders were intensively reworked by Balinese during the interwar period. (Photograph by the author.)

tions that tome (to which she contributed), where Spies's writings and pictures were interleaved with homages by artists, scholars, and celebrities whom Spies had hosted in Bali—among them Charlie Chaplin, Leopold Stokowski, and Margaret Mead. Art historian Claire Holt's contribution is especially telling. She evokes Spies's mystery and paradoxical personality in images she also applied to Bali:

Walter's radiant presence could shrink into . . . almost literal effacement. . . .
He . . . never asserted himself aggressively, whether in delight or disgust—the
two poles in his scale of moods. Was there something in this non-concentrated
ego that was not only peculiar to Spies but also to the people among whom
he lived? And did he efface himself in the presence of authority or officialdom
or strangers just as any Balinese would unless born to rule and exercise his
prerogatives? Did Spies bring to the island within him that sense of just *being*
and not of either becoming or achieving, which are the mainsprings of Western
man? Just to be, like a lake that mirrors the skies . . .? (Rhodius 1965:312–13)

Claire Holt and Jane Belo had shared experiences with Spies when the striking trio explored the islands off Bali's southeast coast in the early 1930s. Holt's
spirited reconnaissance report of that mission prefigured her later testimo-
nial. Belo remained unnamed, tagged as the "family expert" and ethnographer of twinship on the team. Holt's prose style altered when presenting Spies
—the protagonist in a prototypical exotic adventure, presumably constructed
by Holt out of his reported evidence. This patch of indirect discourse and
suspenseful climax stands out in sharp relief from the surrounding rather
routine narrative, based exclusively on Holt's own observations:

About one kilometer north of Swana pass, there lies a tremendous cave, the
Goa Karangsari. Walter Spies descended into it through a small traplike opening and found himself in complete darkness. Walking downward through a narrow passage, he suddenly came into a larger cave and from there into still another one, till, finally, there were large vaulted halls with stalactites hanging
down and all the hollow uncanniness of deep caves. This seemed to be a whole
hollow mountain. After a fair amount of wandering about, the man accom-
panying Spies told him to stop. He was to go no further. Before them lay a small
pool of brilliantly transparent water. "This is the bath of the *dedari* (heavenly
nymphs)," declared the guide. (His name, by the way, was Kichig, and a pre-
ciously helpful soul Kichig proved afterward!) So beyond the bath of the heavenly nymphs no one should pass. (Holt 1936:75)

This obscured epiphany suggests nothing so much as a displaced "Marabar
Caves," that haunting heart of the ambiguities comprising E. M. Forster's *Passage to India* (1924). Evidently, then, Spies's charisma was manifest early on.
Recent commentators have sought—as is proper in "relic-ing"—to restore and
to harness it.

Belo's own "Appreciation of the Artist Walter Spies" in Rhodius' volume
recalls when she, her husband (Colin McPhee), and Spies first met in 1931,
and their years of friendship in their houses in Bali, just six miles apart. She
evokes Spies's profound emotions, boyish buoyancy, and ethereal good looks
"with blue eyes, a longish aquiline nose, beautifully cut and very mobile lips,"
athletic build, restless gestures, and delicate brushwork (Rhodius 1965:317–
18). Others waxed equally eloquent about the person and the painting of Wal-

"Spies himself, then, has been commemorated along with Balinese culture." Walter Spies, photographed by Gregory Bateson. (Courtesy The Institute of Intercultural Studies, Inc.)

ter Spies, and all, including Margaret Mead, affirmed his generosity: "It was Walter who found us a house, it was Walter who found us our first servants, it was Walter who found the carpenter to build our house in the high mountains, and most of all it was Walter who gave us our first sense of the Balinese scene" (Rhodius 1965:359). To judge by Spies's letter of 1938 to Lady Mary Delamere (whom Rhodius identifies as the "Schwester der Countess Mountbatten of Burma and Enkelin von Sir Ernest Cassel"), Belo's esteem was reciprocated; he numbered her among Bali's primary attractions.

Belo's memories of Spies may have been more intricate than anything she states openly in 1968. Mead, as was her wont, revealed evidence that Belo did not. Mead's "Memories of Walter Spies" end with an abrupt exposure, plus a somewhat pat diagnosis to round things off:

> Walter Spies's choice of Bali and of a continuing light involvement with Balinese male youth, seemed part of his repudiation of the kind of dominance and submission, authority and dependence, which he associated with European cultures, and which could be revived in him when he encountered officialdom or rank. . . . The very disassociated impersonality of Bali gave him the kind of freedom that he sought. (Rhodius 1965:359)

Mead's many retrospectives on her life and work were laden with suggestive insights, but so fleetingly conveyed that they can take on an air of insinuation rather than argument (Boon 1985a:345). Some might find it unfitting that such allusions should conclude paragraphs that open by declaring utter indebtedness to Spies for much that Mead and Bateson were to learn of Bali. But twists of this kind often lent a provocative edge to Mead's modes of commemoration.

The complicated facts surrounding Walter Spies's death were outlined in Rhodius' German chapters in *Schönheit und Reichtum* in 1965, and have since been condensed in a translation by John Stowell (Rhodius & Darling 1980). Although none of this information was new, it had not been summarized so clearly or publicly. Those were, of course, the worst of times: occupied Holland insecurely ruling its East Indies; newly promoted officials seeking clout and scapegoats; shifts toward right-wing policies of law, order, and conformity. Specifically, the last viceroy of the Netherlands Indies, a war hero, resuscitated long-lapsed laws against suspect behavior, including homosexuality. Officials well disposed toward Spies were replaced; he was caught in a dragnet and confined on December 31, 1938. After three years of artistically productive imprisonment, he was shipped toward Ceylon with other German internees; on January 19, 1942, near Nias, the *Van Imhoff* was sunk by a Japanese bomb. The last relic of Walter Spies is a *Briefkaart* marked "*gecensureerd.*" In *both* Rhodius' commemorative volume and that of Rhodius and Darling, *both* sides of the fateful postcard are illustrated; the images serve literally as a memento mori.

Rhodius discovered a "blessing in disguise" in Spies's disgrace: the famous prison paintings, which include magical-realist Balinese landscapes drawn from Spies's memory-imagination alone. Appropriately, and perhaps accurately, Rhodius' idealized portrayal of creativity transcending the enemy casts a mantle of innocence back upon details that had been "grossly exaggerated" by "petty-minded" vengeful officials beset by "neurotic hysteria":

> In Bali, friendships between members of the same sex have always been allowed more open and intense expression than is the case in most Western societies, caught in the maze of their own taboos. This attitude was clearly shown by the father of Spies's young friend. When the lawyer asked if he was angry at Mr. Spies's conduct, he replied: "*Kenapa?* (But why?) He is after all our best friend, and it was an honour for my son to be in his company, and if both are in agreement, why fuss?" (Rhodius & Darling 1980:45)

Neither Rhodius' lilting vision nor a more caustic retrospect on Spies's fate was offered by Belo in her 1968 commemoration—at least not explicitly. But biographers of some of our protagonists have shown that Belo had already known the facts that Rhodius revisited in 1964. Indeed Belo herself had possibly been a potential victim of the same wartime forces, and her correspondence reveals that she may have hinged memories of Bali on the trauma of Spies's last years. Relevant material appears in Jane Howard's recent study of Mead's life, colleagues, and times. Howard cites Mead's well-known mention of "a witchhunt against homosexuals" that "broke out in the Pacific [and] echoed from Los Angeles to Singapore" (1984:209). Mead wrote that she and Bateson returned with Belo to Bali, because the situation seemed unsafe for her to go back alone. Howard then cites Belo's letter of February 10, 1939, describing a South Bali official's effort to oust foreigners who could not be kept under surveillance. Another of Belo's letters mentions the government's "clean-up of certain misdemeanors to which residents of these parts were prone. . . . Walter and four others have been in prison in Den Pasar since the first of January" (Howard 1984:209–10). Other fragments from Belo suggest the tenor of those days:

> All of us who lived in a pleasant way have been investigated—police in and out of our houses, all our servants arrested and questioned. Of the 34 dancing girls in my village, all were questioned on my habits, down to a 3-year old . . . Colin had kept it a secret that we were divorced last July. . . . At least half the [European] people living in Bali have been asked to leave, or have left of their own accord, one dares not wonder why . . . the Balinese think the whole white caste has gone mad. . . . Thank heaven for the Batesons and their firm scientific reputations to back us up. (Howard 1984:210)

We have come to a potentially awkward moment in our story. Having cited this much from Howard, we resist interrogating Belo's private side, or Mead's.

Our commemoration leaves such plots to their biographers (e.g., Bateson 1984), in the conviction that "biography" does not *explain* the texts of those whose lives it presumes to reconstruct. Were we here to pursue "the Belo story" or "the Mead story" insofar as each pertains to Balinese studies and anthropology's history, we would strive not to reduce their arts and works to symptoms (of sexuality or anything else), but to weave resonances of their writing—including ethnography, memoirs, and commemorative tomes—into a selection of shifting tonalities: a music not necessarily in a singular key. It is this interpretive procedure that we now pursue through Walter Spies.

Fragment 7: "The relic or the memorial becomes an influence which pushes those who come after to perpetuate the sociological effects of the original event"

To isolate Belo's odd footnote and even to surmise parallels between its references' psychoanalytic narratives and the way Belo may have remembered Walter Spies and company may seem to brush the very brand of diagnosis we seek to avoid. The goal here, however, is not to disentangle but to dissolve any "original event" suspected of lying behind the chains of commemoration whereby Bali, Spies, between-the-wars, Belo, and Bateson's words become "reliced." Yet even with original events and psychosexual symptoms unfixed, sociological effects are nevertheless perpetuated in a transtemporal "charmed circle" of successive memorialists. Through this historical process, moreover, mists do not evaporate but thicken, along with specificities: *obscurum per obscurius.*

Spies's disgrace—and Belo's reluctance versus Mead's relative readiness (which is preferable?) to mention it—reminds us that any commemoration selects strands from a panoply. Such accentuation produces distortions: recognizable kinds of story. In the extreme, tabloids sniff out salacious subcurrents papered over in rosier remembrances. Our more fragmentary aim is otherwise: to rekindle respect for the panoply and resist plumbing for a particular plot line, without, however, repressing the fact that psychoanalytic readings have beckoned several commentators, unsurprisingly.

Walter Spies's public glory was to have embodied the interrelation of the arts that came to betoken "Balinese culture"; his public disgrace arose from his playing into the hands of reactionary forces. The larger-than-life polarities of Spies in Bali (glorious/disgraced) and of Belo and Mead commemorating him may inhibit interpreting indeterminables or reading toward the panoply. If a memorialist—Holt or Mead, for example—even allusively passes the wand of "deviance" over Spies's rich dimensions, those dimensions are magically reduced to compensatory displacement. Similarly, if a memorialist passes the wand of "interwar" over Bali's swirling cycles of influences, they are magically reduced to indices of "aftermath" and "foreshadowing." Both charms may yield engrossing stories, as proved by Mead's enthralling *Blackberry Winter*. But to construe such a "history" as the only story would misrepresent how the past happens, how it becomes constructed—whether in cultures, in cross-cultural studies, or in such movements as "Culture and Personality."

Sensational polarities inform many models of cultures, personalities, and historical periods. We cannot rest content simply to deny the adequacy of polarities, because polarities (exaggerated, reduced contrasts) themselves become social and ideological facts: motives for action. Therefore, polarities must be harnessed: stereotypes must be doubted, questioned, reopened, and turned against each other, particularly when diagnostics start aligning too comfortably across culture types, personality types, and era types.[9] *Zeitgeist*-y notions that "likes attract" are no less objectionable when casually implied. For example, Mead's occasional style of allusion to "sexual preferences" and Abel's style of comparing a culture's standard behavior to "that of the paranoid schizophrenics" can latch onto each other. Under a sometimes tacit rubric of "decadence," further supposed symptoms may then coagulate. Thus, when commemorating interwar Bali (perhaps via Spies), Belo's footnote seems to elide the differences among depolarized gender, male grace, androgyny, homosexuality, hermaphroditism, and other antitheses of twofold male/female distinctions, as if these "symptoms" by nature slosh together. Unquestioned assumptions about normality/breakdown endure in these allusions and arguments, even when tolerance is recommended (sometimes patronizingly).

To counteract or at least displace these familiar and recurrent analytic proclivities, we here attempt an alternative reading of Spies vis-à-vis interwar Bali. The following exercise is ironic and tentative: its surface reroutes or deflects previous hints of affinity; its depths try to dis-spell this very style of analysis, itself included. In the ensuing paragraphs, both Spies and Bali are my relics.

Even if Walter Spies's work—his painting, writing, music, life—stood *for* anything (a dubious proposition), it would not likely have been simply an assault on "proper polarity," such as separate male/female sexual identity. Everything in his canvases projects sensuality, idealized Balinese youths included. The pervasive eroticism stems from interplays of the elements, of hillscape/waterscape/skyscape, of dream/actuality, observation/recollection, and legend/genre painting. He produces near-continuous modulations across different senses, different perspectives, different media, and different ways of knowing/imagining. Spies's art is fundamentally chromatic: not diatonic.[10]

---

9. I learned much about the intricacies and ambivalences of stereotyping at a 1983 Cornell conference on the History of Sexuality, organized by S. Gilman and I. Hull (see Gilman 1985).

10. My analytic metaphor of "chromaticism" stems not just from Debussy and Proust (and other literary modernists, such as the Manns), but from Lévi-Strauss. A drift toward chromaticism of ever finer distinctions, which ultimately "exhaust" sharp mythic contrasts, is a major vector and theme of his *Mythologiques* series (1964–71) and subsequent studies (1983). Lévi-Strauss's

Similar qualities animate Spies's ethnography of performances and his musical interests—particularly a lifelong devotion to several works by Debussy, recently reviewed by G. J. Resink (1984). Spies's first contact with Javanese music in the Yogya court was filtered through previous experience of Debussy, whose own chance hearings of Javanese gamelans in fin-de-siècle Paris is celebrated in the annals of "exotic" influence on European ears. There occurred a spiral of cross-cultural listening—gamelan heard by Debussy, Debussy heard by Spies, preparing the way Spies would later hear gamelan scales, cycles, and notes. His own creations also incorporate Debussian transitions and transpositions: chromatic steps across visual, aural, and tactile codes, or programmatic evocations of their correspondences. Appropriately "Debussy" entered Spies's last recorded words:

> The last mention of Debussy's name occurs in a postcard that Spies mailed in 1942 from his prison camp of Kotatjane, in Aceh . . . : "I sent you today a little painting. . . . It's a fantasy, inspired by the viewpoint we have mornings in the mountains (*brouillard* [mist]). It should be considered only a little prelude, in the fashion of Debussy.". . . Here Spies expresses himself through his fourth "avatar," that of painter. And the word "brouillard" evokes at once the title of Debussy's prelude, "Brouillards," of the *Douze Préludes II* (No. 1). Here Spies, the master of the plastic arts [*plasticien*], comes very close to the composer of the *Images* for orchestra [and] of the two *Images* suites for piano . . . , the instrument of preference for both of them. (Resink 1984:47; my translation)

We return, figuratively now, from musicality to sexuality, or rather gender. Here, readers, is an analogy—musical chromaticism (smallest intervals) : gender ambiguity (sometimes called androgyny). Here is the flip side—diatonic scales : patent polarization of male/female. To schematize—polarized gender : androgyny :: diatonic : chromatic. Androgyny, then, is chromaticism on the keyboard of gender.

To amplify—conventional gender polarization suggests diatonics: more whole steps, fewer keys, restricted clear-cut tonalities. In our scheme androgyny is no periodic or peripheral breakdown from normal, healthy polarity. Rather, the chromatic (paralleling androgyny) contains all the tone differences of the diatonic plus the notes that the diatonic suppresses or makes "accidental." In this dainty dialectic—this music-inspired metaphorical mix—the chromatic (androgyny) contains the diatonic (polarized), even though the diatonic defines the standard against which chromaticism can be heard as subversive

---

long-term attention to chromatic variations has been generally overlooked by critics who reduce his texts (and their reading of them) to an obsessive binarism. A helpful corrective is Bellour and Clément (1979). For some background on connections among Lévi-Strauss, Proust, chromaticism, Debussy/Wagner, and related topics, see Boon (1972; 1982; 1985b). These studies also make tentative suggestions about anthropological texts and musical form—*very* tentative. In regard to the crucial issue of musical preferences, for now, "I have nothing to add."

to tonal propriety. Androgyny, then, tends toward chromatics, providing smaller intervals between the diatonic ones, but also including them. In Western music the history of diatonic/chromatic inscribes a play of suppression and emergence: even when diatonics prevail, the chromatic remains tacit and encompassing (compare Tantrism and heterodoxy).[11] Chromaticism implies ambiguity in matters of tonality (and key) from the perspective of diatonic expectations and norms. Might androgyny be similarly construed in matters of gender?

If one must proclaim affinities of personalities, cultures, and eras (N.B.: one mustn't), then aspects of a culture's, a person's, or an era's musicalities are conceivably as apposite as their sexualities and/or schizophrenias. Alerted to Spies's manifest and public "musical preferences," we diagnose transpositions across small intervals and different sensory arenas. Affinities between Spies and Bali would hinge not simply on his (code word) "androgyny," but on his Debussian arts, or on a theory of chromaticism that could harmonize them with androgyny in the fuller sense suggested above. Recall, then, Debussy:

> By thus drowning or blurring the sense of tonality (*en noyant le ton*) a wider field of expression is ensured and seemingly unrelated harmonies can be approached without awkward detours. . . . Tonality was to be submerged; it was not to disappear. And the purpose of this was to secure expression for a richer, not a shrunken field of associations, transcending the limitations of the mechanical piano like the "immeasurable keyboard" which Marcel Proust was later to describe, the keys of which were to touch upon myriad sensations and which Proust believed was still, even then, almost unknown. (Lockspeiser, 1962:61)

Bali, then, *entre-deux-guerres*, becomes a land-time of chromatic play and intermingling close intervals, occasionally recalled, alas, as a culture period blighted by the breakdown of large-intervalled normality, such as male/female. Such recall is "war"; war is hell (not heaven): sensational, reactionary, unnuanced, unambiguous (and therefore untrue) overpolarity. This sounds like the cadence to our constructed, fragmentary story; but it isn't.

P.S.: Blackberry Tropics

This prolonged "censored postcard" of a paper concludes rather by acknowledging two towering commemorations of interwar ethnology, *Tristes tropiques* (1955) and *Blackberry Winter* (1972), in reverse order. Admittedly, they have been with us from the start.

---

11. On parallels between Tantrism and heterodoxy demonstrated by such scholars as L. Dumont and M. Eliade, and on the desirability of modeling some aspects of anthropological theory after these ritual, religious, and political "alternities," see Boon (1982:178–238).

Balinese houseyard walls, behind which, unless they too have crumbled, domestic activities remain concealed from passers-by. (Photograph by the author.)

Mead's redoubtable autobio-ethnography (an irresistible genre—compare *Variety*'s category of "Bio-pic") flirts with catchword diagnoses of cultures, personalities, and epochs without itself ever committing the most excessive ones (Boon 1985a:354). *Blackberry Winter* shapes a story by converting everything it remembers into personal advantage, a vector of successful career. This style of memoir also characterizes certain kinds of psychotherapy and certain schools of historical narrative (of selves, of times, of cultures). Mead's selective reminiscences aggrandized her profession (and mine), glorified her circle, and justified her research decisions. One extreme example of such tendencies is a passage describing a fieldwork locale in highland Bali. Here Mead's hindsight turned native hardship and medical distress to methodological advantage:

> It was a village in which most courtyard walls consisted of bamboo fencing, instead of the clay walls which, in other villages, shut each courtyard off from sight. I had already learned how much time was consumed in courtesies and gifts of refreshment on every occasion when one entered a courtyard, and I realized that in Bajoeng Gede one could catch a glimpse of what was going on in a courtyard as one walked along a street without actually entering the house. ... The entire population suffered from hypothyroidism, and about 15 percent of the people had a conspicuous goiter. This deficiency of thyroid had the effect of slowing things down so that there was simplification of action, but without a loss of pattern. (Mead 1972:232–33)

It is not that Mead's works were insensitive to misery or suffering. But to construe crumbled house walls and hypothyroidism as a means instantly to acquire slow-motion scenes of private life bespeaks an imagination (and haste) of a distinctive sort. Mead willingly bypassed all that folderol of indigenous courtesies that would have slowed her down. *Blackberry Winter* betrays a similar rush past colleagues and associates, many evoked in quick snatches of stereotype. When Mead's pungently canny remarks start to crowd in on each other, there is no time to opt for a given set of symptoms as determinant, no time for a final cross-cultural or interpersonal diagnosis (Boon 1985a:342–47). Had Mead in fact plumbed for a final, general theory, all possibilities of "thick description" (Geertz 1973)—not to mention reading toward the panoply —would have been thwarted. To her lasting credit, she (strategically, I surmise) did not. Happily, her pace—past broken walls, hypothyroidism, and colleagues—never slackened. Margaret Mead's popular studies, in particular, managed to outrun certain evident deficiencies. This fact helps explain their value and appeal: their adaptability to so many current issues and their continuing capacity to attract readers.

How different was *Tristes tropiques'* restrospective on the paradoxical possibilities of constructing an anthropological tale of anthropology's past. Yet it too gained popularity. *Tristes tropiques'* rhythm of recall is relentless, unmerciful: nonstop transpositions across all codes, which correspond, shift, change places, and ultimately dissolve. The third chapter is symptomatic: a comedy of travel experience "relived," but backwards (as conceived). Proustlike, the text begins in/as memory:

> . . . I was rediscovering with delight a host of vegetable species that were familiar to me since my stay in Amazonia. . . . I reflected on the painful scenes . . . and tried to link them with other experiences of a similar kind . . . (Lévi-Strauss 1955:17)

Step by serial step, we continue reversing:

> Only a little while previously, a few months before the outbreak of war, in the course of my return journey to France, I had visited Bahia . . . a few days earlier I had met with a similar experience . . . (18)

Still more distant pasts cycle through this spiraling return:

> Fortunately, at that time every Brazilian official still had inside him a concealed anarchist, who was kept alive by the shreds of Voltaire and Anatole France which impregnated the national culture even in the depths of the bush. (19)

Memories of experience in reverse lead on to memory of memories in this dispersal toward another "*entre-deux-guerres*":

> But perhaps I would not have behaved so brazenly had I not still been influenced by the memory of an incident which had shown South American policemen in a very comic light. Two months previously . . . (19–20)

Increasingly Proustian, the writing of the account enters the time portrayed, as various memories compound:

> Although up til then I had fared better than my companions, I was none the less preoccupied by a problem to which I must now refer, since the writing of this book depended on its being solved . . . (22)

Sifting his recall of Puerto Rico and Martinique through stereotypes of exiles that others had projected onto himself—Vichy emissary, Jewish Freemason, etc.—the narrator ends "The West Indies" with a parody of Proustian sensibilities that rivals Proust's own parodies:

> And so, it was at Puerto Rico that I first made contact with the United States; for the first time I breathed in the smell of warm car paint and wintergreen (which in French used to be called *thé du Canada*), those two olfactory poles between which stretches the whole range of American comfort, from cars to lavatories, by way of radio sets, sweets, and toothpaste. . . .
>
> The accidents of travel often produce ambiguities such as these. Because I spent my first weeks on United States soil in Puerto Rico, I was in future to find America in Spain. Just as, several years later, through visiting my first English university with a campus surrounded by Neo-Gothic buildings at Dacca in Western Bengal, I now look upon Oxford as a kind of India that has succeeded in controlling the mud, the mildew and the ever-encroaching vegetation. (24–25)

Everything becomes displaced, "West Indianized," including Europe and the U.S. The irony, perhaps even the sarcasm, of Lévi-Strauss's superb punch line is devastating:

> O.K.: I could enter American territory; I was free. (25)

Tristes tropiques "tropes" the flotsam of interwar history, cultures, and states into different chapters, a number of them comic. (Many readers still today want *Tristes tropiques* to be *Blackberry Winter*; it isn't.) Everything is fractured, ruined, and reversible; its mode of rescuing orderability may be likened to "myth." When *Tristes tropiques* was first published in 1955 its plot was the discovery of a metaphorical resemblance between the ways narrated memory and New World mythology arrange metonymies (fragments recollected). The plot remains the same today. In a pivotal chapter, "Crossing the Tropics" (or "crisscrossing the tropes"), different sensory orders, introspection/description, memory/experience, New World and Old, and East and West are all transposed: not confused, but transposed. The prose of concocted metaphors across world-historical metonymies fabricates correspondences. It readies readers to enter the book's tribal evidence through the gate of the chapter on "Sao Paulo," between-the-wars.

At one level Lévi-Strauss's method of multiple analogies across disparate codes avoids nothing. Yet certain costs accrue. We slip too evenly past effects of fixations, repressions, and reductionist symptoms—just the kinds of things Mead often reinsinuated. Such blind spots and coagulations among those transposing "conditions of possibility" *happen*, however untenable this may seem epistemologically. And fixations, reductionisms, and blind spots that *happen* can hurt. *Tristes tropiques* and the concept of myth that it foresees err on the side of smoothing what is rough, leveling what is bumpy, or rendering "spirited" what may feel to practitioners desperate, or perhaps ridiculous. *Tristes tropiques* was the initial entry in Lévi-Strauss's sustained comparison of conceptualized (*conçu*) experience (*vécu*) to a music (a harmonics?) of meanings (*sens*) rather than sounds (*sons*). Like the *Mythologiques* that succeeded it, that text pushed us to the brink of complete chromaticism, where we are apt to forget (to renounce?) the power and effects of chunky polarities and political interests. They seem almost emulsified. Nevertheless, to its political credit, *Tristes tropiques'* tones of conventionalized regret remained nonpatronizing and unmawkish, while many of its critics do not (see Boon 1982:241–62).

One obvious and available antidote to *Tristes tropiques* is *Blackberry Winter* (there are others, perhaps preferable, but less obvious). The two make an odd combination: Lévi-Strauss's transforming as-if lamentations and Mead's mead, her gusto, her semidiagnosis of everything encountered. One might try interweaving these two modalities, providing the former, the "tropics," remains encompassing. Indeed that temporary reconciliation has been one tonality of this essay, though not, I hope, the dominant one.

Concluding Commemoration

What does the feeling for closure fostered by print have to do with the plotting of historical writing, the selection of the kinds of themes that historians use to break into the seamless web of events around them so that a story can be told? (Ong 1982:172)

George Stocking has suggested the occasional relevance of "unilineal descent group" models of intellectual movements to anthropology's history; yet he cautions us not to overextend them (1984:134). Histories of disciplines, even of multimodeled anthropology, tend to imply that issues and isms develop unilineally and from within (Boon n.d.a). An alternative model of movements and transmission highlights the "charmed circle," a constellation of expatriates, émigrés, professionals, and amateurs engaged in dislocated writing and performance. Such assortments of conventional and unconventional scholars and artists are a recurrent context of and for anthropology and cross-cultural studies, as well as cults of the arts. To dwell upon so strikingly nonunilineal (bilateral?) a context of anthropology as interwar Bali helps further unsettle professional convictions of direct influences through the generations of a closed discipline.

"Respecting her right to fall silent . . ." Jane Belo, photographed by Gregory Bateson, 1937. (Courtesy The Institute of Intercultural Studies, Inc.)

Both the charisma of Balinese studies and a sense of the foreordainedness of the approach consolidated as "Culture and Personality" have intensified after the facts, if they were facts. *This* fact underscores the importance of commemoration in anthropology's tales of its past, which can be fruitfully compared to varieties of cultural construction. The intricate arts of selective recall are primary in anthropological accounts of "others" and in histories thereof. "Fieldwork," too, is as much memory as experience, perhaps more retrospective than event. These inescapable issues deserve concerted consideration. They need not be relegated to brief allusions, pseudoprefaces, apologetic digressions, self-congratulatory subjective asides, or even avant-garde treatises too quick to declare themselves "reinvented" (or by now . . . reinvented) and sometimes disdainful of straight academic ethnography. The straight, I submit, is crooked too, as is the crooked. What an opportunity for rereading!

Paradoxically, some historical moments, including some fieldwork contexts, seem almost to happen as memory the moment that they are happening, or so we remember. One general phenomenon that can happen nearly *as memory* (or seem to) the moment that it happens is music. Appropriately, then, certain homages to between-the-wars Bali—a strange interlude storied around Spies, and Belo, and Mead, and Bateson, and . . . —have portrayed it as a musical (see Boon 1977:186–218). Without going so far, it may nevertheless be worthwhile to retune and amplify tonalities and resonances of complex contexts in the history of crossing cultures, particularly where others have inclined to "blackberry" them (my coinage is respectful). As I suggested above, even to "*tristes-tropiques*" such pasts is not altogether adequate either. Hence our provisional alternative: Blackberry tropics.

Jane Belo, "our heroine" in the present commemoration, stopped short of "blackberrying" Bali and Balinists; she had nothing to add to the outré foot-note that we have scrutinized. Respecting her right to fall silent, I have never-theless opened (Michel Foucault might have said) second guessings of Belo's tome/tomb of traditional Balinese culture, in order to intensify readers' aware-ness of the panoplies at play whenever, in Bateson's giftlike words, "events become relics." Such surrealistic possibilities include when "a man is born or dies, or writes a book." Or, I would add, when a woman is born, or dies, or writes a book. . . . Or gives birth. The son can never repay her.

Acknowledgments

I thank Olivian Boon, Robert Smith, George Stocking, Sander Gilman, and also sev-eral colleagues who heard some of these fragments delivered at the University of Min-nesota, for helpful responses. This study has benefited from individuals and resources at Cornell in Anthropology, the Southeast Asia Program, and Comparative Literature.

References Cited

Abel, T. M. 1938. Free designs of limited scope as a personality index. In Belo 1970: 371–83.

Bateson, G. 1937. An old temple and a new myth. In Belo 1970:111–36.

Bateson, G., & M. Mead. 1942. *Balinese character: A Photographic analysis*. New York.

Bateson, M. C. 1984. *With a daughter's eye: A memoir of Margaret Mead and Gregory Bateson*. New York.

Bellour, R., & C. Clément, eds. 1979. *Claude Lévi-Strauss*. Paris.

Belo, J. 1935. A study of customs pertaining to twins in Bali. In Belo 1970:3–56.

————. 1949. *Bali: Rangda and Barong*. Seattle (1966).

————. 1953. *Bali: Temple festival*. New York.

————. 1960. *Trance in Bali*. New York.

————, ed. 1970. *Traditional Balinese culture*. New York.

Benedict, R. 1934. *Patterns of culture*. Boston (1961).

Benjamin, W. 1978. *Reflections: Essays, aphorisms, autobiographical writings*. Trans. E. Jephcott. New York.

Boon, J. A. 1972. *From symbolism to structuralism: Lévi-Strauss in a literary tradition*. Oxford.

————. 1977. *The anthropological romance of Bali, 1597–1972: Dynamic perspectives in marriage and caste, politics and religion*. New York.

————. 1982. *Other tribes, other scribes: Symbolic anthropology in the comparative study of cultures, histories, religions, and texts.* New York.

————. 1984. Folly, Bali, and anthropology, or satire across cultures. In *Text, play, and story,* ed. E. Bruner. Washington, D.C.

————. 1985a. Mead's mediations: Some semiotics from the Sepik, by way of Bateson, on to Bali. In *Semiotic mediations,* ed. E. Mertz & R. Parmentier, 333–57. New York.

————. 1985b. Claude Lévi-Strauss. In *The return of grand theory,* ed. Q. Skinner, 159–76. Cambridge.

————. 1985c. Anthropology and degeneration: Birds, words, and orangutans. In *Degeneration: The dark side of progress,* ed. J. Chamberlin & S. Gilman, 24–48. New York.

————. n.d.a. Anthropology, ethnology, and religion. In *Encyclopedia of religion,* ed. M. Eliade. New York.

————. n.d.b. Balinese twins times two: Gender, birth-order, and "household" in Indonesia and Indo-Europe. In volume from the S.S.R.C. conference on gender in island Southeast Asia, ed. S. Errington & J. Atkinson.

Clifford, J. 1981. On ethnographic surrealism. *Comp. Stud. Soc. Hist.* 23(4):539–64.

Covarrubias, M. 1937. *Island of Bali.* New York.

De Zoete, B., & W. Spies. 1939. *Dance and drama in Bali.* New York.

Forster, E. M. 1924. *A passage to India.* New York.

Foucault, M. 1973. *The order of things.* New York.

Geertz, C. 1973. *The interpretation of cultures.* New York.

————. 1983. *Local knowledge.* New York.

Gilman, S. 1985. *Difference and pathology: Stereotypes of sexuality, race, and madness.* Ithaca, N.Y.

Glenn, J. 1966. Opposite sex twins. *J. Am. Psychoanal. Assn.* 16:736–59.

Holt, C. 1936. "Bandit island": A short exploration trip to Nusa Penida. In Belo 1970: 67–84.

Howard, J. 1984. *Margaret Mead: A life.* New York.

Kallmann, F. J. A. 1952. A comparative twin study on the genetic aspects of male homosexuals (85 homosexual male twin index cases). *J. Nerv. & Mental Disease* 95: 283–98.

Lévi-Strauss, C. 1955. *Tristes tropiques.* Trans. J. & D. Weightman. New York (1977).

————. 1963. *Structural anthropology.* Garden City, N.Y.

————. 1964–71. *Mythologiques.* 4 vols. Paris.

————. 1983. *Le regard éloigné.* Paris.

Lockspeiser, E. 1962. *Debussy: His life and mind.* 2 vols. Cambridge.

Malcomb, J. 1984. *In the Freud archives.* New York.

Mead, M. 1935. *Sex and temperament in three primitive societies.* New York (1963).

————. 1970. Foreword. In Belo 1970:v.

————. 1972. *Blackberry winter: My earlier years.* New York.

Mellow, J. R. 1974. *Charmed circle: Gertrude Stein and company.* New York.

Neiman, C. 1980. Art and anthropology: The crossroads. *October* 14:3–46.

Ong, W. J. 1982. *Orality and literacy: The technologizing of the word.* London.

Resink, G. J. 1984. La musique de Debussy dans la vie de Walter Spies. *Archipel* 27:45–49.

Rhodius, H., ed. 1965 *Schönheit und Reichtum des Lebens Walter Spies (Maler und Musiker auf Bali 1895–1942)*. The Hague.

Rhodius, H., & J. Darling. 1980. *Walter Spies and Balinese art*. Ed. J. Stowell. Amsterdam.

Stocking, G. W., Jr. 1984. Radcliffe-Brown and British social anthropology. *HOA* 2: 131–91.

Taylor, J. R. 1983. *Strangers in paradise: The Hollywood émigrés, 1933–1950*. New York.

Waugh, E. 1945. *Brideshead revisited*. Boston.

INDEX